COACHES CLINICS

INSTANT REVIEW

BASKETBALL NOTEBOOK

VOLUME 8

COACHES CHOICE

ISBN: 157167-206-0
Library of Congress Catalog Card Number: 97-81339

Book Layout and Diagrams: Christy L. Uden
Cover Design: Deborah M. Bellaire
Cover Photos: Photos courtesy of the University of Arizona and the University of Tennessee
Editor: Bob Murrey

Coaches Choice Books is a division of: Sagamore Publishing, Inc.
P.O. Box 647
Champaign, IL 61824-0647
Web Site: http://www.sagamorepub.com

1997 CHAMPIONS

NCAA

MEN'S

WOMEN'S

DIVISION I
UNIVERSITY OF ARIZONA
LUTE OLSON   (25-9)

UNIVERSITY OF TENNESSEE
PAT SUMMITT   (29-10)

DIVISION II
CAL-STATE BAKERSFIELD
PAT DOUGLASS   (29-4)

UNIVERSITY OF NORTH DAKOTA
GENE ROEBUCK   (28-4)

DIVISION III
ILLINOIS WESLEYAN
DENNIE BRIDGES   (29-2)

NEW YORK UNIVERSITY
JANICE QUINN   (29-1)

NAIA

DIVISION I
LIFE UNIVERSITY (GA)
ROGER KAISER   (37-1)

SOUTHERN NAZARENE (OK)
CRAIG WIGINTON   (32-4)

DIVISION II
BETHEL COLLEGE (IN)
MIKE LIGHTFOOT   (34-5)

NORTHWEST NAZARENE (ID)
ROGER SCHMIDT   (27-7)

NJCAA

DIVISION I
INDIAN HILLS CC (IA)
TERRY CARROLL   (38-1)

TRINITY VALLEY (TX)
KURT BUDKE   (34-2)

DIVISION II
BEAVER CO. (PA)
MARK JAVENS   (35-1)

KIRKWOOD CC (IA)
KIM MUHL   (34-2)

DIVISION III
EASTFIELD COLLEGE (TX)
BOB FLICKNER   (25-7)

ANOKA-RAMSEY (MN)
PAUL FESSLER   (25-4)

CONTENTS

CONTENTS

PREFACE

The 1997 season continued to set attendance records as the season closed on an exciting note. In the NCAA Division I Men's Championship game, Arizona defeated Kentucky's defending champions 84-79 in overtime and Tennessee won its second consecutive Women's title as they defeated Old Dominion 68-59.

USA Coaches Clinics is pleased to present Volume 8 of the Instant Review Notebook series. This represents the 34th annual edition and as in the past, efforts are made to cover nearly every phase of basketball. You will find many individual and team drills, organizational ideas, player relationships, offenses and various defenses. These in-depth presentations will provide you with some ideas that can be invaluable as you make plans for your season.

We wish to recognize our dedicated note takers, Burt Droste, Tom Lentsch and Dale Reed for their many hours of recording the original lectures and Mary Jane Grellner for editing and organizing the notes to their final form.

We hope you will enjoy this edition of the Instant Review Notebook and that it will remind you to call us at 1-800-COACH-13 when you plan to attend a clinic or order books and videotapes. With over 45 clinics and 3,000 products, we should be able to help.

Sincerely,

Bob Murrey
President and Editor

QUICK CLIP BIOS

1996-'97

MURRY BARTOW—UAB

One year as head coach at UAB after serving nine years as an assistant under his father Gene Bartow. Began his coaching career as a GA on Bob Knight's staff in 1985, spent two years as an assistant at William and Mary. One of the bright young coaches in the game today.

JOHN BEILEIN—Richmond

Moved to Richmond in April 1997 after five years at Canisius. Prior to that he spent nine years at LeMoyne Jesuit College. A native of western New York, Beilein is the only active coach in the country to have won 20 games at four different levels. (JUCO, NAIA, NCAA Division 1, NCAA Division II) He is 89-62 at Canisius and 271-162 overall.

DAVE BLISS—New Mexico

His team reached the second round of the NCAA Tournament where they lost by one point to Louisville. The team finished 24-8. At New Mexico since '88 and in his 22nd year as a head coach (Oklahoma, SMU). His teams have won 20 or more games 9 of 10 years. Four NCAA and three NIT bids and over 400 wins. Worked with Bob Knight at Army and Indiana and assisted at his alma mater, Cornell.

MIKE BREY—Delaware

Second year at Delaware where he is building a solid and promising program. His team finished in the top half of the league. Assistant at Duke for eight years—two NCAA titles in '91 and '92 and six Final Four appearances. Former assistant and player for the legendary Morgan Wootten at Hyattsville (MD) DeMatha High School.

DON CASEY—New Jersey Nets

John Calipari's first hire was Don Casey, one of the premier NBA assistant coaches. Formerly with the Celtics. From 1974-82, he coached at Temple (151-94). Since 1983, he has been with the Bulls, Clippers (twice), Celtics and now the Nets. His book "Temple of Zones" is a hot item (available through USA Coaches Library).

JIM CLAYTON—Shooting Specialist

Have a problem with your kids improving their shooting techniques? Call Jim Clayton. Excellent instructor. High school for 10 years and spent time working with players on this phase of the game. Now Director of his own Basketball Training School in Huntington, WV. Works with NBA players in individual sessions.

QUICK CLIP BIOS

STEVE CLEVELAND—Brigham Young

Starting his first year at BYU after seven winning seasons at Fresno City College, California's top ranked community college. He led his team to the semifinals of the California State Championships. Every team has been in the playoffs. His seven-year record is 156-72(.672). Coached at Clovis West High School 10 years (180-7). Named Coach of the Year at each level.

KEVIN EASTMAN—Washington State

In his three years as head coach he has accumulated a 48-41 (.539) record and a 23-31 mark in Pacific-10. Is the only WSU coach to take the Cougars to consecutive postseason appearances with a pair of National Invitation Tournament bids in '95 and '96. Career record of 172-116, which includes a head coaching assignment at UNC-Wilmington.

NORM ELLENBERGER—Indiana

Seven years at IU with Bob Knight as assistant coach and administrative assistant. Spent four years with Don Haskins at UTEP and led them to a 16-8 WAC mark and NCAA bid after Haskins was sidelined with laryngitis. Helped coach Tim Hardaway. Head coach at New Mexico seven years (134 wins, two WAC titles, two NCAA and two NIT bids).

ANDY ENFIELD—Shooting Instructor

All-American at Johns Hopkins where he scored over 2,000 points. Milwaukee Bucks shooting coach where he teaches shooting technique and individual offensive moves. Has worked with the Celtics, Heat, Grizzlies and Kings. Best free throw shooter in NCAA history for a career 431 of 466 - 92.5%.

ROB EVANS—Mississippi

When he predicted his young Rebel squad would have an outstanding season, he was right on target. This was the Rebels' best season since 1930 and they reached the NCAA Tournament. Fifth year at Ole Miss. Spent two years at Oklahoma State with Eddie Sutton, 15 years at Texas Tech with Gerald Myers and seven years at his alma mater with Lou Henson.

FRAN FRASCHILLA—St. John's

First year at St. John's after an impressive run for four years at Manhattan. He will need several years of rebuilding to reach the top of the Big East. Led the Jaspers to an 85-35 overall record and four consecutive postseason appearances. NABC Coach of the Year in '94-'95. Assistant 13 years, Providence, Ohio State, Ohio, Rhode Island.

JERRY GREEN—Tennessee

Moved to Tennessee in April 1997 after five years at Oregon. Posted back-to-back winning seasons for the first time in eight years and the first NCAA bid in 34 years in '95 (19-9). Ranked in USA Top 25 in mid-season. Worked with Roy Williams at Kansas. Former coach at UNC-Asheville for nine years (150-109).

QUICK CLIP BIOS

JIM HARRICK—Rhode Island

First year at Rhode Island. He led UCLA to the '95 NCAA Championship, coached there eight years with eight consecutive NCAA appearances plus eight consecutive 20+ seasons. Second winningest UCLA coach behind the legendary John Wooden. Harrick's record was 191-63(.752). At Pepperdine nine years with four NCAA and two NIT bids. 1995 NABC and Naismith National Coach of the Year.

JOE HOLLADAY—Kansas

Holladay just finished his fourth year on the Kansas staff and is involved in all phases of the program. He was a highly successful and respected high school coach, teacher and administrator for 20 years. While at Jenks, OK, the school had 40 state champions in eight years and a record 10 state titles in '90-'91.

MIKE JARVIS—George Washington

Jarvis has been at George Washington since 1990-91 and has led his teams to four NCAA bids. He was the former head coach at Boston University and Cambridge Rindge and Latin. Has become an international recruiter, with six foreign players on his team. He is on the Board of Directors for the NABC.

ANDY LANDERS—Georgia (Women's)

His team was a contender for the number one spot in the polls all year and has been in the top 10 for several seasons. His teams have won over 400 games at Georgia and over 500 total in his career. At Georgia since '79, 10 NCAA bids, one runner-up and two Final Four appearances. National Coach of the year in '86 and '87.

STEVE LAVIN—UCLA

Named interim head coach in October '96 and permanent head coach in February '97. Pac-10 Champions. UCLA ranked in the Top 20. Young and enthusiastic with a solid background in basketball. Had been on the staff five years. He worked three years at Purdue and assisted with the '89 World University Team Trials.

JOYE LEE-MCNELIS—Memphis (Women's)

At Memphis for the past five years, led them to the NCAA Tournament in 1995 with a 21-7 record. Their running style puts points on the board and her post players are even taught to shoot the "3." Stresses an aggressive attitude in her basketball strategy as well as in life.

PHIL MARTELLI—St. Joseph's

Two years at St. Joe. His team reached the third round of the NCAA this year where they lost to Kentucky. 19-13 first year—reached NIT Finals, a first for SJU. Former Assistant at SJU for 10 years under Jim Boyle and John Griffin. Has national reputation as one of the top quipsters in college basketball. Seven years at the HS level—six straight playoff bids.

QUICK CLIP BIOS

JIM MOLINARI—Bradley

1996 MVC Coach of the Year. Since his arrival at Bradley, six years ago, the program has gone 100-78 with streaks of consecutive 20-win seasons, including a postseason appearance at '96 NCAA Tournament. He helped put a Missouri Valley Conference championship banner up and produced an All-American in Anthony Parker.

KEVIN O'NEILL—Northwestern

Few spend more time working or thinking basketball. He tells it like he sees it. Three years at Tennessee, now at Northwestern since April 1997. Has the reputation as a great recruiter. His '93 and '94 Marquette teams led the nation in FG percentage defense. Recipient of the Ray Meyer Award as Conference Coach of the Year. Four teams in postseason tournaments. Former assistant to Lute Olson at Arizona.

TOM PENDERS—Texas

Nine years at Texas. Completely rebuilt the Longhorns' program. Eight trips to NCAA tournament (third round in '97). Teams have averaged 90 points a game and 22+ victories per year. He holds the school record for number of victories. Former coach at Rhode Island, Fordham, Columbia and Tuft. He also coached three years at the high school level.

DAWSON PIKEY—Former Clayton HS (MO)

Highly successful coach for over 25 years. Took a losing program and developed them into a mid-level power. His Rover Defense and Sideline Fast Break led the way to victory. Frequently in State Tournament. Also coached college women's team and led them to a conference title in only one season before retiring.

SKIP PROSSER—Xavier

Three years at Xavier where his teams are 36-20. Ranked in the USA Today Top 25 all season. Midwestern Collegiate Conference Coach of the year in '95. Spent eight years on Pete Gillen's Xavier staff when they won five conference titles and were in seven NCAA Tournaments. Prosser also coached one year at Loyola and 13 years in high school.

STEVE ROBINSON—Florida State

He moved to FSU in June '97 after building a solid program at Tulsa in just two years. This past season he led his team to the second round of the NCAA Tournament after leading his first squad to a 22-8 record, Missouri Valley Conference postseason title and a trip to the NCAA Tournament. At Kansas seven years with Roy Williams.

QUICK CLIP BIOS

KELVIN SAMPSON—Oklahoma

Starting his fourth year at Oklahoma. His teams have made it to the NCAA in each one. In addition to three Coach of the Year Awards, he has been active in international basketball (Jr. National Team and now World University Games). Seven years at Washington State and four at Montana Tech.

JEFF SCHNEIDER—Cal-Poly

In just three seasons, with Schneider as head coach, Cal Poly has had the best turnaround in NCAA Division I. He led the Mustangs into their first season in the Big West, guiding them to 14 wins. Also has the insight necessary in recruiting special student-athletes. He was named the '95-'96 American West Conference Coach of the Year.

LARRY SHYATT—Wyoming

His impressive credentials made it easy for Leo Moon, the Cowboys' athletic director to hire him in April '97. Has coached at six Division I schools (Clemson, Providence, New Mexico, Utah), and is highly respected as a recruiter, bench coach and administrator. Plans to create a love affair between his program, the school and the people of Wyoming.

JERRY WAINWRIGHT—North Carolina (Wilmington)

Third year as head coach who last season took his Seahawks to the brink of an NCAA playoff berth. His team finished fifth in the country in scoring defense. Previously was assistant at Wake Forest under Bob Staak and Dave Odom. Won the Colonial Athletic Association Conference title this year after being picked last.

PAUL WESTHEAD—Golden State Warriors

Recently became an assistant at Golden State, after being at George Mason. Has been head coach for 17 years in college and six in the NBA. His innovative style is designed to produce high-scoring games. A great teacher and motivator, resulting in successful fast break and quick hit plays. Is an active marathon runner and Shakespearean scholar.

ROY WILLIAMS —Kansas

Nine years at KU. National Coach of the Year twice. Second highest winning percentage among active Division I coaches. Won five of last six Big 8 Conference Championships. Holds record for most games in their first eight years. Two Final Four teams in last six years. Assisted Dean Smith at North Carolina. Lost by three to Arizona in third round of NCAA Tournament. Undefeated in first 18 games (34-2) .

UAB ZONE OFFENSE
Key Principles

1. We need good spacing and proper floor balance.

2. We need good inside-outside action. Try to get the ball into the middle of the zone and then see what develops. Getting the ball into the middle of the zone is a major key.

3. Distort the zone, with the dribble. Make two defenders play you. We do not want to just pass the ball around the perimeter without getting any dribble penetration. Look to freeze a defender by driving the ball right at him or driving the ball hard into the gaps of the zone.

4. Look to attack from behind the zone. When the ball is on top, our inside players need to start behind the zone and look to flash up into the lane from behind the defense. When the ball goes to the block, our perimeter player(s) on the off-side is now behind the zone and should be prepared for a skip-pass and shot.

5. On the perimeter, always be "shot-ready." Have your feet ready and be prepared to shoot. Be sure to adjust your position on the perimeter so you are always in the gaps of the zone, which creates some indecision from the two closest defenders in the zone.

6. Make good use of the pass fake and shot fake. Pass fakes and shot fakes will force defenders to straighten up and become out of position, which will create an advantage for the offense. The more we can distort the zone the better chance we will have of getting an open, high percentage shot.

7. The skip-pass is an effective weapon against the zone. We can set solid screens in the zone and look to skip-pass over the top.

8. When on top, receive the ball on the ballside of the floor. We want to cross the mid-line before taking it back to the same side of the floor.

9. We don't want to dribble right at the player we're going to pass to. We have to dribble the ball away from him and then look to bring it back to him for a possible shot. This misdirection action off the dribble is a very effective tool for getting an open shot on the perimeter.

10. Look to pass the ball opposite of where you received it.

11. Alignment of players is important. We can start in a stack to create initial alignment problems for the defense. We can also find a slow-footed defender in the zone and put a quick slasher on his side and look to penetrate past this defender in an effort to distort the zone. We can also start one of our inside players up high to create a 1-3-1 alignment.

12. Our perimeter players should get in the gaps, be "shot-ready" and interchange positions on the floor. We can use audibles, such as "clear" and "shallow" to interchange positions on the perimeter. Cut through the zone and force the defense to make decisions.

13. Look to overload the zone by:

    - Having the two inside players working hi-low on the ballside of the floor, and/or

    - Having the offside perimeter player run the baseline cutting to the ballside corner.

14. Our inside players need to step out on the baseline and work the short corner. A great place to attack the zone is from the baseline. Our inside players have to also look to "take up space" by screening-in and sealing the defense.

15. Always try to reverse the ball to three players on the same side of the floor. On ball reversal, we can look to dribble the ball above the defender closing out on the wing and then look to make a pass to the baseline. We constantly want to create a 2-on-1 offensive advantage on ball reversal.

3-OUT-2-IN ALIGNMENT:

(Diagram 1a)   Perimeter players work together and inside players work together.

Diagram 1a

(Diagram 1b)   Inside-outside action is always a key look.

(Diagram 1c)   4 and 5 look to work the short corners and flash from behind the zone. Perimeter players keep good spacing and they can interchange positions on the perimeter.

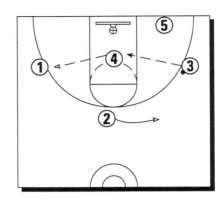

Diagram 1b

Diagram 1c

(Diagram 1d)   Perimeter players can pass to baseline with the low post passing opposite outside.

Diagram 1d

VS. 3-2 ZONE: The shooter (3) works the baseline, corner-to-corner. Bigs look to screen-in and work the paint from behind the zone. (Diagram 2a) (Diagram 2b) (Diagram 2c) (Diagram 2d)

Diagram 2a

Diagram 2b

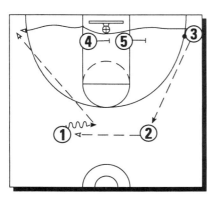

Diagram 2c

Diagram 2d

POWER ZONE ALIGNMENTS: Bigs criss-cross and work high-low. 1, 2, and 3 work together on the perimeter. (Diagram 3a) (Diagram 3b) (Diagram 3c)

Diagram 3a

Diagram 3b

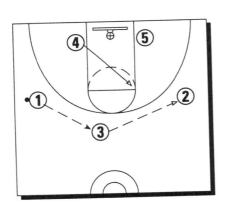

Diagram 3c

(Diagram 4c)   5 works the short corner, side-to-side. Perimeter players keep good spacing and work together.

Diagram 4c

1-3-1 ALIGNMENT: Working to get 4 the ball at the high post and then work from there.
(Diagram 4a)   (Diagram 4b)

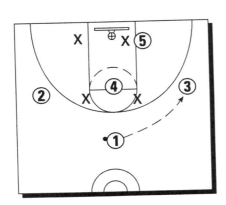

Diagram 4a

3-OUT, 2-IN ALIGNMENT: Looking for a lob to 3 after he touches the ball on the right wing. After 1 receives the ball back on top from 3, 5 flashes hard into the lane and 4 looks to set a backscreen.
(Diagram 5a)   (Diagram 5b)

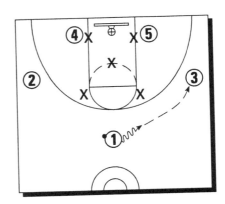

Diagram 5a

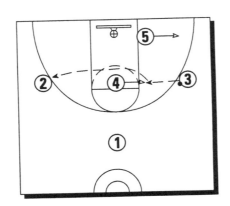

Diagram 4b

Diagram 5b

Diagram 6b

3-OUT, 2-IN ALIGNMENT: We are looking to overload a side. You can look to reverse the ball from side-to-side and overload the zone on both sides of the floor. We don't start the overload action until the second pass to the wing. (Diagram 6a) (Diagram 6b) (Diagram 6c) (Diagram 6d)

Diagram 6c

Diagram 6a

Diagram 6d

MAN DEFENSE

1. Force the player you are guarding to play the way he doesn't want to play. Be tough to play against!

2. Always be in a ready stance.

3. Play defense with your feet—not your hands.

4. Anticipate, anticipate, anticipate!

5. Talk—help each other out.

6. We want all-out, non-stop pressure on the ball. All the time!

7. Priority System:
   - The ball.
   - Your position in relation to the ball and the men you are guarding.
   - Your man.

8. We force everything to the outside—try to push the offense to the sideline and to the corner.

9. Our post defense is critical. Each player on the team needs to work on playing post defense. Stay on the high side of the post player as much as possible. Don't get in a wrestling match. Move your feet and get in position. The best post defense is relentless pressure on the ball!

10. Don't let the player you are guarding do what he wants to do. If he wants to cut through the lane, get in his way. If he is trying to make a cut to the basket, body-up and make him cut somewhere else. Constantly look to take things away!

11. The more penetration we allow, the more our defense will break down. We have to control penetration. Stay in front of your man. Don't let him come to the middle. Push him to the outside.

12. Ours is a team defense! If you are guarding the man with the ball, make him suffocate. Put relentless pressure on him.

If you are not on the ball, and you are on the ballside, be in a contesting position. Don't let your man touch the ball. If you are on the helpside, be in a great position in relation to the ball. Anticipate what is about to happen. Be ready to take something away, talk to your teammates.

DEFENSE WINS GAMES!

1. Mentality:

   - There has to be a sense of urgency.

   - Disposition to dominate.

   - Play defense the way you don't want it played against you.

   - Be tough to play against and take things away.

   - Force the player you are guarding to play the way he doesn't want to play.

   - Ours is a team defense. You need a burning desire to get stops.

2. Transition Defense:

   - Get back—right now—without hesitation.

   - It has to be a dead sprint back.

   - Get back quickly—with a purpose—down in a stance, seeing the ball, in position, ready to get a stop.

- The first man cannot let anyone get behind him. We have to quickly stop the ball—find shooters—bump the bigs at the elbows—and be ready to play—right now.

3. **Half-Court Defense:**

- Stay in a stance at all times—you cannot rest on defense.

- We want disciplined pressure on the ball at all times. "Pressure on the ball—steal away from the ball."

- Never lose sight of the ball. Everything in our defense is centered on seeing the ball and stopping the ball. All five players have to swarm to the ball.

- Influence the ball to the sideline and the baseline. Get the ball on a side and keep it there. We have to keep the ball out of the middle of the floor.

- In our defense, your position in relation to the ball and the man you are guarding is critical. Jump to the ball—when the ball moves, you move. The ball is your first priority and your second priority is your position. Always be in the right position and anticipate for steals (position and vision). Be in position and establish a 5-on-3 defensive advantage. Pressure and position = Good Defense!

- We want to challenge every shot. We don't want the opponent to have any open looks at the basket. We want to get a high hand up on the shooter on every shot attempt.

- Work hard to contest passes. Try to push the offense way out on the floor. Get higher when you contest and force them to back cut.

- Our rotation has to be quick and without hesitation. All five players have to guard the ball. All five players have to rotate down quickly and be in position to stop the ball. Don't just turn and look—swarm to the ball.

- Play defense with your feet—not your hands. Being foul-prone is being a lazy defender. Stay in a stance—don't reach—get your body in the right position and stop the ball.

- A big part of our defense is through help and recover principles. We have to see the ball, be ready to help, then recover quickly. We must get from help to pressure—right now.

- We want good containment. We want to stop the ball and keep the ball in front of us. If we don't have good containment, it will put a major stress on our defense. We want to pressure the ball at all times, but good containment is a must.

- We want to limit post touches, by playing solid post defense. We always want a big-arm up in the passing lane. Stay on the high side as much as possible. Move your feet, break contact, give a cushion, don't get in a wrestling match. Always see the ball and be ready to help.

- We really have to communicate on the defensive end of the court. ("Screen left," "Switch," "I've got your help," "Give me a lane") TALK. Help each other out.

- Jump to the ball and give each other big lanes. Work together and help your teammates.

- In our defense, all five players have to be willing to do the dirty work—take charges, dive on the floor after loose balls, deny the flash, bump cutters, sprint instead of jogging back in transition defense, get the big defensive rebound, etc. Don't wait for someone else to make it happen—get it done.

- Trust in your teammates is important. To pressure the ball as hard as you need to—to contest on the wings—to be as aggressive as we have to be—you have to trust the other four players and have confidence in your help.

- When we switch, it is predetermined. When we switch, switch aggressively and take something away.

- Be disciplined. Do exactly what you are asked to do.

4. **Finalize the Possession:**

- The defensive possession does not end until we have the ball.

We can do this:
(1) By being in position, seeing the ball, and anticipating for steals.
(2) By taking the charge.
(3) By pressuring the defense into making a turnover, and
(4) By rebounding the basketball. We cannot give our opponents more than one shot. We have to block-out, be in position, assume that every shot will be missed, and all five players have to think rebound.

- Good defense leads to good offense—so finalize the defensive possession and we can make things happen at the other end.

Little Things That Make A Big Difference

Note—This presentation was made in a gymnasium with players to demonstrate.

What I have for you are some random digressions, mistakes I have made and a few things for you to think about.

1. You can do anything you want in coaching, but you can't do everything you want. You can't do it all. If you try to go and do it all, you will lose a lot of games. You must keep it simple. You may put in an out-of-bounds play even though all of yours are working.

2. Practice your shooting before you practice your defense. When we start practice, we shoot so hard and so fast. We do this for two reasons. We want to start on a positive note. You can't practice your defense unless your players are warmed up in their shooting. We always do offense first.

3. Loosen up with different drills before stretching. All of us over 40 years of age remember we didn't do any stretching. I have a strength coach who is terrific. But he had my players doing 17 stretches before they lifted weights. It took 20 minutes. Let them stretch for 3 or 4 minutes and if they need more, let them do it on their own time.

    Practice starts at 4 o'clock. We start with 3-3-4. The first three minutes we play catch and move, pass and shoot. When we shoot, we want to keep the ball away from the body. Don't bring the ball in tight. The second three minutes we run out-of-bounds plays at half speed. The four-minute segment is stretching. We will end practice exactly 2 hours and 15 minutes later.

4. (Diagram 1) Shorten every pass. The passer does a good job, but the receiver doesn't always do a good job. It's the receiver's job too. 1 passes to 2, and then 2 to 3. The receiver must know when the passer is going to pass, and the passer must know when the receiver is going to get open. Don't move until the ball sees you.

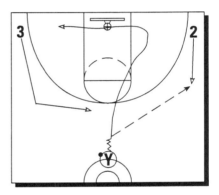

Diagram 1

5. (Diagram 2) Be strong with the ball—show no navels, show no backs. We really work hard at this. This drill is called "Jersey City." 1 bounces the ball to 2 and follows the pass and plays defense. 2 goes strong to the basket. 2 cannot give up the dribble.

Diagram 2

6. Shooting drills. Always have variety in your shooting drills. Make them competitive. If you lose the drill, there is a penalty. This drill has two rebounders, two balls, and one shooter. If he makes 14 in one minute, he doesn't have to run. But if he has to run, everybody runs, the passer and the rebounders. Just to half-court. But I want some kind of penalty if he loses. Put the pressure on.

7. Big man. Body on, ball away. This is the basic rule. Catch the ball, get your foot into the lane. Establish your area but keep the ball away. Have the little jump shot and/or hook shot. Have a move and a counter move. After you catch the ball, quickly make a balance step. Get them to take a quarter turn so they can see.

8. Shooting. It is so mental, don't doubt, believe, be positive. You want the great shooter to have his hands on the ball at the end of the game. You must show your shooters that you love them and have faith in them.

9. (Diagram 3) Along those lines, you must have some idea of who your shooters are. Green light, yellow light, red light. This is a great way to determine who the shooters are. Two balls, two rebounders. Shooter goes left to right around the circle. Chart every shot, and in 25 seconds,

he must make six. If he doesn't, he runs to half-court when he is done. You should get about twelve shots, and if you can't make 50% with no one guarding you, then you don't have the green light.

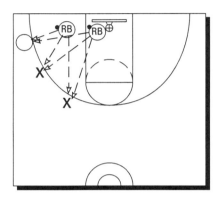

Diagram 3

10. Exchange ideas with other coaches. Don't be afraid of criticism. Have interviews with your ex-players. What did you like and not like about practice? You will learn. I get together with several coaches for a couple of days and just talk basketball.

11. Weight training and basketball. We test them at the beginning of the year and continue training throughout the season and they will be better at the end of the year. After they come out of the weight room, have them shoot for 10 minutes.

12. (Diagram 4) Have a sideline break after foul shots for a change up. 5 takes the ball out-of-bounds. 3 goes to the outlet area. 1 goes to the ballside near mid-court. 2 is a safety valve and then breaks long. 4 runs right to the rim. Ball goes from 5 to 3 to 1 to 4, or else to 2. This is quick and easy. We run it to either side, but we have a call for each side.

13. Prevent defense, no doubles or traps to prevent fouls or 3's. Does your team really know when it is time not to foul?

14. Start a game in a zone and see what the other team does and who should guard who. Do this especially when you are unable to scout. We play zone on the out-of-bounds in the first half just to see how they react. If they have great three-point shooters, just run at them. Do everything that your coaches and my coaches told us not to do. Leave your feet on the perimeter. You'll be surprised how this will bother them.

15. (Diagram 5) 3-on-2, 2-on-1 for a purpose. We all know this drill. But we do it differently. If the offense scores, the Xs come back on offense against 1. If they don't score, they have ten pushups immediately, five for allowing the other three players to score, and five for not scoring against 1. If 1, 2, and 3 didn't score immediately, they have five pushups. If 1 doesn't stop the two X's and didn't score when it was 3-on-2, he has ten pushups at the other end. There is always a winner, and always a loser.

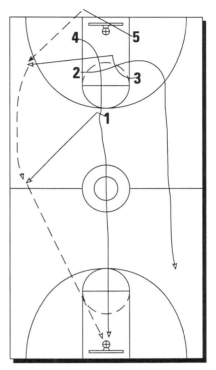

Diagram 4

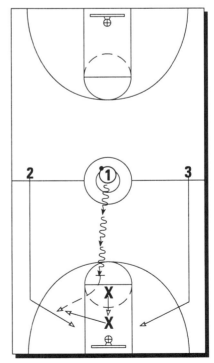

Diagram 4

16. Ultimate basketball is a great drill. This is full-court, no dribbles. The defense knows that they can't dribble so they are playing in the passing lanes. If a team scores, the other team doesn't even take the ball out-of-bounds, they just go the other way. Then you can do this drill with just one dribble.

17. Use of baseball pass vs. zone presses. When the player receives an inbound pass or inbounds the ball, we want the ball put by the ear for a possible baseball pass. My first look is long.

18. (Diagram 6) Defensive slide. Make them shorter, do three shuffles maximum. If you do it longer than half-court, the drill breaks down. Get the ball on the sideline at half-court and then come up and trap. We also practice the shuffle going back and forth across the lane. Teach them to kick out on the first step.

Diagram 7

(Diagram 8) Screening Drill. 2 screens for 1 who fights around the screen. Then 1 screens 3 and 3 screens 2, if 3 passes to 1.

(Diagram 9) Staggered screens. 2 and 3 screen for 1 and 1 closes out on 4. Then 2 and 3 screen again on 1 and he again fights through the screens to close out on 5.

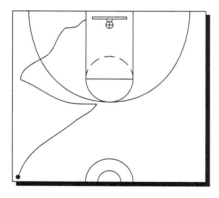

Diagram 6

(Diagram 7) Close-out drill. Make them close out with high hands on the coach. The coach makes a pass and then they shuffle in the direction of the pass. Keep these short, quick, steps. Vary your drills. Have five drills and do each of them once a week.

Diagram 8

19. Making free-throws. We take ten minutes for foul shooting and rest. They must make 20, not shoot 20. If they make 20 out of 21, then they have a five minute rest. And they do five pushups for every miss. Or maybe a ten dribble sprint. They get five dribbles to go the length of the floor, and then back again.

Diagram 9

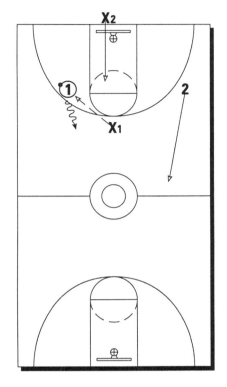

Diagram 10

20. Don't invent too many drills. Your drills must fit your program.

21. Do some type of agility drill three times a week. Example, do three taps and in. Jump rope. Do these all year long.

22. Video every game. You will find that you are never as good as you look or as bad as you look. Video will make you better, it is worth it.

23. (Diagram 10) 2/1 drill full-court. X2 starts on the baseline, the offense starts at the foul line. X2 must catch up. If 1 and 2 score, they play defense and the drill goes the other way.

(Diagram 11)   Here is another version of 2/1. 2 starts at the top of the circle. 1 passes to 2 who breaks out to one side or the other. When 2 gets the pass, 2 drives to the basket and 3 clears to the other side of the lane so that the defense can't play both 2 and 3.

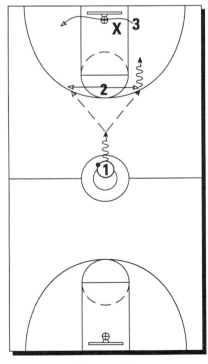

Diagram 11

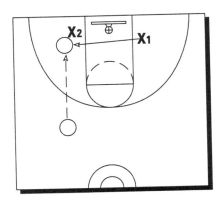

Diagram 13

24. Last-second situations. Put two minutes on the clock and the score is 70 to 70. When one team gets to 74 the clocks starts. In this way, you aren't responsible for one team being behind.

25. (Diagram 12) Play 1-on-1 often. 2 makes the bounce pass and then closes out. Do it from different positions on the floor. Losers will run.

    (Diagram 13) 1-on-1 in the post. The pass is made into the post and then a perimeter player will double-down.

26. Dribble and a half. Don't dribble and then pick up the ball. Dribble, and start to dribble again and then pick up the ball. It will give you an extra step.

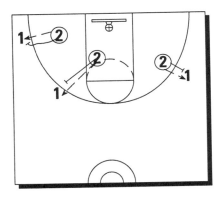

Diagram 12

27. Road Game Preparation. We played loud music at home practices before road games so we had to practice and play with a minimum of verbal communication. We didn't call any plays verbally. We had non-verbal cues. Create chaos!

28. Delay game, don't show it, but do it. Don't take a shot the first time through your offense.

29. Point guards must change speeds, change directions. Do not let them go all out down the floor. They can't make decisions going at break-neck speed.

30. Understand momentum. Stick it to your first team in practice. Make them overcome adversity. Every charge goes against them, every block goes against them. Make them fight for momentum. On the other end of the floor, let the other team get away with fouls.

31. Offensive moves. You need a move and a counter move. You don't have to teach them twenty moves. We tell our players to keep the head over the ball.

Game Management

This is the time of year when all of us are trying to create hope for the coming year. Hopefully, I can give you some food for thought that will help you spark that fire for the coming season.

Over the last couple years we have been 53-14. We have more athleticism coming back this year than we have had in the past two years. Because of this, I have some great expectations for our team next year.

I care a great deal about our profession, so let's start out with what I call "The Art of Solid Coaching." It is very important that young coaches and new coaches realize that the good Lord will put you where you are most capable to have the most influence on young people's lives. Coaches are one of the last bastions of teaching young people respect, discipline, responsibility. Genuine caring is really important in basketball. I say this for several reasons. One is that the kids need it. Second, if you want your team to play well, they have to know how much you really care about them. Players don't care how much you know until they know how much you care! Our goal should be to bring out the best in the players that have been placed in our responsibility.

Here are the points I feel contribute to the Art of Solid Coaching:

- Listen to your players.

- Take additional interest in them, as human beings as well as players.

- Be clear about your expectations of them.

- Be eager to teach them.

- Reinforce positive behavior, discourage unacceptable behavior.

- Develop a trust between them and you.

- Be flexible and open to new ideas.

- Be enthusiastic with them.

- Challenge them and set standards that motivate them to produce the best.

- Show confidence that you can help them because you are prepared.

COACH'S CHECKLIST:

1. Nothing takes the place of your team playing hard. Don't coach caution.

   No matter what your record winds up being, if your team plays hard for you, you've achieved something very special.

2. Avoid losing first. Your philosophy should include playing the percentages. There is a fine line between how much you are going to control your offense and how quickly you are going to shoot. Have an offense that your defense can defend. Don't shoot too quickly if your defense can't stand the pressure.

3. Every coach knows more than he can teach— simplicity, consistency, repetition.

4. Encouragement and enthusiasm—create hope. Everyone has to have hope of something. We all want to have hope for a good year. If we don't really believe it, we can't get our players to grab this hope.

5. Your players become what they believe you think they are. Joe Paterno is the best example of practicing this thought. He also has a sign in his office, "Don't bad mouth your players, they are the only ones we have."

6. Anger is a poor substitute for reason—frustration is an enemy.

7. Some things are within your control while others are not. Know the difference and teach the difference.

8. The game is usually not as important to them, and this isn't always bad. They rebound from crushing losses better than the coaches do.

9. Never second guess yourself on decisions made with integrity, intelligence and the "team-first" attitude.

10. The most essential thing to teach in athletics is to never give up. Today, this is a challenge. We must teach this.

BECOMING A BETTER LEADER:
A. Desire to Be in Charge.
   1. Intrinsic desire to achieve substantial personal recognition despite discouragement, rejection and disappointment.
   2. Courage, creativity and stamina to focus on accomplishing your responsibilities through the directed and delegated efforts of your well-chosen subordinates.
   3. While your success depends on your eagerness to work hard, you must not be over-eager nor impatient.
   4. You must be willing to remain in your natural self.

B. Your Characteristics Determine Your Team's Reputation.
   1. We win with character, not with plays; work hard to keep encouraging and rewarding its development.
   2. We must never build pyramids in our own honor. Self-serving practices will only weaken our effort.

3. Your success will be made possible by the extremes of your personality, but these extremes are always under control.

C. Morale and Discipline.
   1. Morale and discipline are central to unity, but are not always welcomed.
   2. Without discipline, common action is difficult.
   3. Discipline is not suppression and does not mean loss of individuality.

D. Internal Problems.
   1. Beware of those who pledge loyalty in public and spread discontent in private. Anticipate disloyalty and handle appropriately.
   2. Be approachable, listen to both good and bad news.
   3. Be principled, not inflexible—not all will be compatible, but everyone must row in the same direction.

E. Pick Your Enemies Wisely.
   1. Do not expect everyone to agree with you and do not waste energy trying to conform everyone's behavior—unless it affects discipline.
   2. Do not lose your temper without advantageous reasons and do not underestimate the power of an enemy to rise against you on another day.
   3. Do not neglect the opportunity to deceive your enemy. Make him think of you as a friend. Let him act prematurely and never tell him anything.

F. Your Reward System.
   1. The reward is commensurate with the task completed—small for light tasks, large for greater accomplishment.
   2. Praise and feeling of security is sometimes all that is needed.
   3. Sincere concern for and purposeful mingling while still remaining separate will raise spirits and encourage greater effort.

4. Care more for rewarding those under you than for rewarding yourself.

G. There is Another Day After a Loss.
1. Expect your enemies to battle you—don't be surprised, especially if the rewards are considerable.
2. You will not win every encounter regardless of how prepared you are.
3. Should you become aware of impending defeat, face it and take immediate action to minimize its effect and get back to your cause.
4. Momentary loss of self-worth—confidence and determination are normal emotions that accompany personal loss. Lament, if necessary, but do not dwell too long lest the defeat rule your emotions forever.
5. Learn from defeat. Inability to do this clouds your ability to improve for the future.

Here's an interesting idea to consider. Create a wish list for yourself this year. There are things you didn't feel you did especially well this year. List five things defensively and five things offensively you want to change because they're not as good as they should be. Here are the things we have created for the 1997-'98 season.

DEFENSE:
1. Playing hard vs. technique. Are you more concerned about how your players look in executing fundamentals or in how hard they play?
2. Implement defensive scheme earlier—repetition, repetition.
3. Post defense—will we double or trap and rotate on balls into the post?
4. Trap more aggressively.
5. Wide stance when your man has the ball, no reaching. Half of our fouls this year were due to reaching. Here is a drill we'll work on every day to help alleviate this.

(Diagram 1)   You might call this line drill, guard close-out, whatever. You have an offensive player on the foul line extended with a defender in the middle of the lane. The defender throws the ball to the offensive player who drives the baseline. The defender is to get in good defensive position and stop the drive. We encourage the offensive player to drive right into the defender's chest. After making contact with the defender the offensive player executes a back-up dribble and drives to the elbow. The defender has to recover and go with the offensive player without reaching. The players learn they can take a body blow and recover without having to reach.

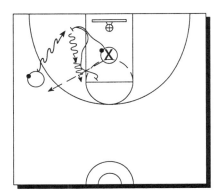

Diagram 1

(Diagram 2)   You can do this same drill with your post men except have them stationed in the middle of the lane. The coach/manager throws the ball to the offensive player. The offensive player turns, chests the defender and shoots. The defender is taught to stand with his arms straight out or up, and take the blow without reaching.

If your players are having a hard time with this drill, it is probably a sign that you need to increase their chest strength.

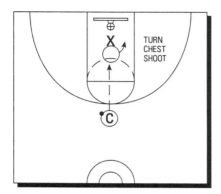

Diagram 2

OFFENSE:

1. Push it—better outlets and run lanes. I love the fast break and especially the way Kansas runs it. They get the ball out quickly and Coach Williams is standing on the sideline waving his arms to get the ball down quickly.

2. Drive to pass—using two or more dribbles. Here are three drills we'll use each day in practice to teach this.

   (Diagram 3) The first is a drive to the elbow and kick drill. As one guard drives toward the elbow, the other guard flares toward the baseline. We make a pass to the guard flaring and he takes the jumper.

Diagram 3

(Diagram 4) In the second drill, we have one guard drive the ball to the baseline. As he does this, his partner cuts to the baseline away. We have this in our offense because we have found that this pass is open 100% of the time. We make that cross-court pass for the shot.

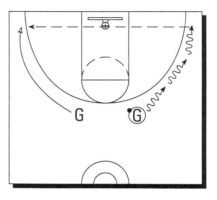

Diagram 4

(Diagram 5) The third drill we call our spin-out drill. This is great for the big men. We have a guard and post. The guard drives the baseline to force a double team or the post defender to come out and stop his drive. The post spins-out toward the three-point line and the guard hits him with the pass. The post doesn't have to shoot a three. If he is comfortable at 15' we encourage him to shoot.

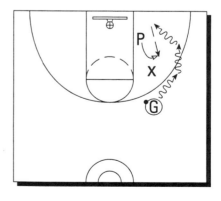

Diagram 5

3. Pressure releases—backcuts, post flash.
4. Shot clock option.

5. Better high-low action with 4 out, 1 in.

STATISTICS:
Keep statistics, but be selective in what you keep. Here are the statistics we keep:

Defensive:
1. Deflections—these are great. If you have someone who can get his hands on the ball consistently, this gives you a chance to make a quick change defensively.

2. Hit the floor—which players are aggressive? Who will go on the floor after the ball?

3. Charges.

4. Types of fouls committed—reaching, rebounding, on the shot, etc.

5. Different defenses—press, trap, zones, etc.

Situational Stats: "Us vs. Them"
1. Free-throw offense vs. defense—are you getting second, third shots, or are they? If you really stress this, you can gain an advantage on the free-throw line.

2. Baseline offense vs. defense—are you getting shots or getting fouled? We scored thirteen times on our baseline offense vs. four times for the opponent.

Offensive:
1. Fast break from misses and turn-overs. How many times are we converting?

2. Fast break from made field goal.

3. Offense from free-throw.

(Diagram 6) Here is a fast break offense from a made free-throw situation that we use at New Mexico. 5 takes the ball out of the basket and quickly steps out-of-bounds. 1 steps to the ballside for the inbounds pass. 2 steps to the outlet on the weakside. 3, after blocking out the shooter, sprints the floor to the corner on the offensive end. 1 brings the ball down the right side. 4 sprints to the box on the right side of the offensive end. 2 fills the weakside lane and comes to a stop at the foul line extended. 5 trails the play and comes to the top of the key on the ballside. 1 can now hit 4 for an inside post-up move. Reverse the ball to 5, who then can hit 2 on the weakside for the three-pointer. We can also make that dribble penetration to the baseline that I talked about earlier and cross-court pass to 3 in the corner for the three.

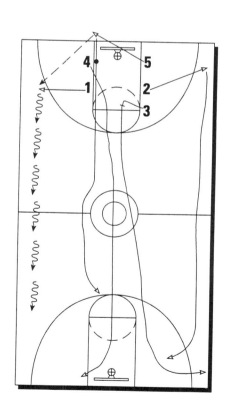

Diagram 6

4. Timeout offense. Do you have a set play or offense you like to use to score off of coming out of a timeout?

5. Shot clock offense.

6. Post feeds—who is good at getting the ball in the post and who can catch the ball in the post?

7. Fouls—charges, offensive rebounding.

Next Year I'm Going To Do It Differently:

(These are things I think we need to improve on or re-evaluate)

A. Starting Point for This Year.
   1. Reasons you lost last year. This becomes a philosophical study of your team. You must realize and accept what your weaknesses were so that now you can work on improving them.

   2. Areas that you want to change. These may be technical, personal or they may be personalities. Maybe you want to be tougher on your team or maybe you have to give them a little more freedom.

   3. Do you fully understand your coaching philosophy? Have your thoughts about the game changed and do you need to analyze what it is that your team needs to do to be successful?

   4. How can you personally become more excited about next year? People don't know how much we all think about coaching.

B. Preparing to be Successful.
   1. Commitment—sense of urgency, priorities. We are lucky to be in coaching. You must realize that this is the moment you must capture.

   2. Organization. You don't have a lot of time, so use it wisely.

   3. Enthusiasm: I, A, S, M, the last four letters of enthusiasm stand for "I Am Sold Myself." If you get enthusiastic about something, you are going to sell it. If you aren't enthusiastic, how can they get enthusiastic about it? Keep the energy level up. Enthusiasm rubs off.

   4. Creativity—visit other coaches and successful people. Explore what makes them successful and adapt it to your system.

   5. Know yourself and your team's strengths and weaknesses. This is really important. My staff helps me assess what we can do, what we can't do and to keep the game within these restrictions.

   6. Don't be afraid of failure. I've seen some very good coaches who, because they were afraid of failure, weren't very good coaches on game night. The ability to handle losses is really critical. A team must be able to learn and benefit from a loss. You will find out more about your team after your first loss than at any other time during the early part of the season.

C. Between Now and The First Practice.
   1. Create Excitement—individual meetings, goals, booklets, include their ideas. We will benefit from how well our players are sold on what we do as a team.

   2. Communication Urgency—leaders are developed, no long meetings. We all have players who want to be good. But, are they willing to work at it now and put a true

effort into it or are they always putting it off until tomorrow or next week?

3. Coach Confidence—know what you want, then teach it through repetition.

4. Critique Performances—your team will be satisfied with what you will tolerate. You must be intense. You must be sensitive to the things that will allow your team to be successful.

5. Continue Pursuit—find those players who want to be successful and will do what it takes to be successful and make them part of your program.

6. Circle of Success—do you deserve to be successful? I learned a lot about this during my time with Coach Knight. We would work so hard that we weren't going to fail. This is a battle of wills. We can't quit before we get done what we must get done.

D. What Coaches Owe The Players
1. Make them overachievers. It is our job to get the best out of our players.

2. Develop their talent within the team frame.

3. Create atmosphere for individual growth—allow your players to develop as individuals, but don't allow the team to be sacrificed for this growth.

4. Be prepared.

5. Create a good feeling. Self-esteem is in short supply. Players must feel good about themselves if they are to succeed.

E. What The Players Owe The Team.
1. No embarrassment. Players must respect the team they are a part of and the school they represent. They must never bring any dishonor to themselves or their teammates.

2. Maximum effort—both physical and mental.

3. Sacrifice for the benefit of the team.

Game management is a term that originated in golf. But, it is really something that can be adapted to any sport. In football, we see situational substitutions, in basketball it is changing defenses, in baseball it means bringing in the reliever or a pinch runner.

Jimmy Johnson once said "If the offense can have a play, why can't the defense?" During a timeout or any stoppage of play, do you take advantage of this and make a change defensively? Do you put to use all the preparation you made for the game? The game, quite often, breaks down into important possessions and you can control these possessions by preparing for them ahead of time. This switch is probably going to benefit our defense more than your offense, but the offense will gain some benefit from it because you will be sensitive to what the opponent's defense does, if anything.

Defensive Menu

*Most Important Defense—Fast Break Defense

1/4 Court	Purpose
1. Man-to-man	Basic, FB defense
2. Zones	
2-3—Bump	Change
—Swarm	Change, Out-of-bounds
3-2—Drop Middle	Change, Out-of-bounds
*1-3-1	
Point Guard Middle	Change, vs. good post
3. Gimmick—Box & Triangle	Change, stop certain player

1/2 Court

4. Half-Court Trap continuous — Change vs. stall & shot clock 1/2 court offensive out-of-bounds end of period

5. Zone 1-3-1 Point Guard middle 1-2-2 — Change vs. most sideline OB Shot clock—end of period Slow team down and force into a 3-2 offense

6. Man-to-Man, face guard — Stop ball from entering into normal areas

3/4 Court

7. Zone Press back into a zone — Slow a team down, force them to use shot clock

8. Dead Ball Face — Side offensive out-of-bounds

Full-Court

9. 1-2-1-1 — Only after made free-throw One trap and back into Man

10. Dead Ball Face —back to a Man — Coming out of a timeout

11. Man-to-Man — Slow team down—Pick up point guard after makes shot

You are trying to get a feel for your defensive philosophy where everything fits into a slot. Our zone rules and man-to-man rules are entirely the same for the player on the ball. We try to do things differently from any other team in our league. We are talking about empty possessions and empty practices. They are getting ready to play you and are spending their time working on your defenses, offenses, etc., not their own. The more you can do to screw up their practice time, the better! If the ball is in the middle when you are playing defense, that's awful. If the ball is in the middle when you are on offense, that's great. The toughest concept to get across is that we are playing defense to stop the opponent. That's where your game preparation comes in. You must have a plan as to how you are going to stop your opponents.

In closing, remember, your players will be satisfied with what the coach will tolerate.

INDIVIDUAL AND TEAM DEFENSE

If you are going to play on a team, man-to-man defense you must sell it. You must continually emphasize it. For example, 80% of the practice, the defensive segment, will come first. Our breakdown drills will come first. You are sending a message to your team if you do this, especially in the first few weeks of the season. You must stay with it, even if you don't feel good about it after several days.

What are some strengths of this defense? One is the adaptability of the defense. We can move our point of pickup because of our opponent or because of our own personnel. "One" is our man defense. If we are going to pick up full-court, we are in "41." If we pick up 3/4 court, that is "31." Half-court is "21," and the three-point line is "11." With this defense you pinpoint responsibility. Positioning is clearly defined and through the repetition of the breakdown drills, they know where they are supposed to be. There are emotional and psychological advantages. Your defense must be something that your team hangs its hat on. Pride. If someone compliments you on the defense, be sure you tell the team. That feedback is part of the selling job. Then, your team will get extreme confidence in the defense.

What are some of the key components?

1. Conditioning. You must be in great shape. We have started including stance and slides in our preseason conditioning.

2. Courage. You must take the charge and dive for loose balls. Playing with no fear is extremely important.

3. Intelligence. You are in a very aggressive frame of mind in this defense. This is difficult to develop. You are in an attack frame of mind. At times it is hard to think and concentrate at the same time.

4. Habits. You're enforcing these through the breakdown drills.

5. Learning. Some need more time to learn than others.

6. Attitude. It is an attack frame of mind. We want to make you react.

7. Confidence. You must have confidence in your teammates. If I get beat, I must know that my teammate is there to help.

What are some key principles?

1. Vision. See the man and the ball. On the perimeter, we don't mind our players losing sight of the ball sometimes and being a little more man oriented if the man is a three-point threat.

2. Move as the ball moves. Move on the pass.

3. Communication. (Diagram 1) This is very hard to develop. You must talk. You must give them a common language, what you want them to say. "Talk to the ball." If X1 is guarding the ball and X2 is contesting on the wing, we want X2 to be talking to X1 while he is contesting. It helps both players. You must emphasize this in your breakdown drills.

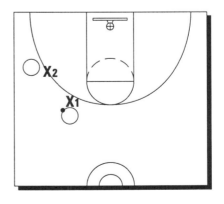

Diagram 1

4. Aggressiveness. Play the defense without fouling. You must educate your players about team fouls. If you have six fouls and a substitute enters the game with no personal fouls, he must know that if he gets just one foul it will send the other team to the line.

5. Influencing outside. We want to keep the ball out of the middle.

6. Denying ball reversal. Get it on the side, keep it on the side. Don't let them reverse the ball.

Breakdown Drills. The key to this is how to pressure the ball. Are you up on the ball, are you making the ballhandler turn his back? Your ball pressure drills all start with your stance. We especially do this with our freshmen. We talk about three defensive steps, individually and with the group. On the practice plan it is listed as "stance and steps." Either the left or right foot is forward. We are rarely in a square stance because we are always influencing the ball somewhere. If you have either the right or left foot forward, you can dictate to the dribbler where you want the ball to go. We may start with all players having their left foot forward. When I say "retreat" I want them to take one step back with the rear foot and slide back with the front foot. With "advance" they are in their stance and move forward just one step. "Swing" means change directions with emphasis on throwing the elbow to help in the turn, pivoting on the rear foot. Then I take a ball and we "guard the dribbler." If I take a step toward them, they retreat, if I back up, they advance. When I pick up the dribble, "used" and they close out on the dribbler.

(Diagram 2)   The zig-zag drill. We go one trip down and back. You can change this drill and make it more gamelike. For example, go zig-zag to half-court and then it is 1/1 live so the defense must influence the ball to the outside when it gets to the half-court line. The good defensive man will be aware of where he is on the court and will begin to influence the ball

even before it gets to half-court. Another variation is to have the offensive man pick up the ball several times so that the defense can react to the "dribble used." We want the defense to "trace the ball." Now the defense is in a square stance.

(Diagram 3)   Influence drill. The defense dribbles hard to half-court and then passes the ball back to the offensive man still using the outside third of the court, the offensive man dribbles as fast as he can down the court and the defense must pick up such a way so as to control the dribbler to the outside. We can pick up "21" or "11." We can also start to work on the footwork of taking a charge. This is a zig-zag series. You can't do all of these every day, just mix them up.

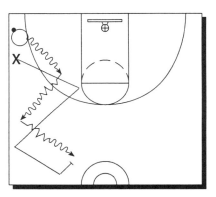

Diagram 2

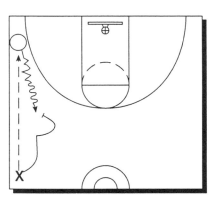

Diagram 3

(Diagram 4) Contesting slides. The key thing in the contesting drills is talking. Emphasize talking. When we contest on the wing, we are splitting the offensive man with our front foot, we have a hand in the passing lane and we are up on him. We must learn the footwork to contest from the foul line extended to the block. As the offense breaks to the block, we want the defensive man to open up to the ball. Don't turn your head away from the ball. The defensive man opens up when he gets to the lane. Coach has the ball and is the passer. The coach can change the drill a little by taking it in a little on the drive and the defensive man must help and recover, or as we call it "fake trap." The coach can also shoot and the defensive player must rebound. All this is done without an offense, 0/1.

Contest the driving lane. This is the same thing except it is 1/1. Work on contesting, influence outside, pressure the ball, trace the ball and keep it out of the middle.

(Diagram 5) If the ball gets to the wing, the stance is more of a square stance. Don't let him get into the middle.

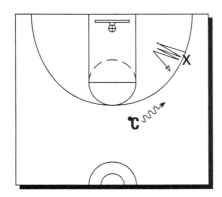

Diagram 4

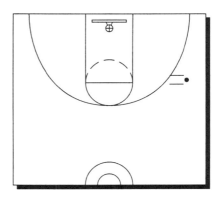

Diagram 5

(Diagram 6) Shallow cut. Now the defensive man must contest on the top when the ball is on the side.

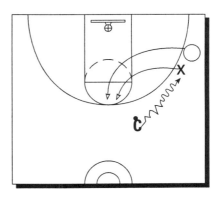

Diagram 6

(Diagram 7) Start with ball on the wing, coach is on top. Start the drill by tracing the ball. No dribble is used. When the ball is passed to the coach, then it is 1/1 deny again.

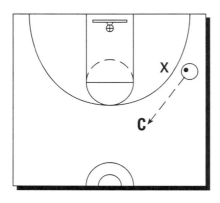

Diagram 7

Diagram 9

(Diagram 8)   Add a post. We work on the footwork for digging into the post. I know this depends to a great extent on how you are playing each player. If you are guarding a good three-point shooter, then you aren't going to be really digging in, but to practice the footwork, we will work on this drill. When the ball goes in, we dig in with our back to the baseline. The defensive man must see both the ball and his man on the perimeter.

(Diagram 9)   Six-point contesting. Coach has the ball. Start with deny the entry. As the offense starts through, deny the backdoor cut. Then open up in the lane in a helpside position.

(Diagram 10)   The fourth point is to take away the flash pivot. The defender must be physical.

(Diagram 11)   The offense then goes to the block and the defense must again deny in post defense. The sixth point is the rebound when the coach shoots.

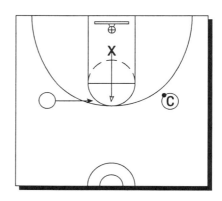

Diagram 10

Diagram 8

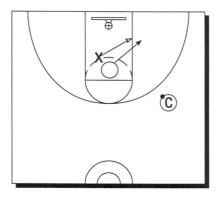

Diagram 11

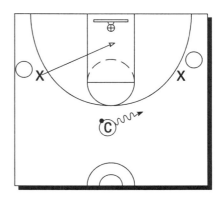

Diagram 13

(Diagram 12)   Close out. On the skip-pass, the defensive player who has opened up in the lane must now close out on the offensive wing and it is now a 1/1 situation. Emphasize that the defense must be under control in the last several steps. The offense is limited to three dribbles.

(Diagram 14)   Start the offense on the block and cross.

(Diagram 15)   Start with 2/2 on top. This drill really shows who cannot control the dribbler.

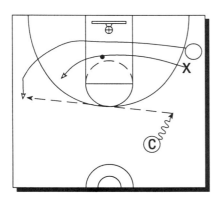

Diagram 12

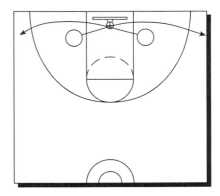

Diagram 14

(Diagram 13)   Two-man drills. Two-man contesting. We are now adding the helpside position. When the ball moves to one side, the ballside is denying the pass, and the other defensive man is in the help position in the lane.

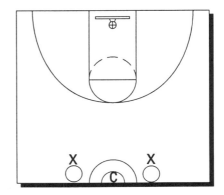

Diagram 15

(Diagram 16)   2/2 on the side with a down-screen. We want X2 to "follow his footsteps." Get tight on him. 2 should curl, X1 will bump 2 who is curling.

(Diagram 17)   Backscreen. Just get through. Give your players some freedom, and let them do it. We don't give them a lot of rules, but we don't switch. We tell them to talk early. Don't allow yourself to be screened. But, the key to all of this is ball pressure. Do you have pressure on the ball. That's where it starts.

Diagram 16

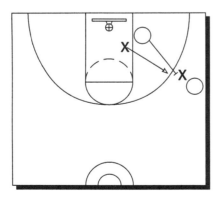

Diagram 17

(Diagram 18)   3/3, contest and interchange. We get more and more gamelike. X2 is denying the wing

pass. The two offensive men on the other side are interchanging. A teaching key for X1 is "don't turn your back." X3 should be the man doing the talking.

(Diagram 19)   How do you defend flex? You are going to play against it, so don't wait until the day before the game. We want to force the cutter low. Jump to the ball.

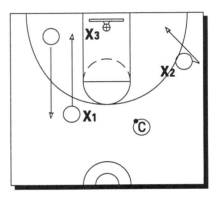

Diagram 18

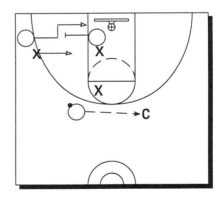

Diagram 19

(Diagram 20)   Post defense. We contest 3/4 on the side of the ball. If the ball is on top, I don't stand next to him, I am off him. I don't think you can give them rules, but you must give them some guidelines. If the ball gets below you, then you get around to the other side. Get some "poke aways." "Break contact" to adjust your position.

(Diagram 21)   You might start with the defense behind the post. This is difficult. If you get caught behind, you must slide with him. You must drill this live, give them some experience.

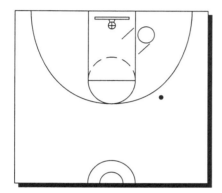

Diagram 20

Diagram 21

(Diagram 22)   High post contesting. We will contest the pass to the high post. We must work on opening up to the ball if the post breaks low. We never start the game playing off the high post. We want to attack. If the high post catches the ball, we get up on him. We want him to put it on the floor.

(Diagram 23)   We trap all ball screens. I don't think you can do it differently for different opponents. Either you trap it or you don't. We do.

Diagram 22

Diagram 23

(Diagram 24)   Shell drill, 4-man jump. We want them jumping in the direction of the pass. We do not allow the ball to reverse. There is the ballside and the helpside.

(Diagram 25)   Now add a coach in the post. Check on the digging technique.

Diagram 24

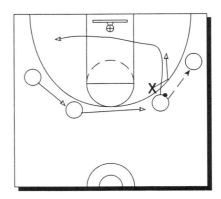

Diagram 26

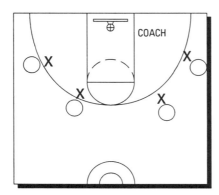
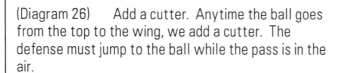

Diagram 25

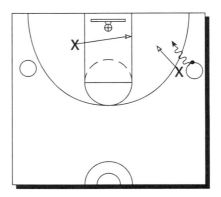

Diagram 27

(Diagram 26)   Add a cutter. Anytime the ball goes from the top to the wing, we add a cutter. The defense must jump to the ball while the pass is in the air.

(Diagram 27)   Same drill except the coach can call "drive it." When that happens, the offense drives it about half speed, and we will check the rotation of the defense.

(Diagram 28)   6/4. Anytime the ball goes to the corner, drive it until you are stopped. Help and recover. They must really talk.

(Diagram 29)   5/5, half-court change. When I yell "change," the ball is placed on the floor. The offense becomes defense, and the defense becomes offense, but on the change you can't guard the same person who was guarding you. This forces your group to talk. Another drill is "random movement." Coach has the ball and it is 5/5. Coach passes the ball to someone and it is live. You can check defensive position. You can roll the ball in, loose ball. You can shoot, check block-out. You can check transition defense if you miss the shot.

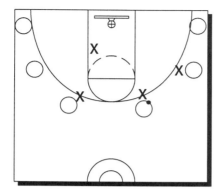

Diagram 28

Diagram 29

(Diagram 31)   You can also double down from the shooter and rotate another perimeter man over to guard the shooter.

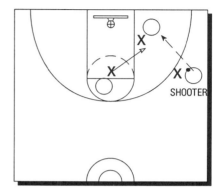

Diagram 30

Diagram 31

In a typical practice, defensively we could run: stance and steps, 5 minutes; contesting live, 5 minutes; two-man contesting, 5 minutes; contest and interchange, 5 minutes; four-man jump checking cutters, 5 minutes; 5/5 random movement 5 minutes. From your random movement, you may go just 10 minutes of 5/5 where you are really emphasizing defense and in transition on the miss.

Question: How do you double on the post if you are defending a good shooter?

Answer: (Diagram 30)   We double down off of the other big man.

TEACHING TRANSITION

Are you going to run? If so, are you going to run on made shots? Certainly you will run on missed ones. We decided that we would run on everything. But you must be careful your team realizes when they have the break. You must work on transition habits. We do a lot with three-man drills.

(Diagram 1)   We do a three-man weave. We weave down, but come back in lanes, the fast break. We are simulating a 3/2 or a 3/1 situation. We come to a jump stop with the ball in the middle, make the pass to the man cutting for the basket.

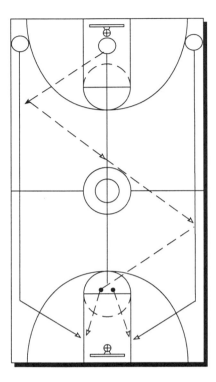

Diagram 2

Diagram 1

(Diagram 2)   We also do three-man passing where each man stays in his lane, ball comes to a jump stop in the middle. We run this both with a layup and also with a jump shot. We emphasize the power layup, square up the shoulders and go up with two feet.

(Diagram 3)   Next we will run this and the ball will be returned to the middle where the middle man gets the shot. We also run a 3/2 in one direction and a 2/1 coming back.

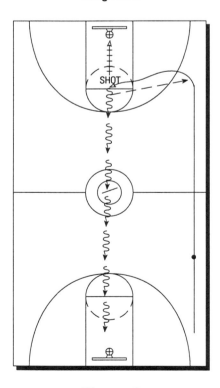

Diagram 3

(Diagram 4)   3/3 recognition. Three A's go against three B's. Then B's come back and a coach will send in one or two D's to play defense at the other end and the B's must recognize the situation. If the coach sends in less than three, then the third D comes in and touches the middle circle when the ball crosses mid-court and then gets into the defense.

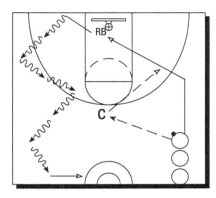

Diagram 5

(Diagram 6)   Dribble to the foul line, stop, jump shot. Then have them work on some dribble moves and drives on the power layup. We like the inside out move where you keep the ball in the same hand. We also use the crossover dribble.

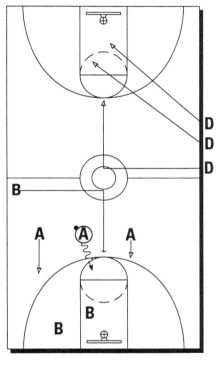

Diagram 4

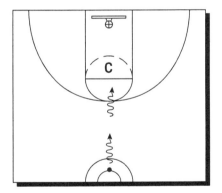

Diagram 6

(Diagram 5)   Individual breakdown, transition shooting. Pass to the coach, get the return pass for the power layup. Get their own rebound, and don't just dribble back, but simulate dribbling against pressure. Next, same thing except shoot a short jump shot. Then take shot fake, one dribble to the middle, jump shot. Then shot fake, and take it to the baseline for a jump shot.

(Diagram 7)   Numbered break. It ends like this. The first big man down goes to the block on the ballside. 2 and 3 stay wide, we call them the sprint men. We call our break "Sprint." 1 is the "handler." The first big man is the "lead," the other big man is the "trail."

(Diagram 8)   A drill for "lead," the first big man down. 4 passes to the coach and is really running. He gets the return pass, many times over his shoulder. He needs to gather himself and go up strong.

Diagram 7

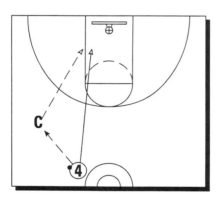

Diagram 8

(Diagram 9)   If he doesn't get the ball on the way down, he will get the ball on the block.

(Diagram 10)   As a "trail," 5 passes to coach and gets a return pass for the three-point shot, if he can. Perhaps he needs to get in closer.

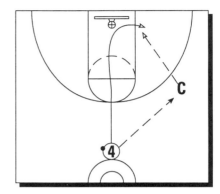

Diagram 9

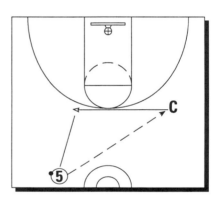

Diagram 10

(Diagram 11)   A rebound and outlet drill. Run it on both sides. Throw the ball off the board, get a two handed rebound, and make the outlet pass to the coach. Coach moves to different spots. You can also use this drill as an offensive rebounding drill. Get the rebound, score, then take it out of bounds to simulate running on the made field goal.

(Diagram 12)   On the finish of "sprint," 1 can dribble to the side and that means that 2 will run a shallow cut. The "handler" will call this as he comes across half-court. 5 will screen for 2.

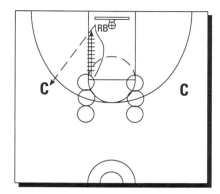

Diagram 11

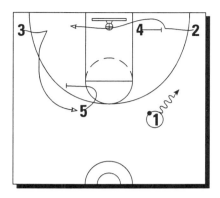

Diagram 13

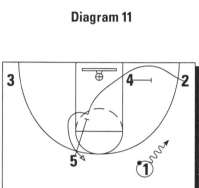

Diagram 12

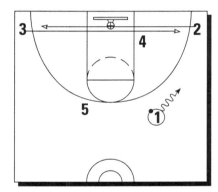

Diagram 14

(Diagram 13)   Or, 2 can run a circle, and 5 will screen away for 3. We can then go into motion from this.

(Diagram 14)   Cross. We cross 2 and 3.

(Diagram 15)   Top. 5 sets the perimeter screen for 1.

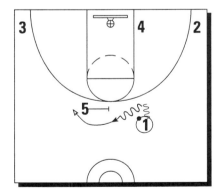

Diagram 15

(Diagram 16)   To get us into our secondary break, we would stagger away. 1 passes to 2, and 5 and 1 then set a staggered screen for 3 who gets the pass from 2. It isolates 4 at the low post. 3 can shoot the three-point shot or curl down the lane.
We will practice this by doing our breakdown drills and adding audibles. We may run a 5-man weave down, and run "sprint" back with an audible.

Diagram 16

(Diagram 17)   You can also run off of a free-throw alignment. One thing we have done is to put 2 and 3 down the floor. We call this "fly." It stretches the defense. 2 and 3 can cross as 1 is pushing it down the floor. We have had teams worry so much about 2 and 3 crossing that 1 dribbled all the way for a layup. You run your offense 5/0. Why not run your break into your motion? It makes it more game like. You can start at half-court if you don't want them running the whole floor. We often do this a little on the pregame session. We actually do a pregame lift. It wakes them up a little. If we have an evening game, we will do it about 4:00 p.m. If we have a 1:00 p.m. game, we will do it in the morning. They dress out in their practice gear for the session and the lift.

Many times we will end practice by running transition instead of sprints. We may have to make fifteen in a row. You are using the transition drill as a conditioner, but the ball is involved.

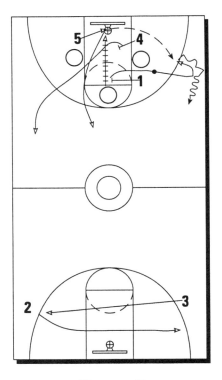

Diagram 17

The Three—Two Zone

You should see the tapes that come in for the draft of the NBA. The 21st pick is very important because either that player has to help you or he must be a tradable player. So you must have a degree of familiarity with players and we just don't see them during the year. You should see the zone offenses on these tapes. Let me give you the general parameters of the zone and then let's go after the zone. Then, if we have time, some of the NBA zone.

There is "playing" a zone, and there is "teaching" a zone. You can teach a zone over a period of time each day with broken down slides, very quickly. You don't abort your man-for-man because the concept of the zone is that the ball on the wing and at the high post is played with man-for-man premise. So, as the ball goes to the wing, how do you want that played in a one-on-one situation, as in a man-to-man? You either make him go into the middle or jam him down the sideline, whatever your concept is, that is how it must be played. It is not just the situation with hand up, jumping around, looking, whatever.

You play this as you would in a man defense, particularly if he takes one dribble, he can't go by you. You aren't swarming him, but you don't want him comfortable so that he can sit there and pick out his receivers. The zone is good, it neutralizes. Think of all of the teams that run motion. They must stop and attack, and they don't seem to be as functional. This is what we see on tape today.

We teach the 3-2 first to get the basic slides down, which are applicable to any zone that you use. Then, we will "tweek it" if the team is coming down with an unusual set.

(Diagram 1) The general rule is the point man is right at the top of the circle. The reason he is at the top of the circle is that he doesn't want to elongate the zone, thereby making it an easy entry into the post. If there is a great three-point shooter, you might edge it up a little, but by and large, he stays at the top of the circle. The wings have their inside foot in the elbow area so that there is a compact view and that the pass must go around the zone or over the zone, which gives the zone time to make the next slide. If the wings stay wide and the zone is pierced with the dribble or a bounce pass or whatever, the zone is now in difficulty. So this compact view seems to take away that type of mind set. Plus, it limits the gaps, where the teams are taught to go at gaps. The gaps don't seem to be as presentable. They are there, but they aren't there.

For the utopian set, let's say that the ball is passed from the top to the wing. This is a drill, this is how it is taught. On the pass, X2 gets out there, he's all the way out. X2 plays him according to your theory. We like to play him on the top shoulder a little because if he dribbles into the elbow area, that is a damage point. If you gave me a choice, I would probably shade him down. I've seen teams play him almost laterally so that he must stay on the side, but that gives him a channel to the baseline. So, I would shade him. That's a big point. As this occurs, X1 shifts to the elbow area. He knows that while he is protecting the elbow area for flash-ups, if that ball is passed back on top, he must be able to recover and come up and play that ball with some reasonable pressure. X3, the weakside, drops to a level where, and this is a basic rule that helps all offside screens, he can go get the rebound and if the ball is skipped over, he can go out and play the wing. That is a crucial slide.

(Diagram 2) The elbow is important because good zone offenses get somebody to the elbow in some fashion. They either start them there, or it is more of a problem for the zone if they bring him there from the opposite side.

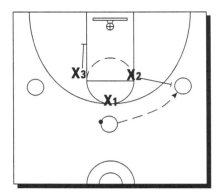

Diagram 1

Diagram 2

coming in and dunks will occur because the other team has brains too. There should be no panic or embarrassment if this occurs. The back men should not be deep because that gives the offense a big area to move between the wing and the back. If you can get them up very high, that would be fantastic because the offense would not be able to force feed it into the post due to the compactness of the zone. But, you must put pressure on the ball, particularly on the wing where most of these dunks come from.

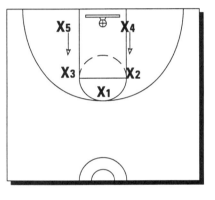

Diagram 3

If you are coaching against a zone, you must get someone to come up and someone to come over, but get someone to that elbow. This causes a problem for the zone because of the movement that takes place after the ball is caught in the high post, because now the zone has shifted to a degree and the movement coming in back of the zone is much more productive to the offense than putting someone there in the first place. So, you must take away the direct route to that elbow area. That is why the point guard is always dropping to the elbow area.

(Diagram 3)   Let's put in the back men. The back men will straddle the line as high up as the offense will allow them. You will occasionally have lobs

(Diagram 4)   This is a walk-through process to get the players to understand their slide positions as the ball is moved. This is the last drill of every practice, about seven or eight minutes. Move the ball around and occasionally try to hit the post. There are seven people positioned against the zone. No shots are taken. But this covers most, if not all, of the situations that could occur. If you had a two-guard front, you would have a 2-3-4. At times you can add a high post to this drill also. If the pass is made to the wing, X2 plays him hard and X1 slides to the elbow. We went down and put this in for Navy when Robinson was there. They didn't want Robinson going out into the corner at all. This is the secret of the zone, that is, making your own adaptions. This drill shows the basic moves. These slides are about 60 years old. They were devised to offset superior talent. They had to do something to survive, so they came up with the zone concept. But, back to this drill. On the pass to the wing, X4 gets into the "cheat" position. He must get ready for the next pass. X5 is protecting the basket area and protecting against the flash up.

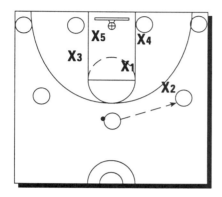

Diagram 4

(Diagram 5)   If there is a gap, it is here, in front of X5. We are alright at the elbow because it is crowded there, but that is the gap that the offside player would look for. So, X5 is there to stop the direct pass into the paint or ride the guy higher if he cuts into the post area. At that time, X4 must not go out too far. X3 drops down on the weakside.

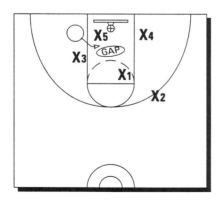

Diagram 5

(Diagram 6)   If there is a skip-pass, the wing, X3, always has the first pass over the defense. This is another drill. You can't ask X5 to protect the middle and protect the corner on the skip-pass. It can't be done. X1 moves from elbow to elbow, X2 drops into the lane, X4 and X5 move to the ballside. How long does X3 stay with the ball? As long as he has it.

Diagram 6

(Diagram 7)   If X5 wants to call off X3, then that is an adjustment that you can make.

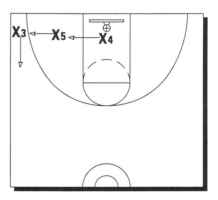

Diagram 7

(Diagram 8)   This is what Navy did. Every pass that went to the corner, either skip or wing to corner, X3, covered. Robinson, X5, never went out.

He bluffed a little. X3 always chased the ball down. They took the 3-2 and turned it into a 2-3. On the other side they did it differently. So, it was a 3-2 on one side and the 2-3 concept on the other.

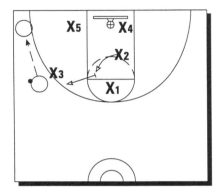

Diagram 8

(Diagram 9)   If the ball goes to the corner from the wing, there are several concepts. X2 can block the lane back. Just get in line so that the pass cannot be passed back.

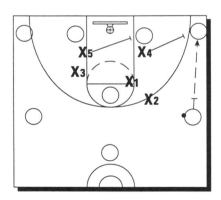

Diagram 9

(Diagram 10)   Or X2 can go into the corner to double-team the ball, especially if he is a good shooter. If X1 takes the wing on the return pass, then X2 runs an "x" move to the elbow area.

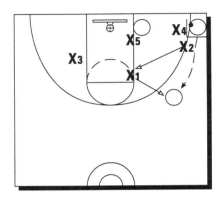

Diagram 10

(Diagram 11)   You can also keep X1 at the elbow and X2 can follow the ball back to the wing.

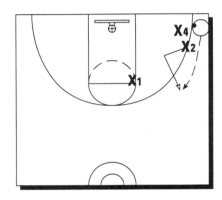

Diagram 11

(Diagram 12)   If the offense has a good post game, X2 can drop almost into the post area and front and it almost becomes a box. X1 moves back and must be in good position to play the man on top. On the quick reversal, the point must be taught to attack to the outside. Don't come straight up. But when the ball gets into the middle of the floor, the wings, X2 and X3, are back where they belong.

Diagram 12

(Diagram 13)   What do you do when the passer cuts? The cutter is honored for at least two steps, and then is checked off. This is where the match-up theory comes in a little.

Diagram 13

(Diagram 14)   Suppose the dribbler comes out and starts to split the zone? As soon as he dribbles, it is a quick double-team. Any splits from the corner or the wing cause a double-team effect.

(Diagram 15)   How about if the dribbler goes down, as more teams should do? There is no one in the corner. This then becomes a switching man-to-man concept. The wing takes him until the base calls him off. The wing then goes high. An

alternative is for the wing to stay with the dribbler all the way and for the base to remain inside.

Diagram 14

Diagram 15

(Diagram 16)   High post coverage. When the ball goes into the high post, one of the base men is the up man. The base men will constantly communicate. In the ideal world, X5 will come up and play the high post man-to-man, with X4 moving into the middle to cover the low post. X4 will have the first pass into the low post area. For the wing men, X2 and X3, this is difficult at first because it is contrary to basketball instincts, if they can steal that ball, yes, do it. But once the ball goes into the high post, don't worry about the high post. Both wings should drop back several steps to be able to handle the first pass that comes out of the high post to the wings.

DON CASEY

This is an unusual move, but necessary to save the zone. The wing has the same rule as for the skip-pass. If the pass is made over you, you chase it down. The point will drop into the high post area.

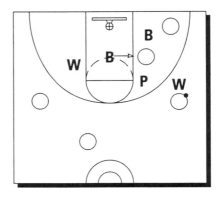

Diagram 18

(Diagram 19) If the ball gets into the side post, he is covered by the back man opposite. Cover both elbows and the weakside box. The slides are built in to meet the problems. This is what we see the most in tapes, somewhat of a high/low situation and a weakside action.

Diagram 16

(Diagram 17) Drill, 6-on-5. The base men must communicate. The wing men must drop and then take the pass into the corner.

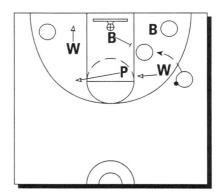

Diagram 19

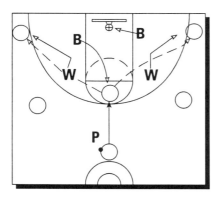

Diagram 17

(Diagram 20) Two-man front. Ball is on the top, out of the middle.

(Diagram 18) Side post, same rule. Play match up at the middle post.

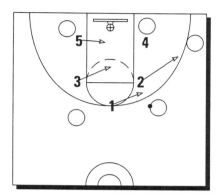

Diagram 20

were pure and the wing would come up with the pass. This did not work too well.

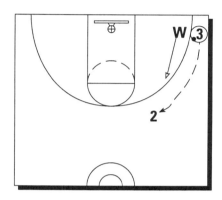

Diagram 22

(Diagram 21)   When the ball is passed from 2 to 3, in days gone by, the point man would drop to the elbow and then as the ball went to 3, would continue on and drop in front of 4. But this has faded out. The offense that players in the past had trouble with was the 2-2-1. So, they had to come up with a move to cover the wing. They invented the match-up. The point will drop back into the high post area with the wing dropping low enough to be able to cover 3 in the corner. The point and the wing are in your basic slide drills that we all do. We don't want the high post area to be vacant.

(Diagram 23)   Now, if 3 ran the baseline, the wing just went with him. It was actually a box and one, but it solved the problem. This is the type of adjustment that you can make.

Diagram 23

Diagram 21

(Diagram 22)   Once 3 made the pass, he would go to the other side of the floor. In the early days, we

(Diagram 24)   How about this? What are you going to do about the high post? If the ball goes into the corner, do you want to send the point man with him and then check him off to one of the baseline men? That seems to be the easier way to handle it.

Diagram 24

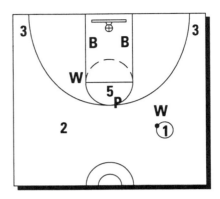

Diagram 26

(Diagram 25)   If the point was on the ball and the ball was swung, then the wing would have to come out and take the ball and the point would take the high post. But the high post is stepping out and screening the point, which becomes a problem.

(Diagram 27)   If the wing had the ball and the ball was dribbled down, you must be concerned about 5 breaking down the lane and 2 coming over to the high post.

The question was asked of me, would you play the zone as much if you were coaching in college? My answer was yes, no, no, yes. I think that you must have some activity to disrupt the rhythm of a man offense.

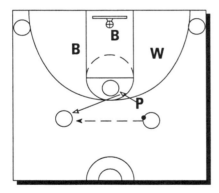

Diagram 25

(Diagram 26)   You can also run this with the wing taking the ball and the point remaining in the high-post area. The point will deny the easy entry pass and influence them not to come in with the dribble.

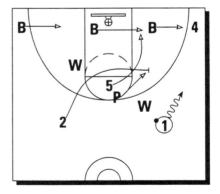

Diagram 27

(Diagram 28)   Here is an adjustment into a 1-1-3. The top man took the ball. If there was an early entry pass, X3 would bluff at the wing, but X2 would come out and take the ball.

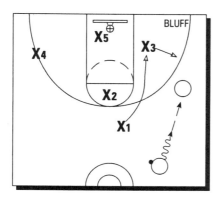

Diagram 28

(Diagram 29)   Against a 1-4. The best part of this is that the defense knows exactly where the offense is going to be. The same rules are in effect. The wing will take the first pass. The higher the baseline men are, the better. If the pass is made to 3, the base man will bluff at 3, but the wing will cover 3. The elbows and the boxes must be covered. If they aren't there, they are coming.

Diagram 29

(Diagram 30)   X4 must give the illusion that he can pick off a pass. All he needs to do is to pick off one. The zone is in a protection area. This is what the 6 or 8 offensive man drill is for. If the wing breaks through, out really isn't a problem. The zone has a chance to react.

What would be your attack against a sloughing, switching man-to-man? That's what you have to put in against a zone. If they are sloughing, I must take the ball to them to freeze them and sneak in from the back and go over the top. That's it. You must get the ball to the player who can make things happen, who has a "game," and put him in where he operates the best.

Diagram 30

(Diagram 31)   This is the universal set. Do you want the ball coming straight down the middle or shift it a little to one side or the other? The offensive player would be one step below the defensive guard. Put your back man behind the zone to elongate it, but don't take him to the corner where he is non-productive. Let's say that the defense is a 2-1-2. If they are matching and they came up at the wingman with the ball, he would have a decision to make. The base man of the offense could step out a little and the wing with the ball could move lower.

(Diagram 32)   The offside wing could flash to the post area and 1 could fill. This means that the middle man on the zone would have to come up and that would give you a chance for some cross court activity so 1 cannot just stand on top.

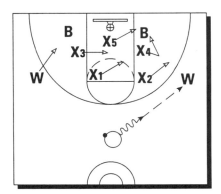

Diagram 31

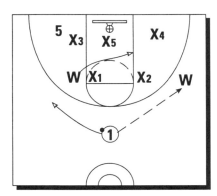

Diagram 32

(Diagram 33)   If the ball gets into the high post, then the point will fill and be ready for the pass back.

Diagram 33

(Diagram 34)   The wings can be tight, almost looking at the ball as it comes up the floor. 4 can make a quick move up the lane. This move will hurt the zone because 4 can pass down to 5 or to the weakside wing sliding down.

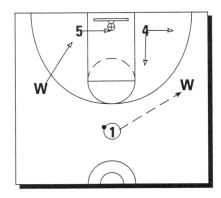

Diagram 34

(Diagram 35)   If you like the 1-3-1, don't put 4 in the middle, put him on the side. It's the 1-3-1 concept but has a high/low opposite each other so the defense doesn't have easy slides.   4 can step out and reverse the ball and then flash low.

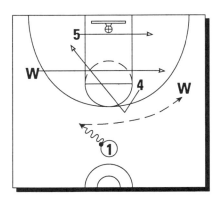

Diagram 35

(Diagram 36)   If 4 gets the pass and the middle man in the zone comes up, your angles are excellent.

The back man on the zone must come out to take the wing and 5 cuts across behind.

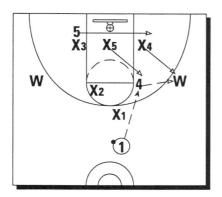

Diagram 36

(Diagram 37)   Quick dribble from a 1-2-2 offense. 1 passes to 3 who dribbles into the corner. What happens? What is the decision-making process? More than likely, they will try to keep the big man in and follow the dribbler all the way down. If 5 comes up, he must be occupied by the middle man. 1 follows the dribbler, 2 goes into the comfort zone.

Diagram 37

(Diagram 38)   What are you trying to accomplish? 4 could step out as 3 comes across. That's fine.

Diagram 38

(Diagram 39)   But you can also dive 4 to the low post and 5 is coming behind 3. 1 fills at the top. There are things happening that should catch the zone.

Diagram 39

(Diagram 40)   What does the dribble move do to the defense? The double dribble where 1 dribbles toward the wing and 2 goes down. 4 comes high and 1 reverses off of 4's screen. You will be surprised how many times 1 can now pass to 2 with 5 breaking across the lane.

Diagram 40

Diagram 42

(Diagram 41)   You can do the same thing from the 1-3-1.

Diagram 43

Diagram 41

(Diagram 44)   The ball is passed back to 1. If the forward passes up, he breaks down. The center comes across, the other forward breaks out.

(Diagram 42)   Here is a variation with 4 coming high and 1 following the dribble of 3.

(Diagram 43)   The All Purpose. What if you have a big player who can't score? You are up high to go low. Break in back of the defense, coming later to the post. Ballside guard down, off side guard over, forward over. When the pass is made, the forward cuts low across the lane. You have turned the 2-3 into a 1-3-1.

Diagram 44

(Diagram 45)   If 2 passes down to the forward, 2 goes across. 5 steps out for the pass and passes to 1. 1 dribbles across the top. 5 follows the ball.

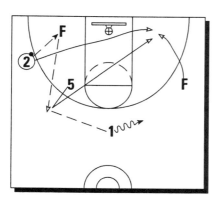

Diagram 45

(Diagram 46)   You want to get some movement out of 1 so when he passes to the forward, 1 and the other forward can interchange.

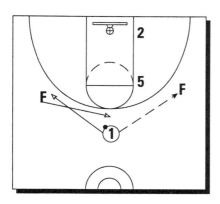

Diagram 46

(Diagram 47)   If it goes into the post, this is a high/low situation. The rule is that if you are on the box and nothing is happening, get to the other box, get away so that there can be some penetration.

(Diagram 48)   If the pass goes into 5 from on top, both forwards fade. This does create movement with timing.

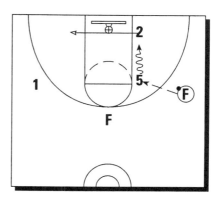

Diagram 47

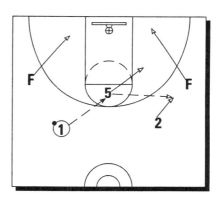

Diagram 48

(Diagram 49)   What do they do in the NBA? Think about your three best players. One of them is probably the player handling the ball. 1 is dribbling up the floor, 4 is trailing, 3 on the wing. 2 will come off of the post.

(Diagram 50)   He will curl, fade, or come straight out. Now the game begins. This is a play set unto itself.

Diagram 49

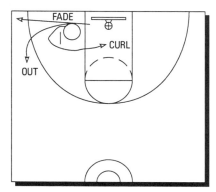

Diagram 50

(Diagram 51)   If he comes out and his man is trailing, rather than going over the top, what does he do? He will curl and have a good chance to get the ball.

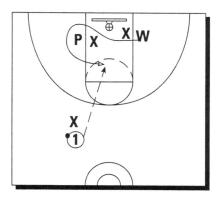

Diagram 51

(Diagram 52)   The other aspect is that if the defensive center steps out to bump the cutter, then the offensive post will screen and seal and 1 can pass into the post.

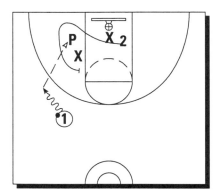

Diagram 52

(Diagram 53)   If 2 breaks out and gets the pass from 1, 1 goes away. 2 and the post have a two-man game.

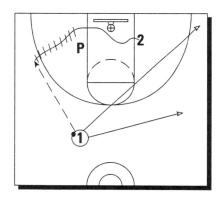

Diagram 53

(Diagram 54)   4 will break to the basket and 2 sees that the defense is under the gun. There is nobody at the elbow. They will drive for the elbow as much as they can. They have the green light for that.

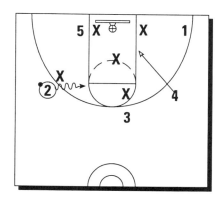

Diagram 54

(Diagram 55)   5 can screen on either side.

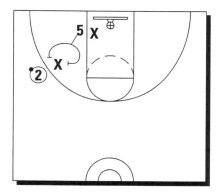

Diagram 55

(Diagram 56)   2 has the ball. 1 will curl around 3 and 3 will pop out. 1 then will sacrifice his body for 5 and screen 5's man so that 5 can come across for a reasonable screen. These are the quick hitters and the decision making factors that are going on in the league.

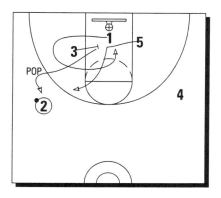

Diagram 56

Shooting—The Lost Art

Note: The following presentation was done in a gymnasium with players to demonstrate. All instructions are for a right-handed shooter.

There has been a serious decline over the last five years in the skill of shooting, both field goals and free-throws, in the basic techniques and skill development. As coaches, we do drills, we do plays, but what we don't do is to look at the root of the problem. You must get to the young players who are eventually going to be in your program and teach them to shoot. When they have baskets that are too high or basketballs that are too heavy, we are setting them up to fail. Do you know why your players can't shoot? The bottom line is that you don't teach them. How many of you have told your players that they must square up on the shot? How many of you have shown them why they don't square up? That's the big thing. You must coach them before they make a mistake. That is the role you are in.

I don't care what offense you run. I don't care what defense you run. Plays don't make the players. Players make the plays. When your players are taught to shoot, make sure that they do the same thing every time. Practice makes permanent. You must change the bad habits and you must be knowledgeable in order to change bad habits.

The name of the game in shooting is alignment. I want to go over what I call my **Top Ten List of Shot Killers:**

1. The index finger is not in the center of the ball. It must be in line with the forearm. If you grip the ball wrong, you can't shoot it correctly.

2. Footwork and stance are not in balance or sequence. Do I want a jump stop? No! I want a jump step, a left-right stop. My left foot is now my pivot foot.

3. Lifting the ball too soon or not to the proper release point.

4. Twisting the lift hand, thumb through the shot. This results in side spin.

5. People jump stop instead of jump step.

6. Not holding the proper follow through. This is what I call "the signature."

7. Watching the ball after the release. Shoot over the front of the rim. Some of the rims have no play in them at all and you must swish it. If you hit the front of the rim it spins the other way and you may get the shot. I really don't want it to hit any rim.

8. Do not lock out the shooting arm. Don't stop with the arm bent.

9. Landing after the shot with no balance. If I come down going forward for two feet, that's how much farther the ball is going to travel.

10. No adjustments, no adjustments, NO ADJUSTMENTS! Some players will take the shot again and again and miss it the same way every time. They will not adjust what they are doing.

I want to go over the three most critical components of the shot.

Three Components of The Shot:

1. Balance.
2. A-line-ment.
3. Judgment.

You must understand these three critical terms. When we talk about balance, we think of a bicycle. You must have balance to ride a bike. We talk about the bicycle stance. We want one foot more forward than the other, just as if you were pedaling a bike. Put your right foot forward. We are talking about little things here. If you turn your foot a little, look what turns with it.

Shooting Sequence:

Stage 1:   Hand Placement—(used a special ball) Put the shooting index finger behind the air valve in center of the ball, lift hand flat on side of ball, cock and lock the wrist to apply proper pressure for grip. Look for wrinkles. You must have your wrist back before you get to the top of the shot. The wrist must already be locked in. The thumbs make a "T." Remember, you must teach this.

Stage 2:   Body Position— Bicycle stance. Foot-knee-elbow-wrist all in alignment to ensure balance. No distortion in body position. Elbow and ball away from the body. Knees flexed, hips square, shoulders square. Sit on the edge of the chair in this position. Make sure to keep the ball and the elbow away from the body.

Stage 3 :   The Lift—Lift the ball to an "L" position. Lift it above your head and just when it goes out of sight, stop! Lock into the "L" position, lift the ball when the jump occurs! Stretch the shooting window up and forward for more control. (You can't see the ball.)

Stage 4:   The Release—Do not watch the ball. The index finger is the last finger to push through the ball. Lock your elbow, roll your wrist over for proper rotation.

Stage 5 :   The Follow Through—Lift the hand straight up with the shooting hand locked over. The follow through is the signature to your shot. Hold it, show it! And value it! When you shoot from the dribble, the left hand goes to the ball, not the ball to the left hand. Now, you have the release, don't watch the ball, push your last finger through the ball, lock your elbows and hold your wrist. Keep your arm straight as long as you can.

Note: The above steps were demonstrated by players. These aspects of the shot were drilled from a sitting position on the edge of a chair. Emphasis was on the lift of the ball into the shooting position. Then the players took three dribbles on the right side of their body (while sitting), and would bring their left hand to the ball, not the ball to the left hand. From the dribble they would lift the ball into shooting position. Then the ball was dribbled with the left hand on the left side and then the ball was changed across the body following the third dribble. In this drill, the ball was taken from the left side of the body to the right hand. Then the ball was lifted to the shooting position.

Drills

(Diagram 1)   Flow Drill. We do about seven or eight things out of this drill. 2 starts at the elbow. 1 has the ball and is on the baseline. Put a cone or a chair in the middle of the lane. Anytime you leave space, you create space. 1 starts to dribble toward 2. 2 will relocate by diving into the lane, and backpedal to the opposite elbow. 1 will make a chest pass or a bounce pass and 2 will go for the layup. 2 will rebound his own shot. I want 2's feet to be facing forward when he finishes backpedaling to the other elbow, and have his inside leg back for the right-handed shooter.

(Diagram 2)   J Block Jumper. We will do the same drill, but now we will take a jumpshot from the area near the first line above the block. We use the glass for this shot. Always shoot for the backboard first, rim second.

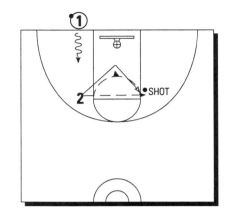

Diagram 3

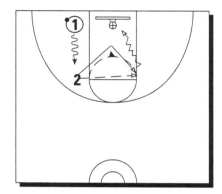

Diagram 1

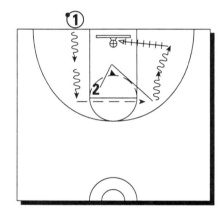

Diagram 4

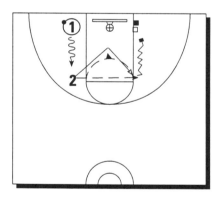

Diagram 2

(Diagram 3)   Wing J. Same drill except that the shot is from the elbow. Step into the shot with the right leg.

(Diagram 4)   Corner shot.

(Diagram 5)   Step out and make the three-point shot.

Diagram 5

(Diagram 6)   If your man can't make the three-point shot, fake the pass and go backdoor. Fake stepping out. Don't have them taking shots that they can't make.

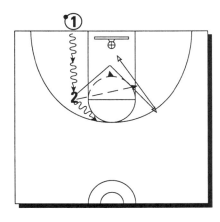

Diagram 6

(Diagram 7)   "1-1-1." One fake, one dribble, one step. Catch the ball, make a jab step, dribble to the center of the free-throw line, shoot. Do this from both sides of the floor.

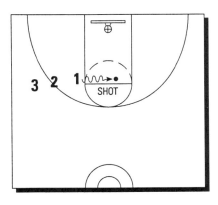

Diagram 7

(Diagram 8)   "Inside pivot motion." 1 passes to 2. 2 steps left, right, and jump shot. 3 then passes to 1. 1 steps right, left, jumpshot. Make the pass to the inside shoulder.

Diagram 8

I have a small court for my young players. I don't want them taking shots beyond their range. I don't want strength to be a factor in the shot. We make all of our players go through all of the drills. We make our big men dribble in the drills just like the guards. There is an old saying, "If you want to keep on getting what you're getting, just keep on doing what you're doing." Things don't happen by chance, they happen by hard work and change. You've got to make change. You have to become the shot doctor.

DEFENSIVE SYSTEM

(Man-to-Man)

Philosophy: Vision, Passion, Commitment, Willingness to work

Four components of a great defender:
1. **Technique**
2. **Communication**
3. **Intensity**
4. **Anticipation**

1. **Technique** is the foundation to reaching full potential.
   - You must demand proper/perfect technique. Repetition/line situations
   - Repetition - Best teacher
   - Game situation - Slippage

2. **Communication** is the key to identifying situations on the court.
   - Key to helping teammates
   - Talking and communicating can cover up physical mistakes (technique)
   - Constant communication
   - If they don't do it in practice, they won't do it in a game
   - You can never talk too much about defense

3. **Intensity**: Teams that play with great intensity are hard to beat!
   - Every play, pass, and shot must be contested!
   - Take pride in how hard you play

4. **Anticipation**:
   - Players must learn or know how to anticipate a play before it happens
   - Players must be able to identify a situation before it happens, act upon it, and perform the task at hand

This is a game of **ACTION VS. REACTION.**
- He who makes the first decision or move usually wins.
- As a defender you want to be the actor and make the offensive player react to you.
- This can only be done if you have the ability to anticipate the next play or pass.

ON BALL

1. Stance:
   - Feet are wide (wider than shoulders)
   - Back is straight with head over the belly button
   - If the ball hasn't been dribbled, hands are up and active (wiping window action)
   - If the ball is dribbled, the inside palm is up with forearm at 90-degree angle:
     —Forearm may make occasional contact with the offensive player to keep spacing
     —Outside hand is active and discouraging any pass

2. **Ball Influence** - sideline/baseline
   - Keep the ball out of the middle
   - Ball above FT line (influence sideline)—feet 45-degree angle, nose on inside shoulder
   - Ball below FT line (influence baseline)—feet parallel to sideline, nose on inside shoulder
   - Ball in middle—"square up," influence sideline (normally to weak hand)

3. **Slides**: Push off foot that is opposite to the direction they want to go (step/slide)

4. **Run-Glide-Run**
   - Player gets beat—Execute RGR
   - Pivot on left heel/right toe
   - Get low, take one long stride, and then pivot back to your stance
   Note: Turn your hips

CLOSE OUTS

They occur a lot if you play our type of defense
Players in proper helpside
Position invites the skip-pass

1. **Above FT**: Run two-thirds distance; get low, throw hands back in air; stutter-step to a wide stance—weight on heels; nose on inside shoulder.

2. **Below FT**: Head up or straight to them; take step to outside to have nose on inside shoulder

3. **Take Away**: Pass to Post
   Direct Drive
   Shot

ONE PASS AWAY

1. Penetrating Pass - Point - Wing
   - Stop this - Advantage
   - Back to the ball, legs bent, one arm-length away from player
   - Ear in chest of offensive player
   - See man and ball
   - Offensive makes quick more backdoor
   - "Close back"—turn head and find ball

2. Non-Penetrating Pass
   - Player to take one step offense
   - The line of the ball and have arm in lane

Depending on match-ups and personnel, you could use this adjustment on a penetrating pass.

HELPSIDE RULES

1. **Two or more passes away**
   - We try to put five defensive players where they put three
   - Split the court
   - Teach low—Point ball—Point man

Head never stops moving (swivel)

Great helpside defenders anticipate! Alert! Active! Talking!

Converting from Ballside to Helpside: "Open up—cross over step—Get there." Move on the pass!

Flash—Cuts—Helpside—Denial Stance

Make contact before mid-point

Anticipate backdoor—close back

CONCLUSION

Defense:
- Teach pressure system rules first
- Don't allow players to deviate

Season progresses:
- You may play certain post players behind, rather than front, and cover down.
- You may play certain shooters in total denial
- You may take one step off on a bad match-up

I want to recruit players who can pressure the ball. We may make adjustments until we have the personnel.

Many of you can't recruit every position, but they can all be taught to defend.

Offensive Concepts

1. What do you want each player to give you offensively?
   a. Define roles
   b. Make a role players role important
      Offensively: Don't waste anyone offensively because the object of the game is to score.
      (1) Pass Ahead for Layup   2 points
      (2) One Offensive Rebound Score   2 points
      (3) Four Free-Throws   <u>4 points</u>
                                        8 points

2. Zone Offense Concepts to Think About:
   a. Bang action
   b. Same side up; weakside over action

3. Concept of Midline for Post Play:
   a. Own the midline
   b. Also look into the mini-lane

4. The Game is Turning into a Penetration Game in College:
   a. Penetration boxes
   b. Spot up game
   c. Shot fake penetration—quick penetration

5. OER Chart or Shot Analysis: Value of the ball is important, but in the game, a, b, c are more important.
   a. P = 10' and in
   b. J = 10' — three-point line
   c. 3 = three-point shot

6. Lines of Attack vs. Half-Court Trap: We see scramble defenses often.
   a. Lane lines
   b. Get to hash mark
   c. Midline

7. Staggered Screen Thoughts:
   a. Make sure BIG is second man
   b. Single—Single
      Double—Single
   c. Baseline Staggers

8. Screen On Ball:
   a. Consider low wing spot
   b. Passer is screener

9. Sprint Break Thoughts:
   a. Do you want pass break or dribble break?
   b. Win sprint to half-court

10. Pro Time:
    a. Game is individual improvement
    b. We spend 15-20 minutes per day shooting
    c. Types of shots we work on:
       (1)   Catch—shoot
       (2)   Shots off cuts
       (3)   Catch—quick penetrate
       (4)   Catch—shot fake penetration
    d. How we practice these:
       (1)   Technique or form shooting
       (2)   Simple contest
       (3)   "Foul" shooting
       (4)   "Chair" shooting

STIMULATE YOUR BASKETBALL THINKING

Shooter's Psyche:
Give them the right to shoot—give them the right to miss.

Don't Fall In Love With Quickness:
Quickness is an advantage, not a necessity.

Motion Offense:
Move ball fast?
Move ball slow?
How do you want to play?

Utilize Tape in Your Teaching:
Importance of midline to post moves and pressing.
Mini-lane.

Free-Throw Shooting:
"Swish" game.
Pressure F.T.'s drill.

Teaching Reading Screens—Verbalize:
"Caught"—45 or straight cut
"High"—Fade
"Trail"—Curl

Teach Screening:
Back to area of attack

Correlation Between Ball Reversals and Defensive Breakdowns:
First three passes are mine, the next are yours!

"Shouldn't Score" Points:
Opening tip
OOB's
Offensive F.T. line play

Best Thing We Have Done in Teaching Offense:
First day of practice: One pass and score
Three Rules of Screening:
- Can't screen air
- Can't screen your teammate
- Can't screen guy guarding you

Practice Problems:
Leave drill and come back to it
Take a time out
Players get three 20-second time outs

What Are Your Worries? Fears?
Press attack
Motion
Sprint break
Special situations
Entries

Four Most Important Words You Must Be Able To Say As A Coach:
"CHANGE, THIS ISN'T WORKING!"

Switching:
Mismatches don't hurt you; open shots do!

Penetration—On Both Sides of Ball:

Defensively:	Teams are denying more and this leaves gaps to drive. Teach penetration
Offensively:	Single biggest thing that hurts a defense. Practice it!

Shooting—Very Important: 15-20 minutes per practice
Types Of Shots:
Catch shot
Shoot off cut
Catch quick penetrate
Catch shot fake penetration
How We Practice Them:
Technique/form
Simple contest
"Foul" shooting
"Chair" shooting

Role Players Interest and Equate the Word Role with Another Four Letter Word:
"SUCK"...I'm not good enough!
Give him some offensive goals:

Pass ahead—1 per half	2 points
Two offensive rebounds—per half	2 points
FTA—3 per half	2 points
	6 points

Conservative Yet Still Want to Press:
Five-Up Press

ESTABLISHING A PROGRAM

1. **Recruiting Work Ethic:**
   High School: Feeder school work ethic

2. **Develop High Morale:**
   ABC's of Success—Attitude, Belief, Chemistry
   Have fun
   Upbeat assistants

3. **Play Development:**
   Pro-Time: Skill development program
   Game Shots—Game Spots—Game Speed
   Eliminate Boredom and Fatigue

4. **Establish Academic Development:**
   Grade checks
   Study hall
   Time management

5. **Establish Communication Lines:**
   Big Eyes—Big Ears—Small Mouth
   Find your mini captains
   How many minutes do you talk to players?
   PAT RILEY: "Must confront reality with today's player."
   Comparative position stats
   We're in the business of ego management and attitude adjustment.

6. **Trust:**
   Yiddish proverb: "Speak as you mean, do as you profess, perform what you promise."

7. **Let Your Locker Room Talk:**
   Would you be proud of your effort and results today if an NBA scout saw you play?
   If your mother, father, teacher, or preacher knew everything you did today, and why, would you be proud of your day?

8. **Edits:**
   Every three—four games for your players

9. **Create Environment For Success:**
   VCR's
   Office
   Locker Room

10. **Public Speaking:**
    Helping others get what they want will help you get what you want!
    Helping others is not an option, it's a must!

11. **Steal Ideas:**
    Books: *Showtime* by Pat Riley
    John Calipari's book
    Pete Carroll's book
    Bill Parcells' book
    Tom Osborne's book
    Seminars

12. **Know Your Level:**
    What to teach.
    EXAM: Defending screens

Match-Up Offense

There are many things players need to learn to run good match-up offense. One bad habit a lot of players have is putting the ball above their heads. Get your players to stay in a triple threat position because when the ball is above their head it limits their options. That player can not penetrate quickly enough and can not ball fake for anything besides a pass.

Another teaching point is to keep the ball out of the corner unless it is for a shot. This is a great place for the defense to trap, so only go there if you know you are going to score.

(Diagram 1)   Shot fakes and pass fakes are very important and must happen so that the zone will move more. Do not let the guards cover the top of the zone, make them keep trying to stop the ball.

Diagram 2

There has to be penetration against the zone either with a pass or a drive. The 3-point line sometimes tends to be like a barrier. But, someone has to expose the ball so that two defenders will come to it and then the offense can pitch it for a shot.

After a player passes the ball, have them take a step in because then when they receive the ball again they can penetrate that much further.

(Diagram 3)   Always reverse the ball to three people. Show the ball to one side with the idea to attack the other side.

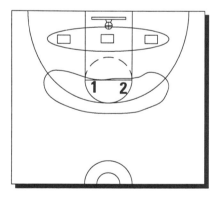

Diagram 1

(Diagram 2)   Keep pressure on the baseline with offense. Do not let the back line move. The defense has trouble guarding the short corner. 3 must be ready to shoot.

Diagram 3

(Diagram 4)   Never pass the ball in the direction of the dribble. Pass fake the way you are going.

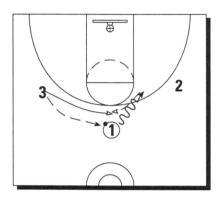

Diagram 4

(Diagram 5)   When 1 receives the ball from 2, attack B's inside foot to freeze the defense. Always have your players ready to shoot and in a pre-shot stance.

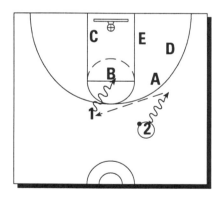

Diagram 5

(Diagram 6)   Look at a match-up zone as a switching man-to-man. And the offense has to attack the check off.

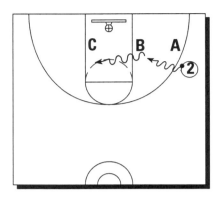

Diagram 6

(Diagram 7)   Do not play with a cutter, play with the screener. Get the ball to 4. Have 4 slip the screen. Always have the cutters cut baseline, do not cut high.

Diagram 7

Scramble Zone Offense

(Diagram 8)   Occupy a spot for two seconds then cut a gap. Cuts are four steps maximum, and we would prefer three, then change direction.

(Diagram 9)   Cut and split two people any time you can.

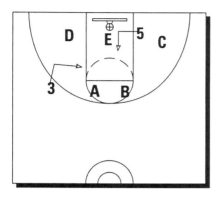

Diagram 8

Diagram 10

Diagram 9

Diagram 11

(Diagram 10)   3 steps then V-cut.

The cutter has to be there the instant the ball is ready to be passed. This is why the players can not make long cuts.

(Diagram 11)   If you start your cut and someone is there, then replace yourself. The short corners must be filled. After two seconds, cut to the middle and read up, because someone has just left this spot. Do not cut two people in the same direction.

As the defense follows a cutting offensive player part of the way they leave openings for someone else to cut to those openings.

(Diagram 12)   If you want your point guard to always be back then tell this player to cut and replace out front every time.

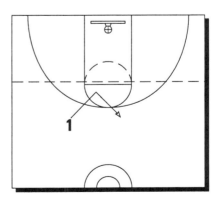

Diagram 12

(Diagram 13)   If you have a post that you don't want on the perimeter, then have this player designated for this area.

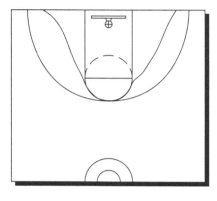

Diagram 13

Any time the ball is caught in the high post area, you have to throw it down low; this means there has to be someone down there. Any time it is caught down low, that player must shoot it.

Refining Post Play

Any team must establish an inside game. Give credit to the players that are always looking for the post feeds. Each team has to get players that will look inside.

The three most greatly exaggerated things in basketball are:

1. Height
2. Fast Break
3. Press

For these things you have to have the right players to do it. But, if you do not have a tall person on your team, you still must throw it inside. Who is a pivot player? Someone you throw the ball into inside. It could be a small guard who knows what to do down

low. If you want to throw it inside, have a second feeder option. 2 throws it to 4 and 4 throws down to 3. 3 must seal. (Diagram 14)

Diagram 14

(Diagram 15)   Know the way the defense is playing the pivot and move them either up or down. Sometimes the offensive player must take a dribble to improve the passing angle.

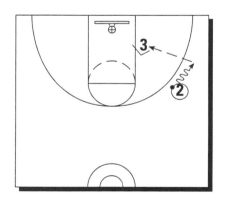

Diagram 15

(Diagram 16)   Whoever is on the other side of the court, know what they are doing and flash, so the team can get a high/low look.

Diagram 16

When a player seals that pivot, he has to own that position. If the defense plays bottom, then get the ball in the middle. If the defense plays above, then get the ball toward the baseline. The pivot has to control the defense's top foot. If the foot gets over, then the hand is to the baseline looking for the lob. If the defense is directly behind the pivot, then that player has to know exactly where the defense is. Find the defense with the upper part of the hips and the weight over the balls of the feet. They must post-up with a half-moon which is little two-inch shovel steps.

(Diagram 17)   Do not lob to the middle. Lob to the corner of the backboard. Lob pass—not throwing it to the man, but rather throwing it away from the defense. Do not bend elbows because it's hard to control and slows down. Instead, throw the ball with a flick of the wrists. The receiver must hold position; do not release until the ball is past your head.

(Diagram 18)   Do not let the post player dribble the ball in the post. Have them learn the hook shot. The hook shot is off the ear not off the eye. Use a head and shoulder fake not a ball fake. Point the toe in the direction the pivot is going and this puts the player into the defense. The purity of the game of basketball is in the feet. Do not move the foot that player fakes to. Do not expose the ball on the fake and do not straighten the knees because the position gained will be lost.

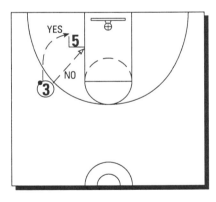

Diagram 17

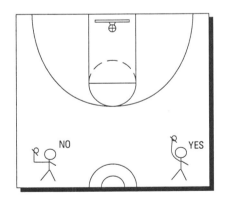

Diagram 18

Never bounce pass to the middle of the court. To the baseline side is okay because there is no one there to get their hands on the ball. Do not have the pivot follow the ball. Have it get there from somewhere else.

Offensive Rebounding

Have your players fight the comfort zone, both mentally and physically, when talking about offensive rebounding. Have the players understand the importance because offensive rebounds wins games.

Body positioning is also very important. The lower the ball is shot toward the baseline, then the more rebounds will be opposite. Refuse to be blocked out. The players must anticipate every shot, which is playing without the ball. Offensive rebounding is just plainly an attitude that a tough player has when he wants to go get every missed shot.

Driving

(Diagram 19)   Every time a player drives the ball, have him get a piece of that defensive player immediately. If the player tends to shy away, then the driver will not get to the basket. Drive to the box. Against a press, go into the defense. Teach your players to finish in traffic. Finishing is nothing more than concentration.

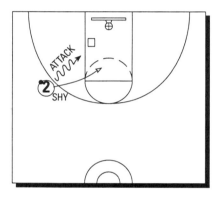

Diagram 19

All-Net Shooting Method

Everyone loves shooters. Unfortunately, there aren't many great shooters in the country today. Why is that? I'll share my theories with you, but first let me say that I've never seen a true player who doesn't want to get better. Shooting is the most worked on skill in basketball. When players come out to practice what do they practice? Shooting. Whether it's good or not is another point.

Why aren't there many great shooters today? I have four theories:

1. **The playground theory**—If you go to a playground, what do you notice? The players are running up and down the court running the fast break. They're not working on individual skills. They don't shoot the outside shot. Why? Because there are no nets on the basket. They can't tell if the ball went through the rim or not so they shoot the layup or take the dunk.

2. **Three-point line**— Not all players have the same shooting technique. Why is the three-point line the same for a fourth grader and a senior in college? This is ridiculous.

3. **Poor instruction**—A lot of the coaches of young players don't know much about teaching the fundamentals of that sport.

4. **Better defense**—Better defense might cause a player to take a bad shot, but it doesn't cause a player to miss an open fifteen footer. There is little evidence to support this theory.

I have what I call the "All Net Shooting Method." The first thing I emphasize is balance and eyes. For a right-handed shooter the right foot is forward, the feet turned a little in, and both eyes are on the rim, which means the ball can't be in the center of the head. I stress aiming for the center of the basket. Some may say the eyes are to be on the rim during the shot. I disagree. After the ball leaves my hand, I look at the ball to see the spin, the arc, etc. so I can see if I shot the ball correctly.

The second thing I emphasize is the shooting hand. Finger tips and pads of the palm, but not the palm, are to be touching the ball. The thumb and index finger of the shooting hand are to be spread apart. The index and middle finger should be the last two fingers to touch the ball and they should be placed in the center of the ball.

Next, I emphasize the "L" position on the shooting arm. The upper arm of the shooting arm stays perpendicular to the shoulder while the lower arm bends a little toward the shoulder on the shot. As you bend your knees to shoot, the shooting arm will lower a little, but this is good because it gives you the range on the shot.

Then, there's the off-hand. The fingertip and pads of the off-hand should be touching the ball, but not the palm. I believe the fingers of the off-hand should be pointed toward the ceiling. I don't want the thumb of the off-hand in what is commonly referred to as the "T" position. I believe this causes you to pinch the ball, rub the ball, whatever, on the shot, which in turn causes the ball to go off line.

I believe there are three types of shooters:

Great Shooters: If you have one of these, then all you want to do with him is just have him work on repetition, repetition, repetition. You do this because they already have the good technique and just need to refine it.

Good Shooters: For these players you want to find one or two things they need help with and make them work on these skills over and over until it becomes second nature.

Streak/Poor Shooters: You need to start with these players in the off-season and have them work on the basics every day. You will be able to make them into good shooters, but I don't know if they'll ever become great shooters.

Let me say something about repetition vs. technique change. People say that if you shoot a little more in practice, this will improve shooting. It just isn't so! Repetition might take you to a certain level, but it won't take you to the highest level. You need to make technique changes and then do repetition, repetition, repetition and you will make that jump to the next level.

As far as gimmicks go, here are my thoughts about them:

- The Big Ball. I'm not a fan of the Big Ball. Number one, it's too big for your hand. Number two, it's not what you shoot with in a game. If you want to do anything, use a smaller rim.

- The ball with the Painted Hands. I believe this ball puts your off-hand in the wrong position and will cause you to push the shot off-line.

The only gimmick I use is the shooting strap. This is to be used on the off-hand to help in the improvement of shooting. You must decide for yourself which of these devices are for you and your players.

Before I move on to some drills that you can use, let me make a comment about jump shooting and free-throws. I think technique is the main problem. Is the dominant foot (right foot for right-handers, left foot for lefties) on the center line? Are the feet turned a little to the left for righties and vice-versa for lefties? I don't think you want your feet parallel to the basket because this causes you to shoot a little across your body. In regard to the jump shot, let me just say that I believe you shoot the ball on the way up, not as you reach the peak of your jump. To shoot at the peak of the jump will cause you to lose your momentum.

Here are some drills that you can use with your players:

Form Drill: This is a one-handed drill. Have your players start three feet from the basket and work on their shooting hand form. Don't allow them to move back until they are consistently shooting with the fingers and pads on the ball.

Off-Hand Drill: This is the same as the form drill, although now you add the off-hand to the ball, but take it off before you release the ball on the shot. Have your players hold their follow through to check their technique. Remember to stress that they'll get the range they need on the shot by bending their knees and bringing the "L" down.

Step-In Drill: Start this drill from fifteen feet on the wing. Have the shooting foot behind the body, ball in triple threat position. Step in with the shooting foot, turning it slightly in, drop the shooting arm, come up, and shoot. Start on the dominant side for each shooter. Right wing for right-handers, left wing for left-handers.

(Diagram 1)   **Two-Man Drill**. This drill is designed to increase quickness on the shot. You have two players involved at a basket. One will be the shooter and the other will act as a shot blocker. Start with the shooter on the free-throw line and the shot blocker 12' away in the lane. The defender passes the ball to the shooter and attacks the shooter, trying to block the shot. You want to eventually work up to the defender being only three to four feet away from the shooter. The shooter has to work on not dropping the shooting arm if he wants to get quicker on his release and not get the shot blocked.

(Diagram 2)   **Two-Ball Rapid Fire Drill**. Here you have three players involved at a basket. One will be the shooter, one the passer, and one the rebounder.

You designate where you want the shot to be taken from. Two balls are involved in this drill. The shooter starts the drill by taking the shot. The passer, who has the second ball, passes to the shooter. The rebounder is to get the first shot and pass it to the passer. You set a time limit on the drill. The objective is to make as many shots as possible within the designated time. Rotate the drill with the passer becoming the shooter, the rebounder becoming the passer and the shooter becoming the rebounder.

(Diagram 3) **Around the World**. Here we designate five spots on the floor the shot is to be taken from. The player stays at the spot until he makes the shot and then rotates to the next spot. The player goes from spot 1 to spot 5 and back. After making the shot from 1 on his return, he goes to the foul line to make a free-throw and ends the drill by making a layup. This is a timed drill.

(Diagram 4) **Follow-the-Leader Drill**. This is similar to Horse, but you have 4 or 5 players in a line. The first player takes two dribbles either to his left or right, pulls up and shoots a jumper. If he makes the shot, the second player has to make it. If the second player makes his shot, the third player has to make his shot. If a player fails to make his shot, he gets a letter

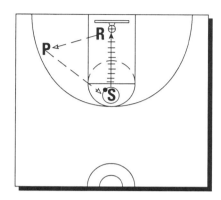

Diagram 2

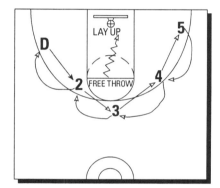

Diagram 3

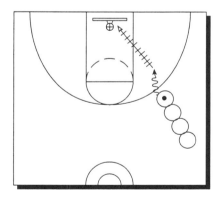

Diagram 4

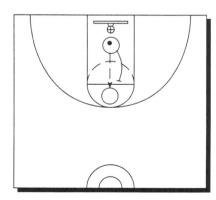

Diagram 1

(Diagram 5) **Consecutive Make Drill**. Here you have twelve players in a line. The first player takes a shot, then the second, then the third, and so on. The player who shoots and misses has to run three laps or whatever the coach designated. The idea is to see how many shots the team can make in succession. The coach designates the spot from which the shot is taken.

(Diagram 6)   **Curl Drill**. Here you have two players involved. One is at the top of the key, acting as a passer. The second player starts at the wing and makes a V-cut to the block and back. The passer hits the wing as he comes back out to the wing. He catches the ball, pivots, and shoots. Look for players to catch, step, and then pivot. This is a move that slows the action down and takes an open shot and turns it into no shot.

(Diagram 7)   **Pop, Pick, Shoot Drill**. In this drill you have a wing, high post, and guard. The guard passes to the wing, makes a ball cut, and then cuts back to the weakside. The post sets a back screen for the cutter. The wing hits the guard for a shot as he hits the weakside guard position. Rotate clockwise on this drill.

(Diagram 8)   **Post Drill**. This is a three-man drill. You have an offensive wing player, a defender, and a low post. The drill starts with the ball at the wing. The defender sets up on the wing, who makes a pass into the post. The defender sinks onto the post as most man defenses teach. After making the pass, the wing cuts to the corner for a return pass from the post and a shot. The defense is to attempt to get out to the corner and put pressure on the shooter. A variation to this drill is to have the shooter make a shot fake on the defense, take one dribble toward the top of the key, pivot, and shoot.

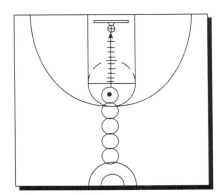

Diagram 5

Diagram 7

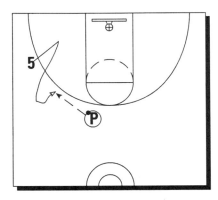

Diagram 6

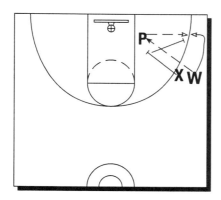

Diagram 8

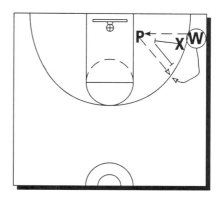

Diagram 9

(Diagram 9)   A variation to the post drill is to have the ball start in the corner and then make the pass and cut to the wing for a return pass and a shot.

In closing, I want to share a one-on-one drill that is a take-off of the old jab step, reverse dribble drill.

(Diagram 10)   **One-on-One Spin Drill.** This is a two-man drill. The offensive player starts with the ball on the block and the defender lines up behind him. The offensive player throws the ball out to the wing with reverse spin on it and cuts to the ball. The defender comes out on the offense to challenge him. The offensive player catches the ball, pivots on the defense, jabs and either drives or shoots, depending on how the defense reacts.

(Diagram 11)   A variation to the one-on-one drill is to have the offensive player catch the ball, reverse pivot, jab, and drive or shoot.

Hopefully, I have given you some things to consider in regard to shooting.

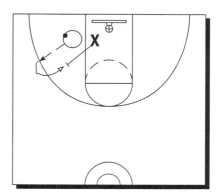

Diagram 10

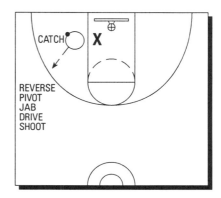

Diagram 11

Man-to-Man Defense

In building a program we had to get respect right away, not only from the fans and our opponents, but also respect from our own players. The attitude they needed to understand came from the defense our program uses.

They way we work with our student-athletes is that they must realize what a mental game basketball is and they have to be willing to give up their summers (because of summer school, working out, etc.).

I pick our captains because we do not want it to be a popularity contest and I make sure to give them some serious responsibilities.

Conditioning

In practice do not expect your players to work hard on something unless it is relevant to what you do in the games. How do you get them to play hard? Demand it! Be careful not to be too technically smart because the players will become stupid. If one player does not play hard, then none of them will. That is why we try to be the best conditioned team in the country. For four weeks we will run on the golf course three times a week up and down the hills. Questions we will ask our players are:

- How committed are you?
- How punctual are you?
- Will you get to bed early enough to run at your best?

The other two days of the week we will run ladders. Running for eight minutes then walk for two. Running for seven minutes then walk for two and so on. The last three weeks of conditioning we will run sprints. One mile must be under six minutes. A half

mile must be under three minutes. And a quarter mile must be under a minute.

In our program we have to get more shots than the opposition. To do this, we must create turnovers and rebound. In all games the best players do not always win!

Principles of Man-to-Man

1. Contain the basketball.
2. Always know where the ball is.
3. Position of the ball dictates your position.
4. Always be in position to help your teammates.
5. Always going to put pressure on the ball.
6. Recognize the side of defense.
7. Perimeter defenders must be ready to help in the post.
8. Contest all shots and all five rebound.
9. Force the ball to baseline.
10. Must communicate on defense.

Defending the Ball

The players must have good balance. Feet should have heel-to-toe alignment. Tail has to be down with feet shoulder-width apart. The back must be straight with the head up.

(Diagram 1) This is a drill that coaches can use to emphasize these points. It teaches getting the head on the ball. Also be sure to teach them how to take a charge. If the player gets beat, they have to turn, run, cut off the dribbler and get into position (Run—slide—run).

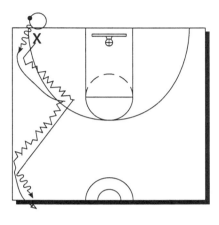

Diagram 1

(Diagram 2)   In this 2-on-2 drill the defenders must help on the strongside while the offense penetrates and pitches. Then the helping defender closes out to the new dribbler.

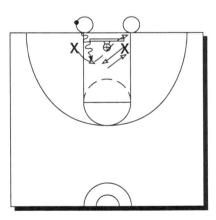

Diagram 2

Most teams need to work on one-on-one defense a lot. Close-outs are one way to do this. When a defender closes out we teach them to take a step back if there is a ball fake. We want the ball to end up in this box (Diagram 3).

Diagram 3

After some of these drills, we will do some 4-on-4 shell defense so the players can get a feel for the positions they need to be in, then we will go live. Some points of emphasis are: To jump in the direction of the pass. Deny the sucker cut. Help across, not up the floor. And work on getting over the top of screens. 5-on-5 can be incorporated to work on blocking out for rebounds.

We need players that are tough. A tough drill that we use is called the "Mr. Iba" drill. (Diagram 4) The coach out top has two basketballs. The coach throws one to the wing and that player goes to the basket while the defender comes over to take the charge. The coach then rolls the other ball and the defender has to dive on the rolling ball. The player picks up the ball and goes to the basket hard while two managers with pads pound on the player until the player makes three shots.

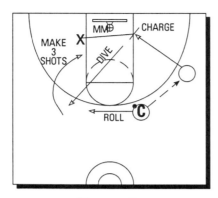

Diagram 4

There must be ball pressure on the basketball so they can not just throw darts to the post. Then it becomes a game of rebounding and our players must go get it and work extremely hard to block-out.

Attacking the Zone Defense

For our system there is a permanent point and a permanent post. The point guard must transport the ball from side-to-side while the post must go from block-to-block. The other three players, called runners, go anywhere they want to go.

We must force the defense to the box mentioned earlier. Do not let the ball come back to the middle because too many good things can happen for the offense. If the ball gets by the defender, they must run to catch up.

We do not want our players switching because we want accountability for our defense. When someone scores we know who to talk to. However, guards may switch late in the game when the offenses are doing hand-offs.

We teach our post defense that if the ball is high the defender is 1/2-man around, and if the ball is low the defender is low (Diagram 5).

Attacking the Zone:
• Alignment
• Movement
• Patience
• Penetration
• Ball Reversal

We will generally start out in a double-stack to make the bottom defender come out and guard. (Diagram 6) We also try to attack the short corner because this flattens out the defense. (Diagram 7) If the post catches the ball in the short corner the first look is at the other post. If a runner passes the ball, then that player must cut through.

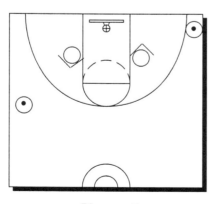

Diagram 5

Diagram 6

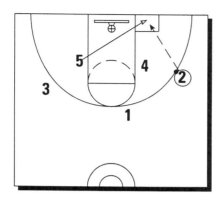

Diagram 7

Diagram 8

Crack Down is a look that can come from a player being in the short corner. (Diagram 8)

Hopefully some of these ideas will help your team attack the zone the next time they step on the court.

Man-to-Man Offense

You've got to do the best with the personnel you have. We all don't have the greatest personnel year in and year out. There are a whole lot of people doing a lot with less. But no matter how good you are, you must also have the personnel. I had my first meeting with my new team. One player walked in with a bag of Wendy's. Two players walked in with headphones on, another with his hat turned sideways. Two others didn't even show for the meeting. So, I said that we would hold our first meeting tomorrow at 7:00 a.m. At 7:00 a.m. there were three players missing. At 7:03, three more come sprinting through the door.

I decided that instead of starting my conditioning program the following week we would start it the next morning at 5:30 a.m. We did. One of the players was late. They quickly got the message. Yesterday morning we had a 6:30 a.m. workout and I just got back from a recruiting trip. I walked in and the players were helping each other, talking, pumping each other up. What a difference a year makes. When I got that job I made up my mind I was not going to tolerate anything less than their best. But, I have learned that you can have discipline and still be flexible.

Lou Holtz said, "Discipline isn't what you do to someone, it's what you do for someone." When you start a new program, you have the hammer and it is up to you to make them come up to your standards. You should never come down to theirs. It is human nature to cut corners. I think that I can watch any fifteen minutes of your practice and know what is important to you as a coach. Good coaches know what they are looking for, bad coaches don't.

In talking about offensive philosophy, what I really want to do is to make you think. As you analyze

these things and get ready for next season, I want you to mull these things over. Our philosophy is, on made or miss, that we go from secondary break to motion to quick hitter. On a dead ball, we run a quick hitter to motion, back to quick hitter. In our game, the shot clock is a factor. Do you have a screening philosophy? We do. Our screening philosophy is big/little screens or little/big screens. Rarely do we screen little/little or big/big. Why? Because the best teams on our schedule are going to switch anything that involves equal size players.

For example, we will switch any big/big across the bottom.

(Diagram 1)   We will switch the 2-3 screen on this play because 2 and 3 are equal size.

Diagram 1

(Diagram 2)   Here is one of America's plays, a 1-4. 1 dribbles to the wing and 2 clears to the box and then up-screens for 5, who goes to the box. As that happens, 4 down-screens for 2. When 2 up-screens for 5, if they want to switch, great. This is a little/big screen and now their 2 is guarding our 5. 4 is then screening for 2. This is a big/little screen. How would you defend that, what is your philosophy? I never used to switch at all.

Diagram 2

Do you have a rebounding philosophy? We try to design our offense with the rebound in mind. If you know that your team is going to miss a lot of shots, then you must make sure that your best rebounders are near the basket.

Diagram 4

(Diagram 3)   Then we came up against something like this. As 3 screened for 2, my players decided that they could switch this and really make it difficult for them to get the ball in the scoring area. So, we did switch it, and we came up with a way to teach switching. But if you switch out of convenience then you will lose some intensity. Here are some ideas about teaching switching.

(Diagram 5)   Winner. We put this play in and did not use it until we needed a basket sometime during the season. Don't use all your best stuff in December. We got to the conference tournament championship with 35 seconds to go and we ran this play. 5 screens for 1, a big/little screen. Very few people will switch that. 3 and 2 stagger double for 4 coming to the block. If 4 is open, 1 passes to 4. After 5 screens for 1, 5 drifts to the top of the key. After 3 sets the first screen, he breaks to the elbow. If 4 isn't open, 1 can pass to 3.

Diagram 3

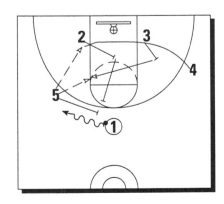

Diagram 5

(Diagram 4)   Switching on a down-screen. 3 and 2 are equal in size. We talk about the "three Ts," talk, touch, and take. 2 down-screens for 3. 2 sees that this is an equal situation and yells "switch." That's the first T. As 2 screens, the defenders come together and touch. Now we take. As 3 comes off the screen, 2's defender will switch to deny.

(Diagram 6)   If 4 gets the ball, 4 must shoot because 2 is back-screening for 5 and 5 is heading to the back side of the rim. If 3 gets the ball, 2 and 5 make the same moves.

Diagram 6

(Diagram 7)   If 1 can't pass to 4 or 3, he reverses to 2, who dribbles to the weakside and makes the pass to 5, who has posted on the block. This play is designed with the miss in mind. Our good rebounders are close to the basket.

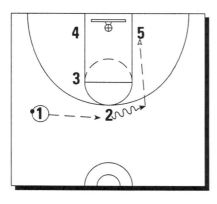

Diagram 7

(Diagram 8)   We were not a good passing team this year, so we didn't run much motion. Quick hitters can get you a shot with one, two, or three passes. You can also design your plays to get your shots for your best players. 5 screens for 1 and 1 takes it to the wing. 2 backscreens for 4, who goes to the block. 1 can pass to 4. 3 and 5 set staggered screens for 2. 1 can pass to 2. Since 5 is at the top of the staggered screen, the defense probably won't switch a big/little screen.

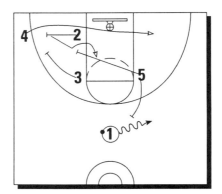

Diagram 8

(Diagram 9)   After 3 screened for 2, 3 went to the wing. 1 can pass to 2 who reverses the ball to 3. 5 posts up for the pass from 3. We call 5's move a second side post up.

Diagram 9

(Diagram 10)   Start from a 1-4. 1 dribbles toward the wing and 2 clears. 5 steps out and screens for 1 as 1 comes back to the middle. 1 and 5 can screen and roll. 3 and 4 set a staggered screen for 2, and then 3 breaks to the corner. 1 can pass to 2 or to 3.

Diagram 10

(Diagram 11)   Another 1-4 play begins with a direct pass to 5. 2 goes backdoor. 3 goes low, 4 sets a down-screen. 5 looks for 3, then 1 cutting off and 3 on the weakside.

Diagram 11

(Diagram 12)   You can run your favorite play out of different sets and disguise it. This is America's play.

1 dribbles to the side, 2 screens across for 4 and then 3 and 5 screen down for 2.

Diagram 12

(Diagram 13)   This is the same play from a different set. The only difference is that 3 and 5 are interchanged.

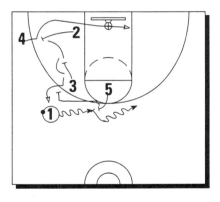

Diagram 13

(Diagram 14)   You can run the screen and roll play (previous Diagram 10) out of a 1-2-2 set. 5 circles away and comes back. 1 comes back off the screen of 5. 3 and 4 set a stagger screen for 2.

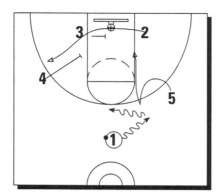

Diagram 14

(Diagram 15)   Our best shooter was 4. After running the previous play several times, we did this. 4 fakes coming off 2's screen, and then uses a stagger screen by 3 and 5.

Diagram 15

(Diagram 16)   Misdirection. Plays that look like they are going in one direction but end up going the other. 1 dribbles to 5 and 5 goes to the block. 4 comes to the top of the circle. 1 dribbles back off of the screen of 4. 3 screens for 2 and then 5 screens for 3. 1 can pass to 4, who steps out for a three-point shot, or to 3 coming off of the screen of 5. The play looks like it is going left, but comes back to the right. 3 and 5 also have a two-man game with 5

posting low. It's almost a double misdirection because the play started to the right, came back to the left, and then back to the right.

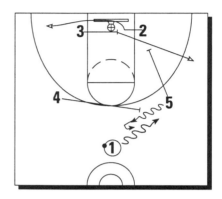

Diagram 16

(Diagram 17)   When the previous play has been scouted, we change it a little. 5 goes down and 4 comes up. 1 comes off of 4's screen and 2 comes off of 3, just like last time. But instead of passing back to 4, as soon as 4 screens for 1, 4 and 5 set a staggered double for 3.

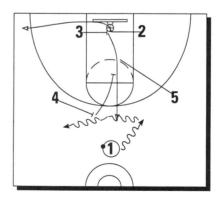

Diagram 17

(Diagram 18)   The interesting thing about this play, if you analyze it, is that it is America's play. 3 screens for 2, 5 and 4 screen for 3.

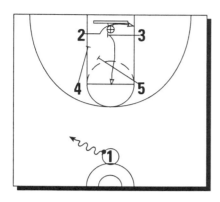

Diagram 18

Diagram 20

(Diagram 19)   Another wrinkle on this play. After 1 comes off of the screen set by 4, 1 passes back to 4. On the pass to 4, 5 keeps going and clears for 4, who is isolated on the weakside.

(Diagram 21)   Second side post-up. Did anyone run or play against a team who ran a double-screen on the ball? From a 1-4, 1 dribbles and passes to 2. 1 clears to the corner and 3 breaks to the middle of the lane. 5 and 4 get ready to screen for 2. It is important that 5 and 4 are below the ball so as 2 comes across he is attacking the basket.

Diagram 19

Diagram 21

(Diagram 20)   Do your plays have a second side post-up? A lot of our plays end up with 4 and 5 on the block, and 1, 2, and 3 on the perimeter. On a dead ball we go from a quick hitter to motion to quick hitter. Our motion is Kansas motion where we screen the passer and change sides of the floor. It's not the Indiana version. We are much closer to the Kansas side than the Indiana side.

(Diagram 22)   3 then backscreens 5's defender and 2 can pass to 5 if 2 cannot drive to the basket.

(Diagram 23)   If 2 can't go to the basket and if 5 is not open, then 2 passes to 3 who comes off of the screen of 4. 3 can shoot if open. If 3 isn't open, the ball goes from 2-3-1-4 on the post. We call this the second side post up. Whenever the ball is shot, we have 4 and 5 in good rebounding position.

Diagram 22

Diagram 23

(Diagram 24)   Shadow. We dummy this stuff every day. The timing and spacing of your offense whether it is motion or man is critical. This is 5/0. We don't call it dummy, we call it shadow. When a shot goes up, we have 3, 4, and 5 rebounding, 2 goes to the foul line, and 1 drops back. When the ball goes through the basket, they turn and sprint to midcourt. So, not only do we run the play, we go through the rebound responsibilities and go through transition. You can also go into your press after a made basket with the coach passing in to a manager.

(Diagram 25)   Side out-of-bounds. You can run some of your plays from out-of-bounds. 4 and 5 are interchangeable. This is a misdirection play. 5 gets 1 open. 1 comes to the ball for pass from 4. 5 turns and rescreens and 1 brings it back on the dribble. 3 screens for 2. 5 steps back and gets the pass from 1. 4 then screens down for 3. Ball goes from 4-1-5-3.

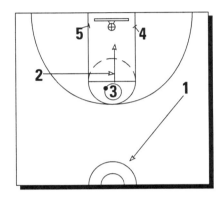

Diagram 24

Diagram 25

(Diagram 26)   An out-of-bounds play from underneath. 2 and 3 break out, ball goes from 1-2-3. 1 backscreens for 5 and then 4 screens across for 1. 3 can pass to 5 or 1.

Diagram 26

(Diagram 27)   I like it when people trap ballscreens. When they do we treat it as a zone press. When you get trapped in a full-court press, you want three outlets and a long diagonal. When trapped we will run the "throw back special."

Diagram 27

(Diagram 28)   1 dribbles to the side, and comes back off of the screen set by 4. When 1 is double-teamed, it becomes a zone press. 1 will back up.

(Diagram 29)   When 1 uses the back-up dribble, he creates space and that creates time. If X4 and X1 are guarding you, attack X4, the slower, bigger man. But there are times that 1 will attack the wide side of the floor. As 1 is trapped, all sets are off. 3 flashes high, 2 goes to the corner, 4 steps out, and 5 goes to the weakside. We have three outlets and a long diagonal. You must have some sort of offense when you get that double-team.

Diagram 28

Diagram 29

Zone Offense

You can look at the zone offense three ways. You can run a continuity, a motion, or set plays. We run a continuity attack into set plays. We run a motion attack into set plays. This is from Gary Williams who got it from Tom Davis. This is particularly good if there is no shot clock. Gary runs it differently than Dr. Tom. This offense stretches the defense from one side to the other and attacks the inside of the zone. We told our players that the reason people play zone is to keep the ball out of the lane. We sold them on the fact that if you can get the ball inside, you can win. So, we wanted to get the ball into the lane. Because of the shot clock, we sometimes had to run the continuity and then go into a quick hitter. But without a shot clock, you can run it all day. We taught the slides of the zone to our team even though we never played zone.

(Diagram 1)   We explained that no matter which zone is being used, when the ball is in the corner it is a 2-3. The base goes out, backside wing goes down, and it is a 2-3. That helped us because our kids needed to know what they were attacking.

Diagram 1

(Diagram 2)   Continuity. 3 pops out, 5 comes up the lane to be used as an outlet. If 1 passes to 3, 5

posts up hard. 1 steps in to the three-point line. 1 looks to 5, and then to 3. If they are in a 2-3 zone, they basically are playing you man-to-man.

Diagram 2

(Diagram 3)   Ball goes from 3-1-2. 4 pops out on a forty-five degree angle to the foul line extended. As 3 passes the ball, he cuts through to the other corner.

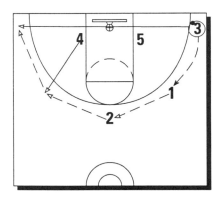

Diagram 3

(Diagram 4)   As 3 catches the pass from 4, 5 comes across low and 4 cuts through high. 4 and 5 are trying to get a 2/1 with X5. 2 and 1 fill. If the guard on the ball side stays out with 2, we have a chance to get the ball to 4 in the middle of the lane. If X5 cheats up the lane, 3 passes to 5.

Diagram 4

(Diagram 5)   If 3 doesn't hit 4 or 5, 4 goes through to the weakside block. We are back to where we were. Once 3 has made the baseline cut through, every other cut from the perimeter is going to come from the wing position. 3 starts the ball reversal and as 2 passes to 1, 2 cuts through to the corner. 3 replaces 2. 4 comes out at the forty-five degree angle again to aid in the ball reversal. After several times, if 1 ball fakes and passes the ball back to 3, 3 can hit 5 in the low post.

Diagram 5

(Diagram 6)   As 4 passes to 2 in the corner, 4 cuts through the lane near the mid-point and 5 again comes across low for the possible 2/1 situation with the middle defensive man. As 4 cuts through, 1 and 3 replace.

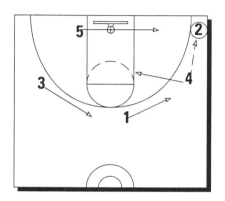

Diagram 6

(Diagram 7)   The continuity continues with 2 starting the reversal. As 1 passes to 3, 1 cuts through and 2 replaces and the ball is reversed again.

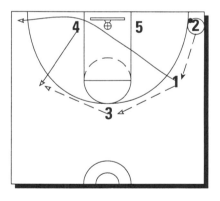

Diagram 7

(Diagram 8)   On the ball reversal, if 4 is overplayed and cannot get the pass from 2, then 2 makes a skip-pass directly to the corner. 4 can get a shot near the mid-post because the defensive man is out too far.

Diagram 8

occupying the weakside guard, 2 is occupying the guard at the top. 3 moves out to the wing. 2 passes back to 3 and on that pass 4 comes to the dead spot.

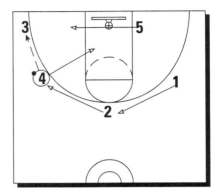

Diagram 10

(Diagram 9)   Tom Davis (Iowa) does it this way. As 4 passes to 3 and cuts through, 1 comes across and fills 4's spot. 2 stays at the top of the circle. 2 is a very good shooter.

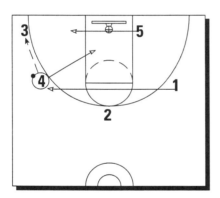

Diagram 9

Diagram 11

(Diagram 10)   You can also keep 3 on the baseline and fill with 2 and 1 as 4 cuts through.

(Diagram 11)   Quick hitter. We start the same way. The ball goes from 1-3-1-2-4-3. 4 cuts through and 5 comes over. 1 and 2 fill.

(Diagram 12)   3 passes to 2 who dribbles toward the top of the key as 1 drifts away. 5 rolls to the middle of the lane against this 2/3 zone. 1 is

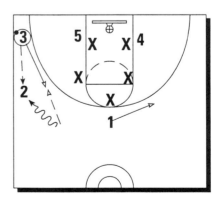

Diagram 12

(Diagram 13)   We now have a 2/1 vs. the backside forward. 3 can also skip-pass to 1 if the weakside back defender goes across to cover 4. 5 flashes to the weakside block.

(Diagram 16)   Vs. a match-up. As the ball is reversed against a match-up, 3 has run the baseline to the corner.

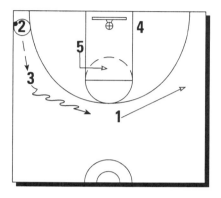

Diagram 15

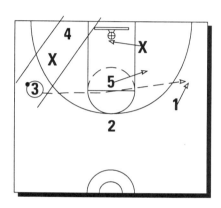

Diagram 13

(Diagram 14)   You can run this same thing out of a motion set. 1 passes to 2 who passes back to 1. 2 cuts to the weakside corner and the ball is passed from 1 to 3 to 2 for the shot.

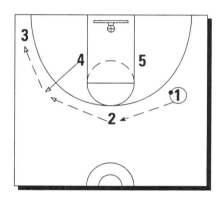

Diagram 16

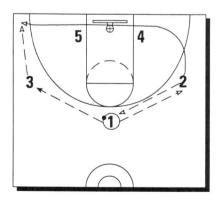

Diagram 14

(Diagram 17)   As 4 passes to 3 in the corner, he cuts to the dead spot and 3 dribbles it out into the gap. 2 holds. 5 delays, but flashes middle as 3 is dribbling. 3 can pass to 5 and 5 to 4.

(Diagram 18)   Or, 3 can dribble out and pass to 4, who passes to 5 cutting to the basket.

(Diagram 15)   If 2 doesn't get the shot, 2 passes to 3 and 3 dribbles out as 1 slides away 5 comes across the lane, and 4 breaks to the dead spot.

Diagram 17

Diagram 18

(Diagram 19)   If 3 can't make the pass directly to 4 or to 5, the ball is reversed from 3 to 2 to 1, who can pass to 5 flashing to the mid-post. 1 can pass to 4 on the baseline where 4 can shoot or pass to 5 breaking down the lane.

Diagram 19

(Diagram 20)   You can run this with a three-out/two-in set. We call this "corner." 1 dribbles toward 3 and hits 3, who hits 4 in the corner. 3 goes to the dead spot, 5 flashes. 4 can pass to 3 or to 5

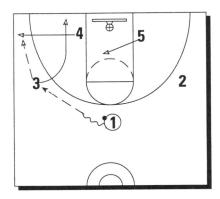

Diagram 20

(Diagram 21)   Inbounds under. 5 screens the top man on the zone. 2 breaks to the corner. 3 comes high. 1 inbounds and steps to the dead spot. Many times 1 is open.

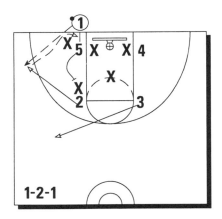

Diagram 21

Quick Hitter Offense

Before I get into discussing our quick hitter offenses, let me share several things with you. First of all, I came in early today so I could hear Don Casey speak on defense. Defense is the key to any team's success and we're no different at St. John's. The best basketball book on defense I ever read was titled, *Multiple Defenses for Winning Basketball*. This book was written in 1971 by a coach at Earlham College in Indiana. The coach's name was Del Harris. While everything in it is not applicable to every level of play and situation, we can all get one or two things that would be applicable to our level of play.

Second, I would like to share a story with you. In 1993, while coaching at Manhattan, I had a very good team. We played Columbia University and were up by 17 at half-time and wound up winning by 37. The next day my athletic director calls me into the office and says, "What would you do if you were beaten by 37?" I know he wants me to admit I had run up the score, but this was just not true. I had played my freshmen quite a bit in the game and it happened that I had a very good freshmen class that year. So I said to him, "Honestly, I'd go get better players." This year at St. John's we played Miami, Villanova, Michigan, and Minnesota, all in a row. We played at Minnesota on a Sunday and got annihilated. We were down 33-5 at one time and were beaten 78-39. This was one of the worst defeats in St. John's history and as the game is going on, all I'm thinking is "We've got to get better players." The moral of this story is that all the things you're learning at this clinic is great, but if you don't have the players to execute it, it isn't going to work.

Third, at St. John's we switch equals on defense. This philosophy came about during my first year at Manhattan. We had a very good, smart group of players at Manhattan my first year. I came in with the mind set that we were never going to switch, we'd fight through, or over, every screen. My players knew the other team's personnel as well as I did and they would switch certain situations. They didn't switch every time, but they were switching what I described as equals (players of equal ability). Being the bright coach I am, I told my coaching staff we had to incorporate this into our system. So, we borrowed what we call "talk, touch, take" from Del Harris.

(Diagram 1)   We only switch equals. By this we mean that we do not allow a small player to switch onto a big player or vice versa. X2 is at the high post and X3 is at the low post. On the screen down, X2 tells X3 of the screen, the two defenders touch each other to eliminate a slip screen, and then X2 takes X3's man and vice versa. The bottom man being screened is always responsible for calling the switch. I tell you this because our quick hitters are responsible for calling the switch. Also, our quick hitter is based in part on creating big man-little man screens and causing mismatches.

Diagram 1

Our total **offensive philosophy** is:

- On all made or missed FG's we run a secondary break to motion to quick hitter as the shot clock winds down.

- On all dead balls, after timeouts or turnovers, we run quick hitters to motion to a quick hitter as the shot clock winds down. Usually, we start our quick hitter when there are twelve seconds or less on the shot clock.

Our philosophy on quick hitters is based on **eight principles**:

1. We want to be able to run a group of plays from the same set.

2. We want to get the ball into our best player's hand.

3. We want to take the first great shot we can.

4. We want to run misdirection.

5. We want to have a pass and dribble entry option for each of our quick hitters.

6. We want to run big-little man screens.

7. We want to have designated offensive rebounding responsibilities.

8. We have a "pull and kick" opportunity to each play. This means we want to be able to drive the ball, pull a defender off a teammate, and hit the open teammate for an open shot.

(Diagram 2)   The first quick hitter I'll share is what we call "winner." We run this when we really need a basket. We don't run all our good things early in the season. We save some of our better quick hitters for later in the season when we really need a few surprises for our opponents. 1 dribbles toward 4, 4 sets a backscreen for 1 (big-little screen). After 4 has set the backscreen for 1, he moves down to set

a screen for 2 (big-little screen). While 4 was setting a backscreen for 1, 2 and 3 have run a staggered double for 5. 5 has continued across to the ballside block. 3 has screened and come to the ballside elbow. 2 comes off 4's screen to the point and 4 has cut to the offside post. If 1 can get the ball to 4, he does. Upon getting the ball, 4 must take the shot.

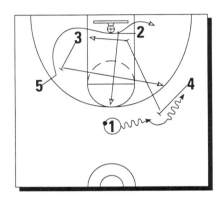

Diagram 2

(Diagram 3)   If 1 couldn't get the ball to 4 or 3 on the elbow, 1 reverses the ball to 2 who dribbles to the offside wing and looks to hit 4 in what we call the "second-side post-up."

Diagram 3

Before we go on, let me share two more things with you. One, do you have a rebound philosophy in your offense? Even if you're running motion, do you have a rebounding philosophy? We believe every shot will be missed, so we run all our quick hitters with the philosophy that we need to rebound. Two, do your plays have a screening philosophy? About all our plays are centered around big man - little man screens. This ensures that the opposition will not switch on our screens or that if they do, the switch will result in mismatches.

(Diagram 4)   Here is a play we run to get a quick three-pointer or an open post-up. 5 screens for 1 as he dribbles to the wing. As this happens, 2 screens for 4 coming to the block. Both of these screens are big-little screens. As 2 screens for 4, 3 and 5 are setting a stagger double for 2, who comes off these two screens for the open three.

Diagram 4

(Diagram 5)   If 2 isn't open for the three or 5 for the post-up, 1 reverses the ball to 2, who hits 3 as he pops out to the wing. 3 looks for the second side post-up by 5. On any shot we have 4 and 5 in good rebound position.

Can your quick hitters get you a shot on one or two passes? Here is an example of a quick hitter. We call this "America's Play." Why? Because everybody in America runs it.

Diagram 5

(Diagram 6)   2 screens across for 4. 3 and 5 double down for 2. 1 can pass to 4 for a post-up or to 2 for the three-pointer. If you're not a good passing team, this minimizes your losing the ball because of a bad pass.

Do you have favorite plays? If you do, can you run them out of different sets? If you do this, you can disguise a play and also make it tougher for the opposition to prepare. Here is an example of a screen and roll play that is pretty popular right now from two different sets.

(Diagram 7)   From a 1-2-2 set, 1 dribbles toward 5 and then reverses back to the top of the key. 5 screens for 1 on the reversal. As 1 reverses his dribble, 3 sets a cross-screen for 2 and 4 sets a down-screen for 2. Here is our stagger double-screening action. 1 can hit 2 for the open jumper or look to dump it inside for 4. Some of you might wonder what 5 does after setting the screen for 1. Depending on his ability, 5 can roll to the basket, step back out for the open jumper, etc.

Diagram 6

that are so loud your players can't hear you over the noise. Here's how we practice our hand signals. We got this idea from Gary Williams. The coach stands on the baseline facing the offense. The defense must have their back to the coach, facing their offensive man. The coach gives the signal and the offense runs the appropriate play.

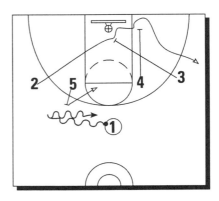

Diagram 8

Diagram 7

(Diagram 9)   Here is a good 1-4 high continuity play. 1 passes to 3 and cuts off a backscreen set by 4. If the lob is there to 1 we get the ball to him. As 1 passes to 3, 5 rolls down the lane to post-up.

(Diagram 8)   Here is the same play from a 1-4 high set. 1 dribbles toward 5. 2 breaks to the basket. 1 reverses his dribble, coming off 5's screen. As 1 comes off 5's screen, 3 breaks to the basket to screen for 2. 4 rolls down the lane to set the second screen and we have the same options as before.

I like to run a lot of plays out of one set. We like the 1-4 high set. We have over 31 plays that can be run out of this set. We won't run all these in a season, but I like to have them in our arsenal. For all our plays we have a verbal and a hand signal call. We do this because there are certain gyms where you play

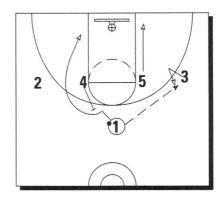

Diagram 9

(Diagram 10)   If 5 or 1 aren't open, 3 passes to 4 at the top of the key. At the same time, 2, on the weakside wing, cuts hard to the basket, bypassing 1 who is coming out to the vacant wing, and sets a screen for 5. 4 passes to 1, who looks to dump the ball inside to 5 on the post-up. After passing the ball to 1, 4 cuts down the lane to down-screen for 2, who cuts to the top of the key. 1 can look to hit 2 for the three-pointer.

(Diagram 12)   An option on this 1-4 set is for 2 to dribble to the wing. 3, who was on the wing, cuts to the block. 2 passes to 4 at the high-post, 1 cuts off 4 for the fake hand-off. 4 dribbles toward the weakside and 5 slides down the lane to set a screen for 3, who comes hard off it looking for the quick ten-footer.

Diagram 12

Diagram 10

(Diagram 11)   If no shot materializes, 4 and 5 come back up to the high-post area and we start over.

(Diagram 13)   Another play we run off the 1-4 high set is: 1 passes to 2 and cuts to the ballside corner. 3, the offside wing, cuts across the lane and comes to the mid-post area.

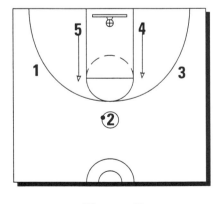

Diagram 11

Diagram 13

(Diagram 14)   4 and 5 set a stagger double-screen for 2 on the dribble. As 2 comes off the screens, he looks to see if he can turn the corner and take the ball to the basket. If not, he takes the ball to offside elbow. After setting his screen, 5 looks for a tough screen from 3 and cuts to the basket. 2 looks to hit 5 on this cut.

Diagram 14

(Diagram 15)   After setting his screen for 2, 4 continues across the lane and sets a screen for 3. 2 looks to hit 3 for a three-pointer. If 3 isn't open for a shot, he passes to 1 at the wing. 1 can now look to dump the ball into 4, who has rolled to replace 5 at the block. We actually don't teach our post players to cut to the block, but to the basket. We do this because we don't believe there is an official who will call three seconds that quickly.

This is one of my favorite plays. Why? For several reasons: One, it's an unusual play that opponents probably haven't seen before. Two, we have big-little screens all the way through. Three, we have ball reversal. Four, we have second side post-up. Five, we have rebound position. And finally, we run it out of a 1-4 set and unless you know our signals, you don't know what is coming.

We run all our quick hitters dummy during practice and we have specific responsibilities for rebounding. On any shot, 3, 4, and 5 form a triangle in the lane. 2 always goes to the foul line for the long rebound, and 1 always cuts to the mid-court circle. If the shot is missed on the dummy play, 3, 4, and 5 must put the ball back in the basket and then all 5 players have to turn and sprint to the defensive paint on the opposite end of the floor.

In closing, let me quote something from Vince Lombardi. He said: "A coach knows what he's looking for in a play." As a coach, you know what your play should look like when it ends. If you don't hold your players to a very high standard, you'll break down when it counts most.

Diagram 15

The Passing Game

We break the passing game down into two different settings. One is with the center open and this is used to combat pressure. This is usually good at the end of a game. The passing game is done without a lot of screens, but with a lot of movement and the more pressure you get the better. The other is the screening game where you constantly set screens. By the first of December, we like to be somewhere between these two offenses. You must decide where the scoring is going to come from. How many posts do you want? You may have only one post, or the luxury of having as many as three. If you are from the old school where you need to know where the ball is every time that it is passed, I'm not so sure this is for you. We can go into the passing game directly or we can run the secondary break through, which takes 17 seconds. But this isn't a concern with the high school coaches. The longer you run the game, the better you are going to be.

(Diagram 1)   The idea is that the ball is in one person's hands and the other four people are working to get it. 1 passes to 2 and gets a rear screen from 3. 5 screens away for 4. The ball remains stationary and the other four people have worked together. And that's exactly what you want.

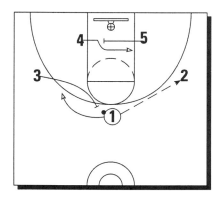

Diagram 1

(Diagram 2)   2 passes to 3 and gets a rear screen from 4. 1 down screens for 5.

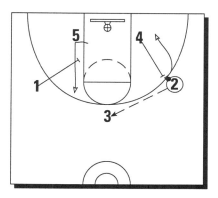

Diagram 2

(Diagram 3)   3 passes to the other side and 4 sets a rear screen for the passer. This is a good idea because that keeps 3 from standing and waiting to get a return pass.

Diagram 3

(Diagram 4)   5 can pass back to the top of the key, get a backscreen from 1 while 3 downscreens for 2. This is actually a pattern that tells each person where to go and what to do and leads them into the passing game. Now some teams switch all screens and some will switch the perimeter screens but not the perimeter/post screens. When we catch the ball, we don't want it in the triple threat position. We want the ball above our head, looking at the goal. Some people will try to guard us belly-to-belly to get us to turn away from the goal. We work on what we call the "rip through." We move the ball hard, with the weight out and away from the pivot foot. We don't want the jab foot going backwards because then you can only see 180 degrees. We can't be backed up. If we are going to drive it, then we get in the triple threat position with the ball on the hip.

Diagram 4

Here is a fundamental. Make the first easy pass. Every time someone has the ball, there will be an easy pass, two medium risk passes and one that can't be made. Make the easy one. I think that playing defense is tough when two things are moving. First, the ball must move. The other thing is that the players must move. Now, the defense is not only looking at the ball, but must see two different objects as he is playing. If you can't make a pass, you must think about driving into the old broken line area of the lane. We call that "power." It doesn't mean dribbling anywhere else. It means dribbling into the lane. And when you get there, gather and go up for the shot. So if the strength of the defense is on the outside and you can't make a pass, then drive the ball. If you are overplayed, don't fight the pressure

to the sideline or to half-court. Just make the quick backdoor move and go all the way to the basket. Don't fake this move.

Our rule is "one step, every step." If you make the first step, you are going backdoor. The other idea is to keep the ball out of the corners because you are so limited as to what you can do with it. We look at the top of the key as a swing area. We can look inside, but we are really looking to swing the ball to the opposite side. So, make the easy pass, make the backdoor cut, and swing it across the top of the key. If you are going through the lane, it can't be a shuffle, it must be a sprint. Not only are you cutting through the lane, the defensive man is cutting through the lane. So cut through crisply. Discourage making a pass and asking for the return pass. Point guards have a tendency to do that.

We need communication among the four people who don't have the ball, the screeners and the cutters. Everybody is a screener and everybody is a cutter. We give a visual sign, the fist up, and we also have a verbal sign, which is calling the name of the person who you are screening for. The farther the screen is set away from the defender, the better chance he has in getting around it. The communication must be good. You can't sway when you set the screen, they'll call that. We get our arms up and the elbows out and this makes kind of a "V." It is up to the man for whom the screen is being set to rub his man off on the screen.

(Diagram 5)   The ball is on the wing and 3 is going to set a backscreen for 4. Where is the defender? 3 wants to have 4 clear to go to the goal. In that case 3's back should be to the goal when the screen is set.

(Diagram 6)   On the down-screen that is not necessarily true. Then the screen would be whereever 2 wants 3 to get the ball. 2's back should be facing the area that he is trying to clear for 3.

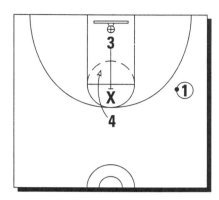

Diagram 5

Diagram 7

Diagram 6

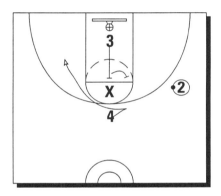

Diagram 8

(Diagram 7)   Backscreen. If 4's man gets on the inside of the screen then 4 would bump and fade and then 3 should rescreen. This means that if 4's man initially gets by 3's screen, then 3 should turn and screen 4's man again as he tries to get back out to guard 4.

(Diagram 8)   If 3 sets the screen and 4's man gets to the ballside, 3 would rescreen him as 4 cuts away. 4 must make the move to get his man hung up on the screen. This is what we call the V-cut.

(Diagram 9)   If 4 wants to go to the right, his initial V-cut move is to the left so that the screen is set up for 3.

(Diagram 10)   This is a double-edged sword. Whichever way the cutter goes, the screener goes the other way. 3 becomes an outlet at the top of the key. If 4 bumps and fades out to the top of the key, 3, the screener, should cut to the goal. One goes one way, the other goes the other way.

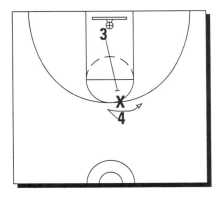

Diagram 9

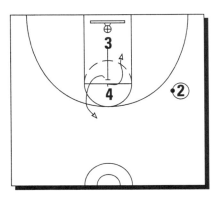

Diagram 10

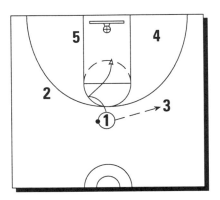

Diagram 11

(Diagram 12)   Keep away. This is a competitive drill. Anytime we have a competitive drill, the team that loses will run at the end of practice. This is 5-on-5. The only time you can dribble is on the entry as you come across the mid-court line. Once the first pass is made, there is no more dribbling. Every time you make a pass you get one point. You play to 25. The only way that you can score is an uncontested layup. The players can go anywhere they want. If you are overplayed, you go backdoor. When the defense stops the offense, it is their turn to be on offense. Keep the ball out of the corners. If the ball is caught in the corner, it is a violation. In this drill you will find people leaning backwards to get away from the defense. You can call this a violation too.

(Diagram 11)   Balance. This is what most coaches want. But this is a bad part of the passing game because if they go there every time, the defense knows where they are going to be. Then, the passing game is predictable. The player making the cut must have a purpose. We need movement with a purpose, not just movement. If a player doesn't know what to do, widen out and find the ball. And you also find a couple of other things. You find where your teammates are and you find where the goal is. 1 doesn't have to set a screen. He can fake and cut to the basket. 2 and 5 will fill. There is a tendency for post people to hang in the post area. There is a tendency for the point guards to hold the ball. That will not make your offense unpredictable.

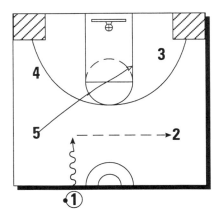

Diagram 12

We do not want any assistant to question a player's shot. It is a shooter's mentality. You must swallow your words. We don't want a player to start to take a shot and then start thinking "should I take it or should I not?" If you claim to be a shooter, let it fly. If you don't shoot it and you are open, you come sit beside me. How would you like to play with those rules? They know that if they don't shoot it they are coming out, and if they do shoot I won't say anything. Shooters have a mentality that is very delicate. Kids love to play our style. So far we have just been covering general guidelines.

(Diagram 13) Four around one. This is 5's area of movement. 5 must be between the ball and the goal. He can post up anytime that he wants to. If 2 passes and cuts, 2 does not want to jam up the middle.

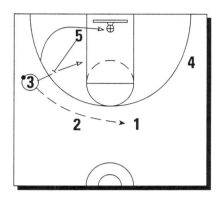

Diagram 14

(Diagram 15) If 4 is a very good passer, this is his area, and 5's area remains the same. 1, 2, and 3 will play on the perimeter.

Diagram 13

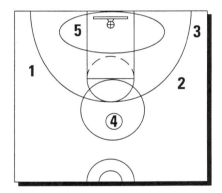

Diagram 15

(Diagram 14) If the ball is reversed, such as a skip-pass from 3 to 1, 5 does not have to seal and follow the ball. 5 can set a backscreen for 3 and let 3 cut through. But then 5 must go back inside.

(Diagram 16) The high post (4) can set screens for the perimeter players. 4 sets the screen for 3.

(Diagram 17) 3 comes off the screen and cuts down the middle. 5 will fade to the corner to give 3 room.

Diagram 16

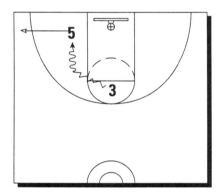

Diagram 17

game. You must also work with your center to get open. He should have a favorite move, a counter move, and a power move. When two people pass each other, they should never pass without setting a screen. Never pass up a screening opportunity.

Diagram 18

Diagram 19

(Diagram 18)   4's rule is when he catches the ball he looks low and then looks opposite. He does not look back to the same side. 5 will post between 4 and the goal.

(Diagram 19)   You can run a 3 post offense with 3, 4, and 5 screening for each other. 3 can start by setting a down-screen for either 4 or 5.

(Diagram 20)   3 can down-screen for 5 or 4 can cross-screen for 5. 1 and 2 can get a screen from the man in the high post position. But basically you are trying to get the ball inside because that is where the strength must be if you are running a 3-post offense. Eventually what you want is to combine both the passing and screening games. If you are working against pressure, you open it up a little, if the defense is sagging, then you run the screening

Diagram 20

Secondary Break

I want to take you all the way through the break and then get into some of the drills that we do. From 33% to 40% of our scoring comes off our primary or secondary break. This is based on the North Carolina break.

(Diagram 1)   Whether there is a miss or a make, we only have one outlet. We want him on the side of the floor where the ball is, and he must get the ball. When 1 gets the ball, we do not want to see 2, 3, or 4 in the picture. As soon as the ball is in 5's hands, 2, 3, and 4 start to run. The key is in the first three steps. If 1 can turn this into a primary break by passing to 2, he does it. By primary, I mean 1/1, 2/1, 3/2 or until the defense has the ball stopped. Then we get into the secondary break.

(Diagram 2)   1 takes the ball to the side, 5 goes to the top of the key, 4 shadows the ball low, 2 and 3 can run either side. If 1 passes to 2, we do not want 2 to make the return pass to 1. 2 should look to 4, and then pass to 5. Look what that does to the man guarding 4. 5 can hit 4 or pass to 3. 3 must get open.

(Diagram 3)   4 shadows the ball. 2 steps in and rear-screens for 5 who breaks down the lane for the pass from 3.

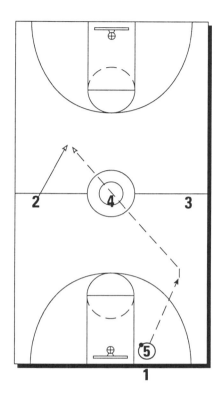

Diagram 1

Diagram 2

Diagram 3

(Diagram 4)   2's angle is important. The tendency is for 2 to run straight at 5. That's a bad angle. Remember what I said, put your back to the area that you are trying to clear the man to.

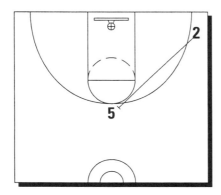

Diagram 4

(Diagram 5)   If 5 doesn't get the pass from 3, 3 will pass back to 2. 5 will continue across the lane and set the screen for 4. 4 usually cuts low so 5 knows how to set the screen. 4 and 5 both duck into the lane for a possible pass from 2. 2 can also catch and drive. The options are that anyone on the outside can pass into the low block. Then there is the possible dunk by 5. The third option is for 2 to break into the middle, and then there is the duck-in

move by 4 and 5. It takes 17 seconds from the time that 5 gets the rebound until 5 screens for 4. We then go into the passing game or a set play.

Diagram 5

(Diagram 6)   A counter move. There is a tendency for the point guard to stay on the side. However, we want some variation. We want the "slice" move where he changes into the middle or to the other side. He can even start into the middle and come back to the original side. The point is that he must be unpredictable. As he is coming down he is looking for 2, 3 and 4.

(Diagram 7)   4 must give a little to the side for the angle pass. If 1 can get the ball ahead to 2 and 2 can dunk it, that's exciting basketball. But the main point is that he should not put the ball in jeopardy while going from one end to the other. A good point guard will have a two-to-one ratio of assists to turnovers. 1's eyes are down court. He must see 2, 3, and 4.

(Diagram 8)   Let's say there are two defenders back. We will also allow 1 to take the ball to the corner. 1, 2, and 3 become interchangeable. 1 then passes to 2, and takes good angle to set the backscreen for 5.

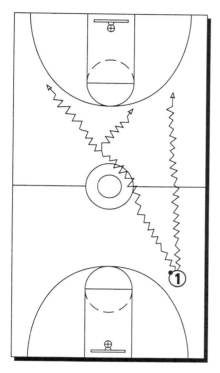

Diagram 6

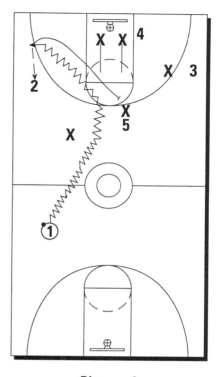

Diagram 8

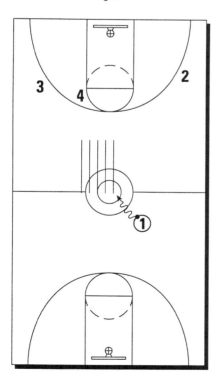

Diagram 7

(Diagram 9)   We have several sets off of this. This is the secondary flex. This must be called. 1 hits 5, and 2 makes a shuffle cut off of 4. 5 will pass to 2 or to 4, who ducks into the lane. It is a secondary break setup with a flex cut out of the corner with the ball in a high/low situation; if we don't get that, we go into a set play or the passing game.

(Diagram 10)   Double. 2 is your good shooter. Run this to the side of your shooter. 1 to 2, and 2 skip-passes to 5, who passes to 3. 4 follows the ball. 1 cuts in and sets a screen for 2 with his back to the top of the key. 5 follows and he also screens for 2 with his back to the top of the key.

Diagram 9

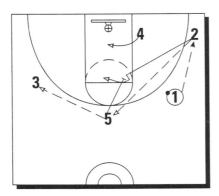

Diagram 10

(Diagram 11)   3 passes to 2 coming off of the staggered screen.

Diagram 11

(Diagram 12)   Backdoor. If 1 passes to 5, then 4 must stay and 3 can go backdoor.

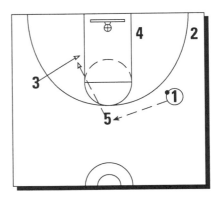

Diagram 12

(Diagram 13)   If 5 can't pass to 3, 5 dribbles toward the wing. 3 continues into the lane and screens for 4. 4 can cut high or low. 1 moves in and down and screens for 3. So the options are 3 going backdoor, 3 screening for 4, and 1 screening for 3 coming to the top of the key. If you don't have those, the play is over.

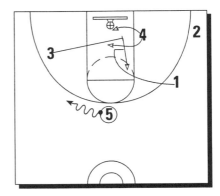

Diagram 13

(Diagram 14)   Kickback. If 5 can't swing the ball to 3, 5 passes back to 1. 2 moves in and then sets a backscreen for 5. 5 comes off the screen and if he doesn't get the ball, 5 will come across and screen for 4.

Diagram 14

(Diagram 15)   2 steps out and can get the pass from 1 and then 2 looks inside to 5 and 4 who have ducked into the lane.

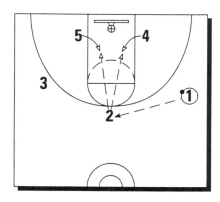

Diagram 15

Drills: We have 5 main drills and a secondary break game. Anytime that we use the word "game" after a drill it means that it is competitive. We make them score on the secondary break. If the defense stops the ball, blow the whistle. Keep score. Don't do a lot of teaching. This is the only way that I know to run one secondary break after another. A foul counts as a basket.

(Diagram 16)   Drill #1. Point guards in the middle. Ball starts on the side. 2 passes to 1 and they are sprinting to the other end. 1 can pass to either 2 or 3 but should have the ball when he comes under control at the other end at the free-throw line. He makes a bounce pass to 3, who is sprinting to the basket.

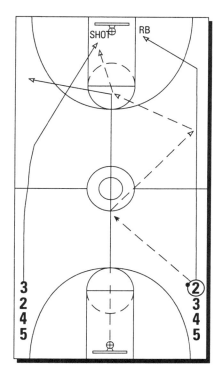

Diagram 16

(Diagram 17)   2 will rebound and make the outlet pass to 1, who is now in the outlet area on the side. If the shot is made, 2 will not take the ball out-of-bounds because 2 never takes the out-of-bounds during a game. 1 will make a baseball pass the length of the floor to the first man in the next line.

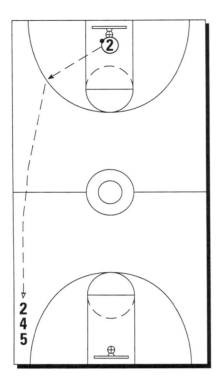

Diagram 17

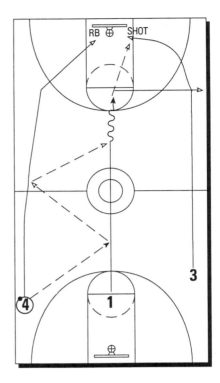

Diagram 18

(Diagram 18)   Now the drill is run on the other side. If 4 and 5 are the rebounders and the shot is made, they will take the ball out-of-bounds. Don't let them cheat when they inbound the ball. Don't let them flick it in without looking. We want the shoulders, hips and feet turned. We will run this game for about one or two minutes.

(Diagram 19)   Once your kids know how to do it, we will use two balls. 2 and 3 both have a ball. As the first three people get to the top of the key, the next three start.

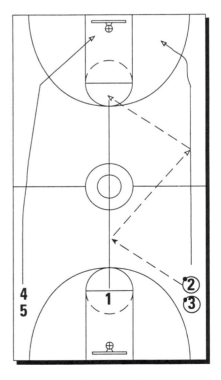

Diagram 19

(Diagram 20)   Drill #2, dribble bust out. 2 will rebound the ball, and look for the outlet and act as if the outlet is not open. 2 will swing the ball low, and dribble to the outside toward his partner. 3 doesn't leave until 2 catches the ball. 2 will pass ahead to 3 and 3 will take the layup. Meanwhile, at the other end 4 and 5 are running the same drill coming the other way.

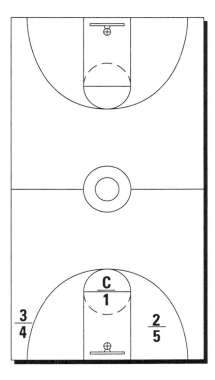

Diagram 21

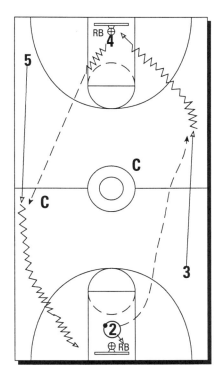

Diagram 20

(Diagram 21)   Drill #3, the box out. 1, 4, and 5 are on defense. The coach shoots and they box out.

(Diagram 22)   1 was boxing-out the coach so now he is a free outlet. 5 or 4 will rebound and make the outlet pass to 1. Players X and Y are on defense at the middle of the floor. On the outlet pass, X and Y will drop back on defense. We want a score on one or two passes. It is 3-on-2 and we don't want to take all day to score. We prefer a layup.

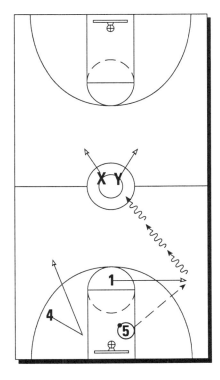

Diagram 22

(Diagram 23)   Regardless of what happens at the other end, X and Y will come back 2-on-1 against 1.

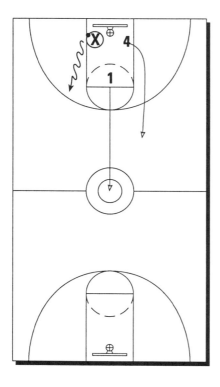

Diagram 23

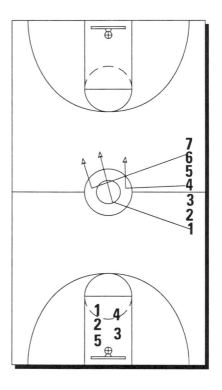

Diagram 24

(Diagram 24)   Drill #4, recognition. There are five offensive players in the lane. Another group of players is on the sideline near mid-court with another coach. The ball is rebounded and the play starts with five offensive players going full-court. The coach on the sideline will send out either one, two, three, four, or five players to play defense. The defensive players must run out and touch the floor in the center circle and then drop back to play defense. The offense must recognize how many people are back on defense and then find the open man. The timing is such that the defense should be backpedaling and not set up at the other end.

(Diagram 25)   Drill #5, 5-man weave. Each player touches the ball once, and the ball never touches the floor. The ball goes from 1-4-2-3-5.

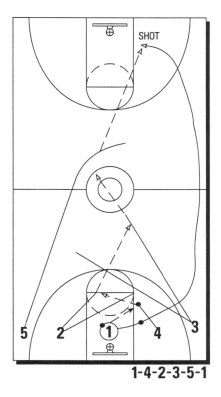

1-4-2-3-5-1

Diagram 25

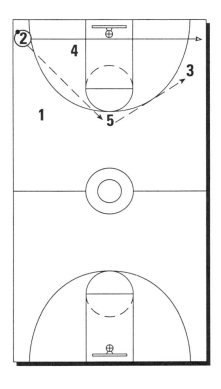

Diagram 26

Question: How about against a zone?

Answer: (Diagram 26)   If they were to get into a zone every time, we would have 2 skip-pass to 5 and then run the baseline as 5 reverses the ball to 3.

Developing the Fast Break

I think that we ran as well as anybody, but I have never seen anyone teach the fast break part-to-whole. I've run John Wooden's fast break at all levels. I tell our players that the number one skill is listening. Number two, you better have good hands or I won't throw you the ball. When you get on the court I want you to have five basic things. I call it the "Big Five."

1. **Stance**. I want you in a stance at all times, feet as wide as the shoulders, chest out, back straight, head up, bent at the knees and never at the waist. I don't think it makes a lot of difference how you hold your arms, but it does make a difference how you are in the rest of your stance.

2. **Concentration**. Concentrate on everything you do. When you get on the floor, give me everything you've got for a couple of hours.

3. **Quickness**. We work on quickness every day, both hands and feet. We want to be quick in everything we do. Be quick, but don't hurry. Have your players go as fast as they can under balance and under control.

4. **Balance** means that the head is at the mid-point between the two feet on everything that you do. If I am shooting, dribbling, rebounding, I want the head on the mid-point between the two feet. They say don't reach. What are they saying? Don't take the head out of the mid-point of the two feet. Balanced players play, unbalanced players sit.

    Quickness and Balance are the two most important things in basketball.

5. **Hard Play**. I just came from an NBA tryout camp. We had one player who played so hard that it made everybody else look like they were standing still. He energized the others on our team.

The Seven Fundamental Areas: We teach this every day.

1. Acknowledge a good pass. When a player passes you the ball and you score, you thank him in some way.

2. The ball goes on the chest, under the chin, elbows out. While in the stance, I want the ball touching the chest. If you do that, no one will take it away from you.

3. The two-foot jump stop. When I stop while dribbling, I want a two-foot stop, balanced, under control, head at the mid-point ready to pass, or shoot. Make a two-handed pass. Then fake a pass, make a pass.

4. V-cut, and ask for the ball. Everything we do on offense starts with the V-cut. If the receiver doesn't ask for the ball, don't give it to him.

5. Step back, crossover on the dribble. This will eliminate the reverse pivot where someone can come from the weakside and steal the ball. Don't turn your back on the defense. Keep the ball no higher than the knee.

6. When the ball goes up, the hands go up. Make your players pinpoint the ball.

7. Follow the shot, with your hands up.

Let's talk about building the fast break. In the NBA, the good teams all run, because you get easy baskets. Young players like to do it and it teaches them to pass and dribble while on the move. It allows you to catch up when you are behind. Certainly you must control it, and you must be patient. You are going to have a few more turnovers. You must understand and teach good shot selection, and where the shots come from.

Why do we fast break? It teaches you to push the ball. It is the greatest conditioner of all time. If players cannot run the floor and change ends, then they are not able to go on to the next level. The most misused part of basketball is blocking out and transition defense. I want to score 1/3 of the time on my half-court set offense, 1/3 of the time from the fast break, and 1/3 of the time off of the defense. That makes you hard to beat. Before you can run, you have to rebound.

(Diagram 1)   Rebound, pass out. Each man must make a V-cut. 1 passes to 2. 1 fakes away and comes to the foul line and gets the return pass from 2. 1 then underhands the ball off the glass above the rectangle. 2 rebounds and as he is coming down he makes a half turn and makes the outlet pass to 3. We run this on both sides. The ball goes from 1-2-1-2-3.

Diagram 1

(Diagram 2)   Two line rebounding. 1 underhands the ball off of the board and gets his own rebound. He makes the outlet pass to 2, who passes to 3. The rebounder makes a half-turn while in the air. Run this on both sides at the same time. Change lines.

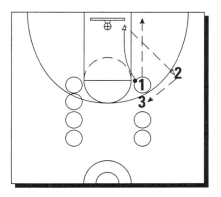

Diagram 2

(Diagram 3)   Flanker. This is a technique fast break drill. Go back to the seven fundamental areas. 2 and 3 go as fast as they can to half-court. There they slow with balance and under control and go to the free-throw line extended, plant the outside foot and go to the corners of the board in balance and under control. 1 takes three or four hard dribbles and inside of the top of the key he makes a two-foot jump stop. He can make the pass or shoot the jumper. After 1 makes the pass, he moves to the elbow on the side of the ball. He is ready to receive the return pass. The outside man usually shoots the bank jumpshot. The offside player goes to the block. He coils, hands up, ready to rebound.

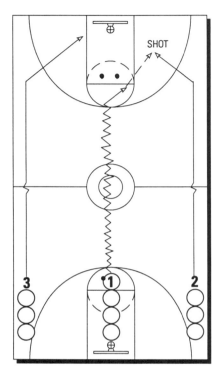

Diagram 3

(Diagram 4)   The shooter goes to the middle to rebound, 1 moves to the ballside block.

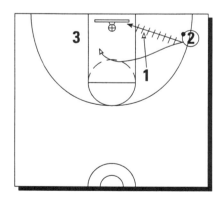

Diagram 4

(Diagram 5)   4/0. The coach shoots. Guards are

responsible for the long rebound. The outlet pass is always made on the ballside. Rebounder is the trailer on the outlet side. Rebounder outlets to the ballside guard, and the pass is then made to the other guard breaking in the middle. The pass is made near the top of the key because there will always be a defender at half-court. The same principles apply at the other end.

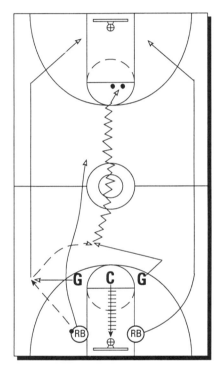

Diagram 5

(Diagram 6)   If you run it 5/0, the other big man will take the trail position on the ballside and the rebounder will stop at half-court.

(Diagram 7)   3/2 conditioner. It is a 3/2 drill with a third defensive man coming in at mid-court, touching the floor, and then playing defense to make it 3/3. The back man takes the first pass, the front man takes the cross-court pass and we hope our trailer picks up the reverse pass. That's how we defend the fast break. This is a continuous drill.

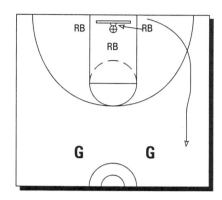

Diagram 6

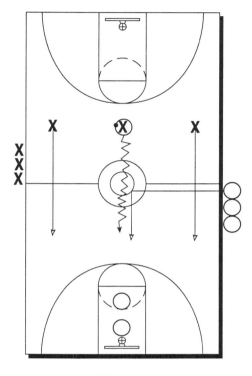

Diagram 8

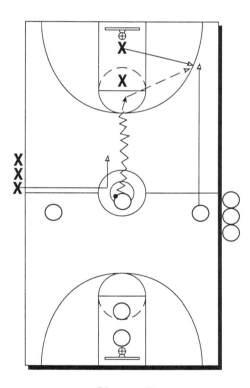

Diagram 7

(Diagram 9)   3 lanes, 1 weave. Rebound the ball off the glass and then make three bounce passes weaving to half-court. At half-court the middle man makes one or two dribbles and we are into the fast break. We do it so that each man has a chance to be in the middle. We do the same drill using a chest pass instead of a bounce pass. The third drill is a one-pass break. The ball is rebounded and the outlet pass is made. Then the ball is dribbled the length of the floor with the same fast break principles. The entire team goes one way, then the entire team goes the other way. I don't like to have nine guys standing while three go down and back.

(Diagram 10)   2/1. The middle man is the defense.

(Diagram 8)   When the defense gets the ball either after a turnover or after a made basket, they become the offense and go to the other end where the same thing happens. The third man comes out to play defense as they cross mid-court.

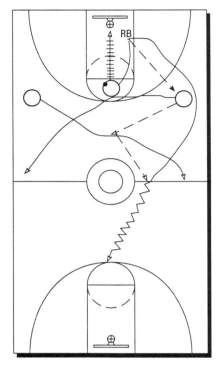

Diagram 9

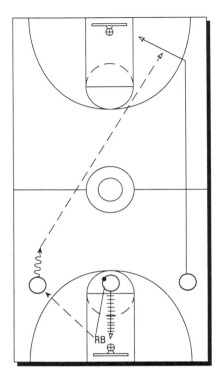

Diagram 11

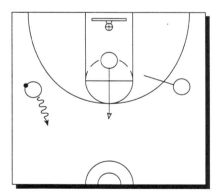

Diagram 10

(Diagram 14)   4/2 continuous, three teams, red, white, and blue. White starts with the ball at mid-court going 4/2. R1 and R2 are not in this. When you go 4 on 2, you should score. When red gets the ball after a make or a miss, then the red team goes 4 on 2 against the blue at the other end. B1 and B2 are not in this until the blue team gets the ball after a make or a miss. This is continuous action. The only bad thing about this is that it takes twelve players.

(Diagram 11)   The ball is rebounded off the glass and outlet. The wing man makes a one-bounce dribble and makes a high lob cross-court pass to the other wing. This is not a baseball pass. It is a two-handed pass with a backspin that will go straight up when it bounces.

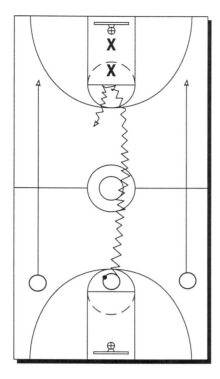

Diagram 12

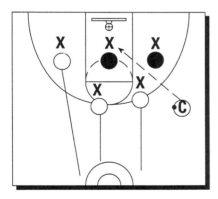

Diagram 13

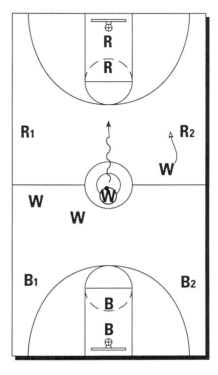

Diagram 14

(Diagram 15)   5/5 control. This is not a fast break drill, but it is a fast break drill. The numbers go man-to-man offense, the X's play man-to-man defense. If the numbers score, then they press. If the X's are scored on, they run the press offense. If the numbers don't score, then they are in transition defense. If the X's stopped the numbers, then they fast break. After we go down and back, we change. X's go on offense to start. Sometimes we just let them go and scrimmage, but usually we control it this way. And we also control the scrimmage with a time and score factor. We may start from a foul shot. You can do more teaching in a 5/5 control. You are a teacher of basketball and the court is an extension of the classroom. You have your methods, discipline, and you know what you are doing. Teach what you know, and know what you teach. You win games by teaching from three to five in the afternoon. You don't teach during the games, you are coaching then. But you are teaching 90% of the time.

Don't get your priorities mixed up. Hopefully you will help your team win by covering all aspects of the game in practice.

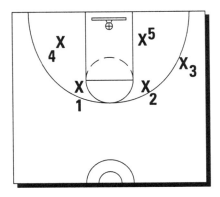

Diagram 15

Balanced Court High-Post Offense

I ran this offense for years, and changed parts of it from time to time, but I've never changed the basics. I watched John Wooden run this for years and I said to myself why should I change anything after he has experimented with it for 28 years? But you must adapt it to your system and your team. I want to start with some drills. We teach everything from part to the whole. We show them what we want and why we are doing it.

(Diagram 1)   Side-post. Do this on both sides of the floor. 5 sets a screen at the high-post with one foot in the top of the circle and the other foot on the line. He is not facing straight ahead, he is turned. 1 passes to 5, makes a V-cut, gets the ball back and comes off the screen and 1 and 5 run the screen and roll with the one bounce dribble. The second drill is the dribble, screen and roll. 1 dribbles into the middle, uses 5 for the screen and then they screen and roll.

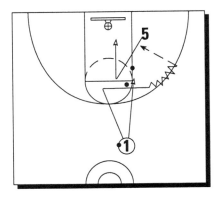

Diagram 1

(Diagram 2)   Side-post delay. 1 passes to 5 and cuts to the outside but doesn't get the ball. 1 comes back for the pass from 5. 1 can shoot or pass to 5 going down the lane.

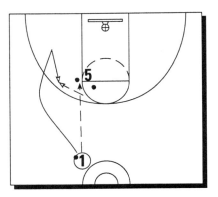

Diagram 2

(Diagram 3)   Inside screen. 1 passes to 5, and sets a screen in the lane. 5 comes off the screen and 1 flares out. 5 makes a one bounce dribble, has a shot or a pass to 1.

(Diagram 4)   Flatten or curl. 5 must be able to read what the defense does. 4 sets a screen for 5. If the defense trails, curl.

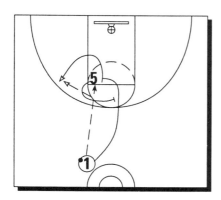

Diagram 3

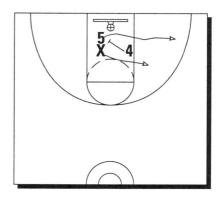

Diagram 5

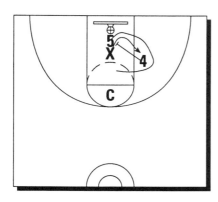

Diagram 4

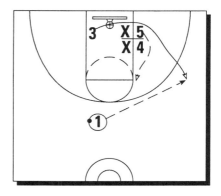

Diagram 6

(Diagram 5)   If the defensive man goes over the top, then 5 must flatten out along the baseline.

(Diagram 6)   Pop the stack. 4 and 5 set a double-screen for 3. If 3, coming off the double-screen, gets the ball, then 4 screens down for 5, who breaks to the high-post. 4 then posts up low.

(Diagram 7)   3 can shoot, or pass to 4 at the low-post or to 5, who can pass in to 4.

(Diagram 8)   If 3 comes off the stack and does not get the ball, that means that we are running a side-post on the other side of the floor.

(Diagram 9)   Everything ends like this. This is a great offense if you don't have a big player.

(Diagram 10)   Continuity. 3 and 4 go down to the blocks. What happens if your play breaks down? You go into the continuity.

Diagram 7

Diagram 8

Diagram 9

Diagram 10

(Diagram 11)   Guard cut. 2 passes to 3, comes off of 5's screen and goes to the corner.

Diagram 11

(Diagram 12)   If 3 doesn't hit 2, 3 passes to 5 and screens down for 2. 1 goes away and 4 ducks into the lane for high/low action.

(Diagram 13)   5's first option is to 4, then 3, and then 2. If they aren't open, he passes to 1.

(Diagram 14)   After passing to 1, 5 screens down for 3. This is an offense within itself. 1 can pass to 4 or to 3, who then looks low for 5.

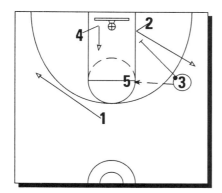

Diagram 12

Diagram 13

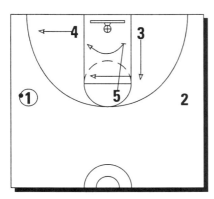

Diagram 14

(Diagram 15)   An option is 3 and 5 set a double-screen for 2.

(Diagram 16)   Another option, 4 comes up and screens for 1, and 1 runs a screen and roll.

Diagram 15

Diagram 16

(Diagram 17)   Another option. 4 can set the backscreen for 5. 3 passes to 2, who looks for 5. The beauty of this offense is that you can design any kind of play that you want to run and adapt it to your personnel. You really don't need anything else.

(Diagram 18)   Here's how you alleviate half-court pressure with this offense. 5 breaks low, and 4 comes high for the pass from 1. 5 and 3 form a double-screen.

Diagram 17

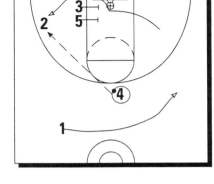

Diagram 19

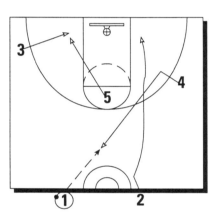

Diagram 18

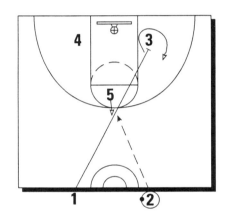

Diagram 20

(Diagram 19)   2 cuts low and comes off the double-screen for the pass from 4.

(Diagram 20)   An option is for 5 to break high for the pass from 2. 1 breaks off and sets a screen for 3. Or, 1 can curl around 3 and come back for the pass from 5.

(Diagram 21)   Guard dribble. 3 V-cuts high and then goes low for the backdoor cut.

(Diagram 22)   Guard screen. 2 is our good player. 1 passes to 3 and screens for 2. 2 comes off the staggered screens set by 1 and 5.

(Diagram 23)   Option. 3 and 5 set a double-screen low. 2 comes off the screen set by 4 and comes to the top of the key as 5 breaks high.

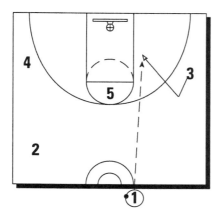

Diagram 21

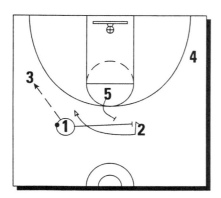

Diagram 22

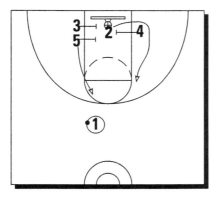

Diagram 23

(Diagram 24)   Guard follow. 1 passes to 4 and goes behind 4 for the return pass. 5 sets a screen at the high-post and 3 breaks to the low-post.

Diagram 24

(Diagram 25)   4 comes off the screen set by 5 for the lob from 1.

Diagram 25

(Diagram 26)   If 4 doesn't get the lob pass, 1 has 3 dribbles off of 5. 5 then screens down for 3. 2 screens down for 4 on the other side.

Diagram 26

Diagram 28

(Diagram 27)   Guard around. 1 passes to 3 and breaks around and goes low. 1 and 5 set a double-screen as 3 passes to 2. 3 breaks low and then comes over the top of the double-screen as 4 uses the double-screen in the other direction and breaks to the corner.

(Diagram 29)   If 4 passes to 1, 3 and 4 set a double-screen for 5.

Diagram 27

Diagram 29

(Diagram 28)   Low-post set. Low-post is ballside. 2 passes to 4 and goes away. 3 cuts to the high-post. 1 moves to the top of the circle. 4 looks to 5. If 4 can't hit 5, 4 hits 3, who looks in to 5. 5 seals.

(Diagram 30)   Backdoor. 4 clears, 1 passes to 3 at the high-post and cuts to the basket. You can also run this play by cutting 5 to the high-post.

(Diagram 31)   This is a 1-2-2 set. 1 passes to 3. 4 breaks high and 1 comes off 4's screen and goes to the corner. 2 replaces at the top of circle. What happens is that when you finish you are in a 1-3-1 set with 1 on the baseline.

Diagram 30

Diagram 32

Diagram 31

Diagram 33

(Diagram 32)   Guard dribble. 1 can dribble to the wing and 3 goes away. 4 breaks to the high-post, 5 comes ballside. 2 screens for 3. 1 can pass to 3 or to 4.

(Diagram 33)   1 can pass to 5 breaking to the high-post.

(Diagram 34)   Screen the screener. 1 passes to 2, and screens down for 5. 3 then screens down for 1.

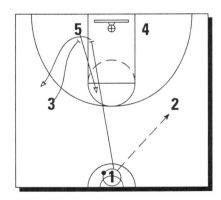

Diagram 34

(Diagram 35)   As the ball is swung from 2 to 5 to 1, 3 continues across the lane and screens 4. 5 then screens down for 3, who comes off the screen for the pass from 1.

Diagram 35

(Diagram 36)   We start this with a fast break after a made basket. 5 inbounds to 1, who dribbles. If the break isn't there, we go into this.

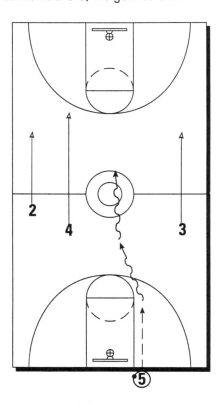

Diagram 36

(Diagram 37)   1 passes to 3 and goes away. 2 goes low.

(Diagram 38)   2 sets a screen for 4, who is on the ballside block. 5 sets the screen for 2, who breaks up the lane.

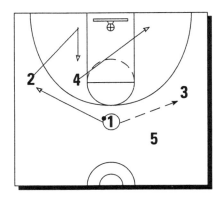

Diagram 37

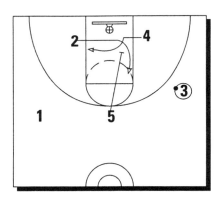

Diagram 38

(Diagram 39)   Drills. We run this on Monday. High-post screen. 1 passes to 5, who breaks to the high-post. 1 comes off the screen set by 5. Run this to both sides.

(Diagram 40)   Backdoor, Tuesday. The wing works to get open and then goes backdoor and gets the pass from 1.

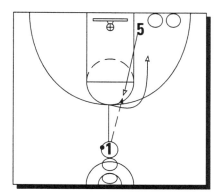

Diagram 39

Diagram 40

(Diagram 41)   Add the high-post. 1 passes to 5 and 3 works to get open and goes backdoor.

Diagram 41

(Diagram 42)   Wednesday. The ball is passed from the wing to the top of the circle. The high-post and wing will set a double-screen for the baseline man. If he gets the ball we pop the stack.

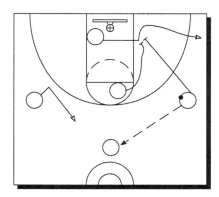

Diagram 42

(Diagram 43)   Thursday. 5/0. We run this late in the week for the timing and the spacing. You must start the offense with a guard-to-guard pass. Next the guard dribble, etc. We do the fundamentals every day.

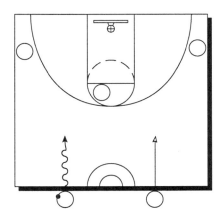

Diagram 43

Offensive Concepts

I've been a high school coach for 23 years so I know some of your problems. I have been through some of the things that you are going through. I know your time is very limited, teach all day and then coach. This year our team was 34-2. I think we had the best team for the overall season. Several years ago we thought we were weak physically and we really worked on our strength program. Last year, we thought that our outside shooting had cost us. So, we did some things on our outside shot. We put a limit on them. We made sure the right players were shooting the ball, we worked hard on our outside shooting and we did improve in those areas.

Next year we are really going to work on our quickness. How do you teach quickness? Maybe for us it is recruiting more quickness, or more off season work. We struggled against Arizona both inside and outside with their quickness. They beat us to the ball. Coach Williams is everything that you read about. Our seniors were asked about him, and two things kept coming up; he is hard working and honest. He is a tireless worker, always doing something for Kansas basketball. I think one of his greatest strengths is giving his players confidence. At half-time, there are not a lot of blood and guts speeches. He works on their confidence. That's one if his greatest strengths. Another great strength is the way that he changes every year to fit the personnel.

Some of us can get hung up on a system, but if you watch, you will see that we change from year to year. You must be careful about this yourself. We don't have anything written out. Coach doesn't like that because we are constantly changing. Before the season starts, our staff gets together for a couple of days and we just talk basketball, this year's team and what we think that they can do. We decide what we want to work on the first week of practice, the second week, and the third. Those are our goals.

Our offensive goals are rather elementary. We say we are going to fast break. The two types of break we have are the secondary break (this means there are more than two defenders back) and the primary break. In the first week, we are going to work on the secondary break and finishing it.

(Diagram 1)   Our regular secondary break ends up like this. As we reverse the ball, every player looks inside first. The ball is being reversed from 2-1-5-3. 2 then sets the rear screen for 5.

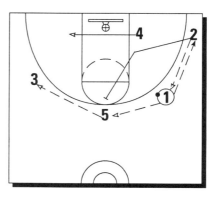

Diagram 1

(Diagram 2)   Finishing the break means 5 comes across the lane to the offside block. 5 then screens for 4 as 3 reverses the ball back to 2. We set some goals for the secondary break. Three-point shots for our big players are not okay, even if the defense is set. Coach Williams only let one player shoot the ball off the break this year. This is a complete change of philosophy for this year as compared to last. With the primary break, if there is one defender you have to shoot a layup, you cannot shoot an outside shot. If there are two defenders back, we are going to shoot the ball in two passes or less.

Free lance offense. This means either a screening game or a passing game. We screen when people sag against us and we pass when people pressure us. Coach Williams wants this written down to make it very definite. This is what we want to do. And he wants to stick to that. He will make changes, but by setting goals, that reinforces it. We will then plan the second and third weeks of practice. That's as far as we would plan. It's important for you to have a plan that fits your players for that year, and stay with it. We run these drills to teach the primary and secondary break. We use two or three of these every day in practice.

left receives a bounce pass for the layup. The other outside player gets the rebound, and passes to the middle man who has broken out to the outlet position. If the shot is made, and this is a 4 or 5 man, he will take the ball out-of-bounds and make the quick inbounds pass. The outlet then makes a baseball pass the length of the floor to the next man in line. If the layup is missed, the shooter must go to the top of the field house and touch. We don't care how the layup is shot.

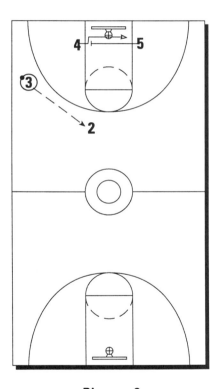

Diagram 2

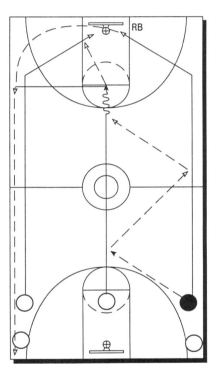

Diagram 3

(Diagram 3)   Fast Break Drill #1. Start with three lines with the ball on the side. The players make chest passes with the ball ending up in the middle at the other end of the floor. The outside players make a 45 degree cut to the basket and the player on the

(Diagram 4)   Fast Break Drill #2. 1 tosses the ball against the backboard, and rebounds the ball out in front of him. We pull the rebound down through low to the floor and take one dribble. 2 has released and will receive a long pass for the layup. This is run at both ends at the same time.

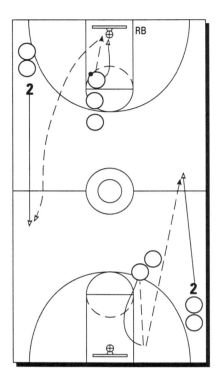

Diagram 4

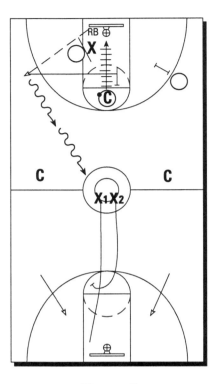

Diagram 5

(Diagram 5)   Fast Break Drill #3. The coach shoots the ball, and it's a 3-on-3 block-out. There are two other coaches at mid-court. After 1 blocks out the shooter, he becomes the outlet. There are two defenders starting at half-court. X1 stops the ball, and the other defensive man takes the first pass. It is 3-on-2. When the defense gets the ball, either after a made basket or a rebound or turnover, then the point man comes back on defense and the two defensive men become offense, and it is 2-on-1 in the other direction.

(Diagram 6)   When it becomes 2-on-1 in the other direction, the outlet pass must be made to a coach. The coach will return the pass and it is now 2-on-1.

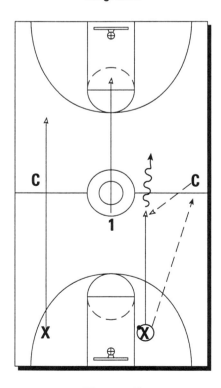

Diagram 6

(Diagram 7)   Fast Break Drill #4. This is a recognition drill. Put six players on the side with a coach. Each has a number. Coach shoots the ball and the drill starts 5-on-0. The coach on the side has designated any number of players (from 1 to 5) to step out and play defense. The point guard must recognize whether it is a secondary break or primary break. If there are two defenders or less, it is primary break and the ball is in the middle. If there are more than two defenders, it is a secondary break and the ball should go to the corner.

of the offense will receive passes from the end line players. So there are three offensive players shooting about the same time. The player who shot the layup takes his own ball out of the net and starts back in the other direction along with the two players who made the passes from the end line. So, they have four minutes and 20 seconds to make 100 shots. This is a continuous drill.

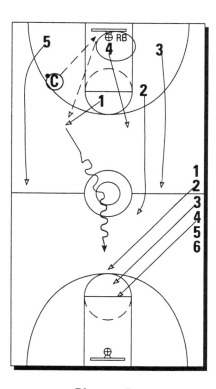

Diagram 7

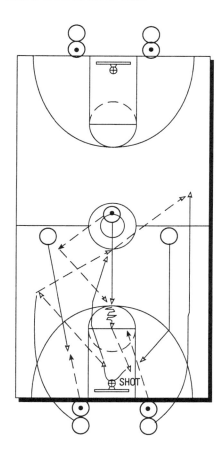

Diagram 8

(Diagram 8)   Sonics Drill. We put four minutes and 20 seconds on the clock. Three players start at mid-court, the middle man has a ball. There are four other balls, one for each line at the ends of the floor. The drill begins with a 3/0 fast break, the outside men filling the lanes. The ball is passed back and forth until someone gets a layup. The other two men

(Diagram 9)   5 vs. 5. This is a competitive drill and we go to ten points. Coach starts the drill by shooting the ball. This is a good conditioner, and we are working on the secondary break.

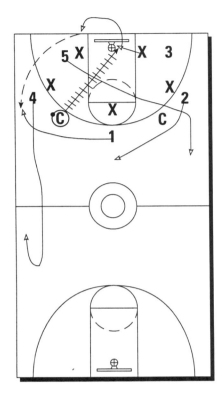

Diagram 9

the other team gets it. Any time we play 5-on-5, it is recorded by the managers and that's where coach gets his running at the end of practice. We run every day, but coach also rewards the players during practice. They can pick up "plus points." Anytime you run to the other end and back, a ten-second drill, that is a plus point. If you do it twice, that is 22 seconds, three times 33 seconds, etc. So, if you have some plus points, you can use them in lieu of running. At the end of the season some seniors have plus points left over at the end of their careers and they can will them to somebody. Our returning players are already bargaining for them. Next year at our preseason meeting, these will be mentioned. The coach takes into account the inflation factor so they may not get all of them.

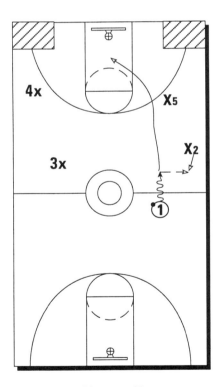

Diagram 10

(Diagram 10) "Keep Away." We have two kinds of offenses, both free lance. We have one where there is pressure on the ball, and the other when people sag. The offense we use against pressure is "one game." We keep everybody wide and high, and we pass the ball. We don't set any screens. To teach this we play a little game of keep away. Only 1 can dribble the ball and once he comes across half-court and makes a pass, he cannot dribble either. This is how we teach the passing game. This gets your players open, moving, and looking for the open man. We do this early in the year.

Rules: No dribbles. Keep ball out of the corners— it is a violation. Can't pass and get a pass back from the same player. You always let the player who makes the pass cut first. Cut all the way through. We play to 50. On the first day, only the passes count, one point each. When you turn the ball over,

Back to the drill. On the second day, we add ten points for a layup, and five points for a foul and still get one point for each pass. On the third day, we add a "one dribble for a layup."

We don't do box-out drills. When someone misses a box-out, we don't make a big deal of it. We just sprint to half-court and back.

(Diagram 11)   The screening game, "three game." We like a lot of free lance things. We do have some set plays on a dead ball situation, but most of it is free lance. The screening game and the passing game are completely separate. If the defense is sagging, we are going to try to screen these people down even more inside the lane. We have several rules. We want to make at least three passes unless we have a layup. We want to change sides of the floor with the ball. We want to give the defense a chance to make a mistake.

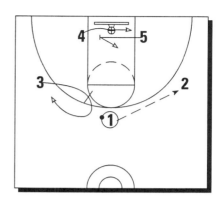

Diagram 12

(Diagram 13)   2 passes back to the top of the circle to 3. 1 will down-screen for 5, and 4 will rear-screen the passer.

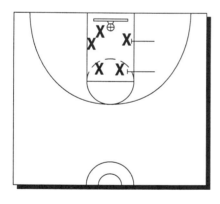

Diagram 11

Diagram 13

(Diagram 12)   There are four different types of screens that we use; lateral, side (flare), down, rear. We use the whole method, all five players. 1 passes to 2. When 2 gets the ball, 5 makes a lateral screen for 4. 4 always goes low. 3 will set a flare screen for the passer.

(Diagram 14)   3 reverses the ball to 5, 1 sets the lateral screen for 2, and 4 sets the side-screen for the passer. If you do this five times, you will be back where you started and your players have played all five positions and set all types of screens.

Coach doesn't like to get an offensive foul because of an illegal screen. He doesn't like physical basketball, he is more of a finesse coach. We teach our players to put one hand on the other wrist at waist level when setting a screen. Inside, sometimes our players set a butt-screen and then look for the ball. We don't run this as an offense, this is just the way that we teach it. We talk about being on the buddy system. Find a buddy to screen. It doesn't have to be the logical screen. We like to screen for the passer. Most people like to pass and go away. But we like to screen the passer. If the defense fights over it, we will cut to the basket.

Your offense must communicate. We use visual and verbal signals. We call out the name, and also when we are going to screen, the screener puts his fist in the air. We don't want two players to screen the same man or have two men go to screen each other. I am either going to get a screen or give a screen. I must make eye contact with my teammate and a fist in the air means that I am screening for you. I also call out his name. Our favorite screens are little for big, big for little. If we can get big for little where little is coming out for the shot, now big must come out and cover him and that is what we want. If we can get little for big, then inside, they have a little man on our big man.

(Diagram 16)   If the ball is passed back from the wing to the coach, that means that 4 can come out and set a rear screen for 1. 4 could also set a side-screen and 1 could flare to the corner.

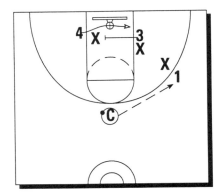

Diagram 15

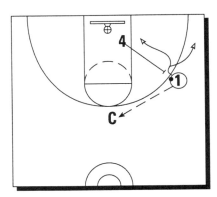

Diagram 16

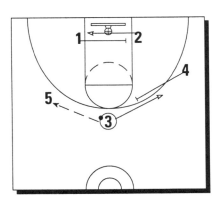

Diagram 14

(Diagram 15)   This is a drill where we work on setting legal screens and getting the ball inside. Put a man on each block and one on the wing and the coach is an outlet. So it is 3-on-3. The coach can be used as an outlet at any time.

(Diagram 17)   Coach could also be on the wing. 4 can rear-screen for 1 or 3 set a side-screen for 1. You need to do a little teaching first; the angle of the screen and where you want to set it. As long as the defensive player can see you, you can set a screen as close as you can get. When he can't see you, you have to give him one step.

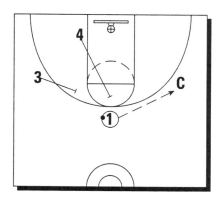

Diagram 17

PRACTICE PLAN

This was our practice plan for the first practice of the season.

Emphasis of The Day:
    Offense—Sprint to offense.
    Defense—Sprint back on defense.

Thought For The Day:
It's amazing how much can be accomplished when no one cares who gets the credit.

Stations:
A: Stretching   B: Jump Rope
C: Shooting Form   D: Individual Work

Perimeter:
Beginning Dribble   Post—Favorite & Counter

TIME	SUBJECTS
6:40	On track—stretching
7:00	On court—shooting form
7:08	Individual Work (This is time to improve individually)
7:22	Discussion
7:24	Fast Break Drills #1 - #4 (Pacers Drill)
7:30	Defensive Stance & Step-Slide (3 min)
7:35	Defensive Stations (3 min) 1. Guarding ball—middle—JH 2. Deny—MD 3. Close out & challenge shot — ND
7:45	**Free Throws and Water** (At every basket)
7:49	Group Work: I—Shooting—Group A (Continue shooting form) II—Defense—Group B & C (one man front shell)
7:55	Rotate
8:01	Rotate
8:07	**Shooting and Water Break** (3 min)
8:13	Fast Break Drill #3 (3-on-2, 2-on-1)
8:17	Secondary Break—5-on-0 (Corner option—Finish it) (Dribble option)
8:25	Half Court Offense (Quick passes)
8:35	Controlled secondary break game (Secondary into quick passes) (Look for drive)
8:55	Conditioning

Blue: Robertson, Haase, Ransom, Williams, Pollard
Red: McGrath, Thomas, Pierce, LaFrentz, (Branstrom), Pugh
Injured: Vaughn, Bradford

The above will be posted in the locker room at 2 o'clock. The players will have to know the emphasis of the day and the thought for the day. What group they are going to be in is listed at the bottom. The groups change every day for about the first month. We started on the track because the women had the gym from 4 p.m. to 7 p.m. We practice a lot in the evenings. That lets our kids go to classes with labs in the afternoons on Tuesdays and Thursdays. On Mondays, Wednesdays and Fridays we usually go from 4 p.m. to 7 p.m. With the shooting form, that is exactly what it means. We have a coach at each basket. We have shown everybody how we want them to shoot. We do this every day, for reinforcement. You can see that the discussion part is very short. Coach brings the team together to talk about what he wants to get accomplished that day. He will then ask about the emphasis of the day. If he gives them something, he wants them to know it. We have covered the drills listed. Overall this will be similar from year to year, except that Coach Williams will make the changes to fit the personnel.

(Diagram 18)   We also did this. Coach stands in front of the line. Man with the ball takes one dribble and makes a pass to a man breaking to the center of the floor. The third man fakes up and then goes backdoor. We are working on the lob pass, looking down the floor, and the bounce pass. We don't throw any backdoor passes unless called.

Question: How much will you change the new players' shooting form?

Answer: Obviously we recruit good athletes. But some of them have just gotten by on their athletic ability and they really can't shoot. We will change some shooting forms. We are allowed to work with our players two hours a week in the off-season during the academic year. We can have as many as three players at a time. This is when we work to change the shot.

Question: How about the secondary break against the zone?

Answer: (Diagram 19)   We will run almost the same thing against man or zone. We want to change sides of the floor. The ball is passed from 1-5-3 and 4 rolls to the block.

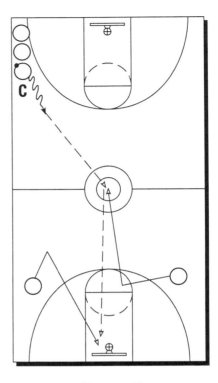

Diagram 18

Diagram 19

(Diagram 20)   Here is a tip. Against the man defense, when 2 starts to set the backscreen for 5, have him come to the block first. The angle is better for the screen.

(Diagram 21)   Against the zone, the only thing that is different is that 2 will not screen. He will look for a hole in the zone. But if X3 is a small man, we will screen him with 2 and 3 will make the lob pass to 5 going for the rim.

Diagram 20

Diagram 21

Diagram 22

Diagram 23

Diagram 24

(Diagram 22)   We have a set play to get the ball inside. There is always a man on the opposite side. 1 is a good player with the ball, 4 is a good post player. 2 and 5 set staggered screens for 3, who breaks out.

(Diagram 23)   1 has the ball, 4 and 5 are screening inside. A screen is set on the defense and the lob is made cross-court to a shooter.

(Diagram 24)   Many times X5 will not guard 5 if 5 comes out. Coach Williams wants our big men to handle the ball out on the floor. If X5 does not cover 5, 5 will not rear-screen, but will set a side-screen. As 3 comes off the screen, 5 will step out and get the shot. If your big man isn't a good passer, give him some parameters. Maybe he is not allowed to pass the ball inside to the post area. And our big players don't shoot three-pointers very often. They should shoot the shots that they can hit.

Defensive Philosophy

What is your defensive philosophy? Defense is an attitude. You can't teach it if you don't believe in it. Defense is the truest team aspect in basketball. Defense wins games, defense wins championships. There are certain things that make each person special in life. My special ability is that I can get young men to want to play to their fullest potential. You can't win with losers, you win with winners. In the end, losers will lose and winners will win. Defense will eventually come down to be a half-court game. When the teams are equal in ability, the team whose players play the best team defense will win.

Defense must be adjustable, adaptable, and flexible. We were 15 - 14 this year; it was one of my worst years in coaching. We were one scorer short of being good. Thus, the games we won were due to our defensive play.

There are five "C's" that we talk about in teaching our defensive system at George Washington University. They are:

1. Conditioning: Players must believe they are in better condition than any team they will play.

2. Confidence: Players must have confidence in themselves, their teammates, and the coaches.

3. Consistency

4. Communication: Players must learn to communicate constantly during a game. The old Celtics of K.C. Jones, Sam Jones, Satch Sanders, etc. were known for the constant talking they did while on the court.

5. Commitment

Our defensive system is very simple and very basic. Teaching and adjusting in man defense is just like pitching. If you have three pitches and learn to throw each pitch at three different speeds you now have nine different pitches. This is the concept we try to use in dealing with our defense.

Before we start teaching our defensive system, we make sure our players are in good physical shape. We have a list of basic fundamental drills we use to condition our players. One such drill is what we call the "Command Drill." This deals with stance and movement.

(Diagram 1)   Line your players up in rows with the coach on the baseline, facing the players. The coach gives a command, the players give the command back, and then they execute the command. Such commands are "stance, right, left, back, up, drop, 10." On the command of "10" the players drop and do 10 pushups, then jump back to their feet. This teaches the players to execute properly and to communicate. At the high school level you might want to start with three minutes and build up to eight minutes. If any player isn't communicating or executing properly, start over.

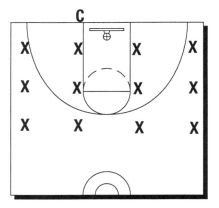

Diagram 1

A teaching point that we emphasize in our 1-on-1 drills: If you are guarding a right-hander, the left foot is up and slightly outside the opponent's right foot, forcing him to the left side of the court. As the opponent goes left, the defender gets into a head-to-head alignment.

In defending the ball, we tell our players if they are in the backcourt, they are to turn the ball as many times as possible; similar to what you do in your zig-zag drill. When the ball enters the front court, we want to face the ballhandler and force him to use his weak hand.

While I was at Cambridge Latin, I allowed my freshman, sophomore, and JV coaches to teach whatever offense they wanted because offense changes every year based on the personnel available. However, they all had to teach the same defensive system, as this was a constant from year to year. We would send our players home with a sheet (or sheets) that covered what we were going to cover the next day in regard to defense. At practice the next day, we would explain what we wanted our players to do—visually showed them what we wanted, had the players walk through the skill, then perform it at half-speed, and finally, execute it at full speed.

Red Defense

(Diagram 2)   This is the defense that Bob Knight has lived with his whole coaching career. This defense is where you have a ballside and weakside area.

In talking about man-to-man defense, you must start out with pressure on the basketball. All defense must start out with this concept. We force opponents to their weak hand, not to the middle or the sideline. We don't worry about this because we don't guard passes that go laterally. We will deny and contest all penetrating passes. We will not allow teams to make passes into the post either.

We always force any player to his weak hand, but when he gets ready to shoot we have the hand nearest the shooter's hand raised just above the shoulder, with the elbow bent.

Diagram 2

Basic Concepts of Red Defense:

- Force the dribbler to use his weak hand. Most often, this means forcing left.

- Prevent all passes—guard to forward, guard to post, forward to post.

- Side the post—near hand and foot between your man and the ball.

- Side the mid- and low-post when your man is below the line of the ball.

- Move behind your man and establish baseline siding position when the ball is in line or below the post man. Attempt to move him off the lane with your body.

- 1/2 way rule when you are not denying; in "weakside" defense; two or more passes away. We should be close enough to put a foot on the mid-point line.

- Adhere to "line of the ball" rule, which states that you should always be below the line of the ball, enabling you to always see your man and ball.

- Stay between your man and the ball.

- Fight over the top or "slide vs. screens" on the ball.

(Diagram 3) On cross-screens, we will actually lose sight of the ball momentarily. The defensive man whose offensive man is going away to screen has one responsibility—to make sure his teammates get through the screen. When X4 hears X5 yell "screen," he wants to get as close to his man as possible, chest to chest, and slide through the screen. X5 must position himself above the screen and be in a position to see the ball and the offensive and defensive men coming to the ball. X5 must also leave some space between himself and his man. We do this in case X4 can't stay chest to chest with his man. X4 must then go over the top of 5's screen and through the space that X5 left between him and his man. We actually tell X5 to pull his teammate through the space.

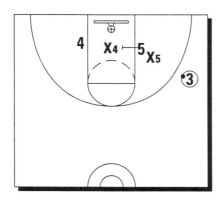

Diagram 3

- Communicate: Talk! Talk! Talk!

- No inside cuts. No one ever cuts between you and the ball.

- Take away the baseline drive by placing your foot on or over the end line vs. the drive.

- Call "5" on the discontinued dribble.

- Call "shot" on the shot.

- Call "box" to emphasize the importance of boxing out.

- Call "ball" on the rebound, then look to outlet the ball either by the pass or dribble.

White Defense

(Diagram 4) This defense begins where the red defense ends, and that is when we force the offensive player to pick up the dribble. Now, all five players will deny all passes, even lateral passes (guard to guard). We now do something different from red in that we switch all screens.

Diagram 4

Basic Concepts of White Defense:

- As long as we control the ball, we want everyone to be close enough to touch their man.

- Attempt to deny all passes—guard to guard, guard to forward, and all post passes.

- Near hand and foot in the passing lane against everyone.

- We will use our red post defense rules, except we will not "double" the ball.

- Force the dribbler to use his weak hand.

- Switch vs. screens on the ball.

- The "switch" call should be made by the man nearest the basket. He should physically push his teammate into the passing lane. Players come together, touch, push and talk.

- If we are beaten backdoor or off the dribble, we will switch.

- Try to see man and ball at all times and follow ball-you-man principle.

- Create steal, turnover, "5" and speed up tempo.

- Everyone must release to the ball if teammate is beaten.

- If beaten call "help."

- Call "shot", "box", "ball."

Diagram 5

Blue Defense

(Diagram 5)   This is a soft man defense. It is our closest answer to a zone. Everyone but the man on the ball has a foot on or in the lane. This won't actually be possible because this assumes that a team has no shooter.

(Diagram 6)   The adjustment we do is if our defender is playing a shooter on the ballside, he will have both feet just inside the three-point line. Everyone else has a foot on, or in, the lane.

(Diagram 7)   The post rule for this defense is whenever your man is in the mid- or low-post and the ball is below the foul line extended, we front the post.

Diagram 6

Diagram 7

(Diagram 8)   Another adjustment we make in the defense is that on all screens on the basketball, we double-team the dribbler.

Diagram 8

On cross-screens we follow the Red Defense rule for cross-screens.

Basic Concepts of Blue Defense:

- Everyone except the man playing the ball has at least one foot on, or in, the key hole and is in the help position. Against three-point shooters we want to be just inside the three-point line.

- Follow post defensive principles and "double" rules on pass into post, same as the Red Defense.

- The man playing the ball plays regular defense, forcing the ball to be dribbled with the weak hand or hand predetermined by scouting report.

- Do not deny the guard-to-forward pass. Have both feet and hands between man and the basket.

- Body shall be positioned so the hand and foot nearest to the ball is in the advanced position so you can see man and ball.

- Move to the ball on the pass.

- We will "double" team screens on the ball unless we decide to do otherwise. Maintain the double-team until the dribble is discontinued. When this occurs, the man who left the screener to double recovers to his original man, "help and recover."

- Call "shot," "box," "ball."

"Combo" Defense

Here we combine the three defenses according to the opponent's strengths and weaknesses. We usually go into this defense after a timeout, we never try to switch to it on the run if at all possible. This provides us with our version of a box-and-one, triangle-and-two, etc.

Instead of having to teach a box-and-one against a team that has one great player, we go to our combination defense. Now, we combine our white and blue defense. We put one player on their great player and tell him that all he has to do is deny him the ball. He doesn't even have to worry about losing sight of the ball. All his other teammates are following the blue defensive principles and he will have help at all times.

Basic Concepts of Combo Defense:

- Playing the dribble—force to the weak hand.

- Post defense—side the post, double passes into the post. Follow Red principles.

- Defending screens on the ball—the man playing the screen will determine what we do when a screen is set for the ball. If the defender is in Red, we will fight over or slide; if he is in White, we will "switch," and if he is in Blue, we will double.

- Defending the dribble hand off—we will follow our Red principles and stay with our own men.

- Call "shot," "box," "ball."

If you want to be a winner in your field, you must assume the characteristics of a winner. You must be ready to try new things and new projects. You must face each new problem as a challenge to be overcome. You must welcome competition with respect, rather than fear. If you make mistakes, you must admit them and use them as foundation stones on which to build success. You must be decisive and your decisions must be backed by your personal commitment. Finally, you must be positive at all times, especially when things get rough. You must think positively, act positively, and live positively. Continue to strive for excellence and remember that "We are what we repeatedly do."

Full-Court Pressure Defense

Some people press to create tempo. Others press to control tempo. Some people press to force turnovers. We press because you don't. We will agree with you that you will be most efficient on defense if you play within a 20' radius of the basket. If you could back it up to a 12' radius, you would be more efficient if they can't shoot from the outside. If your defensive philosophy is don't let them get a good shot, you can do that. If your defensive philosophy is to force turnovers and create tempo, then that changes things.

There is one time when we think every coach in here would agree to press. That's a time and score situation when you are behind. What goes through the players' minds if they haven't pressed in the past three weeks and they end up in this situation and now have to press? How comfortable do these players feel about pressing? We always like to press in the first half to see what you do against our pressure so we can address that at half-time. The biggest reason we don't press is that it looks bad when we are down on the wrong end of the floor playing defense, somehow the ball comes out of the trap and you get beat and they "lay you up."

Here's the other scenario. If you score, you sprint back to the defensive end, defend the ball for 30 seconds and then the other team scores. Good defense. The other team scored. It just didn't look bad. The first thing we tell our players is that we are going to give up layups. We are going to get more than we give up. They don't get to walk it down the floor. When the ball comes in, you are going to be fighting for your life when you play us.

(Diagram 1)   We have our spacing rule, our pressure rule. Now we tell X1 to cut the floor, keep the ball on the sideline. X2 works on knowing when

to rotate up. It doesn't matter if it is a trap or just a jump. Again, spacing becomes important. But this goes hand in hand with surprise. 2 should sprint deep and that would force X2 to guard her, but usually the player in this position has the tendency to slowly filter out looking back over her shoulder. If she filters down the floor, X2 should go with her, but don't match her step for step. Give the ball-handler the illusion that you are going, but take half steps.

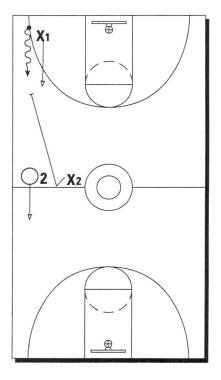

Diagram 1

(Diagram 2)   We have a dribbler who thinks that she has beaten their defense. But, X2 isn't really going with 2. X2 is going to come back and surprise. To do this, X2 must be relatively close. How close? How quick are you? We are really working on run and jump rotation. As X2 jumps, X1 rotates in the direction that the jump came from. Dribble, jump, rotate. Do this drill on both sides of the floor.

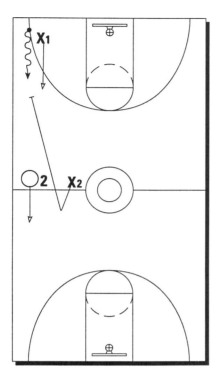

Diagram 2

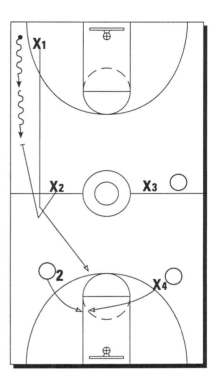

Diagram 3

(Diagram 3)   Now do it 4-on-4. X2 jumps to the dribbler. X4 takes the middle as 2 filters into the middle. Here is our rule for pressing. When you decide to do something, do it. Go with your instincts. Don't change your mind because this causes changes in your teammates.

(Diagram 4)   We are gambling when we press so if you decide to rotate, then rotate. We are gambling that 1 won't be able to pass the ball to 4, who is the open player. Rotate in the direction that the help came from and pick up the first open player.

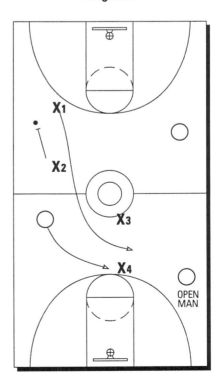

Diagram 4

(Diagram 5)   Let's simplify this. 1 is the dribbler. X2 jumps to the dribbler. X3 will rotate up to the open player. X1 must then drop back to the support position.

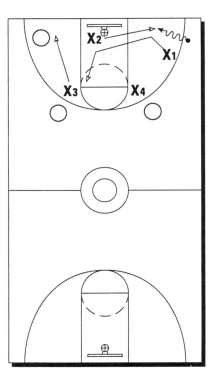

Diagram 6

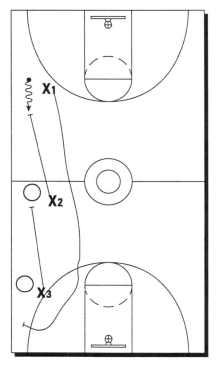

Diagram 5

(Diagram 6)   Put it in a shell drill at half-court. X2 comes to the dribbler. X3 rotated down so X1 keeps going to find the open man.

(Diagram 7)   2-2-1 Press. All presses are really the same. They just have different points of emphasis. There are two ways to play the front. You can stay under the ball and make it hard for the ball to go down the floor at all. Or you can channel the ball toward the sidelines and hope to trap. You can trap either way really. But the front has two different looks.

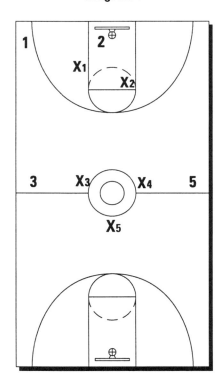

Diagram 7

(Diagram 8)   Let's not let it go down the floor. The ball is passed to 1. This is 2-on-2 support.

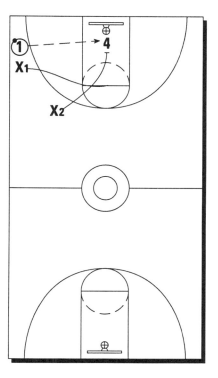

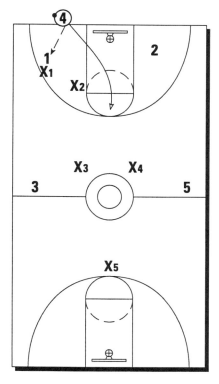

Diagram 8

(Diagram 9)   If the ball is returned to 4, "quick man to the ball." Who takes this pass? Whoever can get there first. Or, if 4 can't dribble, don't guard her. Just let her stand there.

(Diagram 10)   How about the person ballside at mid-court? What do you tell X3? If she breaks up, let her go. If she filters deep, take a half-step with her. There is somebody behind you who will pick her up. Always have serious pressure on the ball. If the dribbler gets away, we will have support for you.

Diagram 9

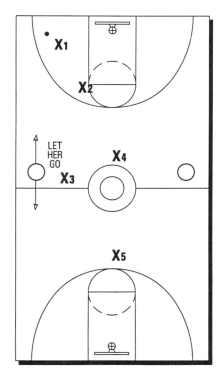

Diagram 10

(Diagram 11)   What about ball reversal? X2 comes up on the first pass. X1 drops to support position and then takes the ball on the second pass.

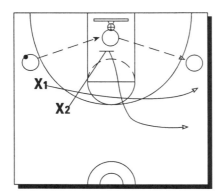

Diagram 11

(Diagram 12)   It's possible that X1 will be "quick man to the ball" on both passes. In that case, X2 remains in support position.

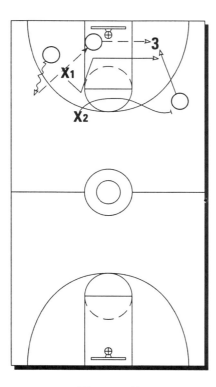

Diagram 12

(Diagram 13)   The ball is passed down the sideline. "Quick man to the ball." When our kids understand they can hustle without worrying about rules, somebody is on the ball and somebody is in support. How aggressive are they? Regardless of which two people you put up there, one of them assumes more responsibility than the other. Every person doesn't have the exact same rules. This will depend on their aggressiveness and their quickness. Don't make it an equal responsibility situation.

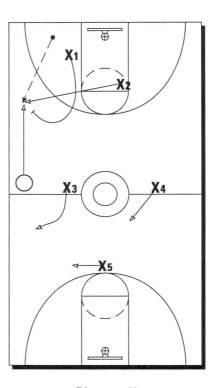

Diagram 13

(Diagram 14)   We can also trap. X3 half-steps back and comes to trap. X1 has cut the floor and the support man is in the passing lane when the trap is set. The player in the trap will not try to split that trap because the support player is in the way. When this is happening X5 must stay even with the ball. Keep your nose on the ball. X5 has the pass down the sideline out of the trap.

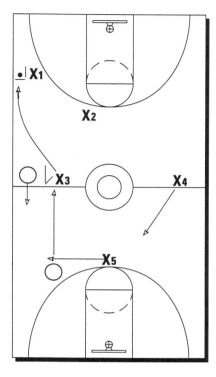

Diagram 14

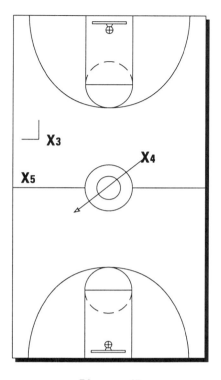

Diagram 15

(Diagram 15)   Anytime the trap is sprung, the person who started at mid-court on the weakside, X4, must rotate long. She must rotate away from the ball. This is difficult to teach.

(Diagram 16)   It looks like this.

(Diagram 17)   We will give you the pass back. When it occurs, X4 rotates up through the middle.

(Diagram 18)   Man-to-Man Pressure.

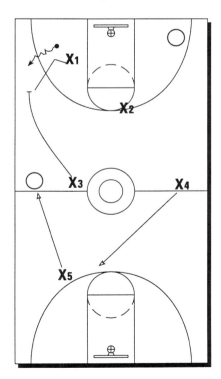

Diagram 16

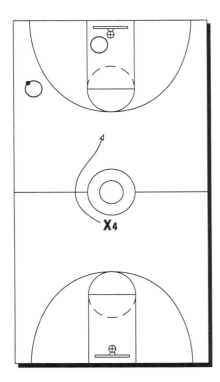

Diagram 17

(Diagram 19)   How about a run and jump? No problem. X1 runs in the direction that the help came from and picks up the first open player. I'd like three or more players involved in the rotation. The last thing you want is for someone to stand on the backside, matched up, when passes are being thrown and they should be rotating.

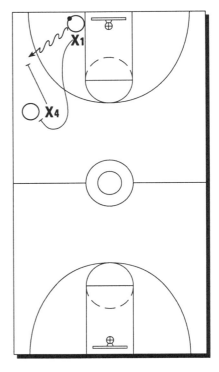

Diagram 19

(Diagram 20)   Charlie Press. We can face guard you. X4 is the critical man.

(Diagram 21)   We want to get the quick trap. Influence the inbounds pass. Do we rotate or not? Depends on our spacing. If we are too far away we don't rotate.

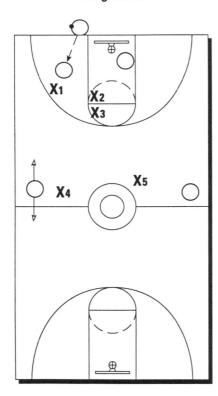

Diagram 18

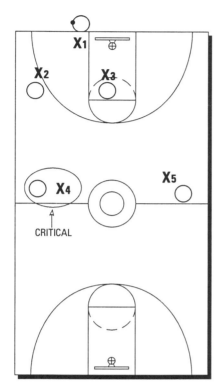

Diagram 20

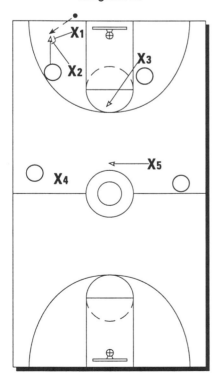

Diagram 21

Question: If the ball crosses mid-court, are you going to continue trapping?

(Diagram 22)   Answer: No. We will jump it.

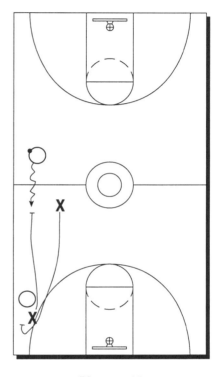

Diagram 22

Question: What do you do if you are pressuring the inbounds pass and the offense screens across?

(Diagram 23)   Answer: We switch and X2 must drop to the ball.

(Diagram 24)   If we are pressuring the inbounder, the inbounder will have these three looks.

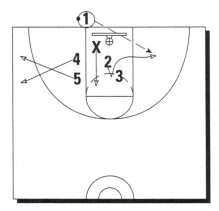

Diagram 23

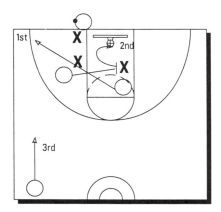

Diagram 24

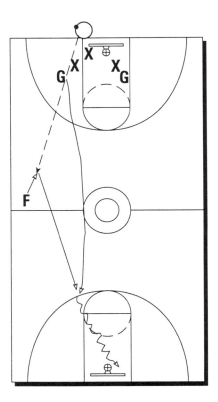

Diagram 25

(Diagram 25)   Here's how we handle this offensively. The pass is made to the forward breaking up. On the flight of the ball, our guard breaks long for the pass. It's so easy.

(Diagram 26)   If the defense denies the up-cut, the forward reverses long and the inbounder makes the long pass. We don't make a pass to the man breaking long. We make the pass out on the floor and let the player run it down.

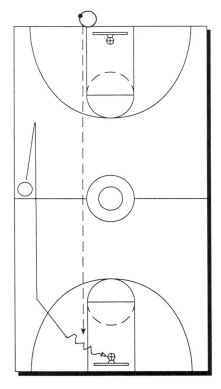

Diagram 26

(Diagram 27)   When all of this is happening, 5 cuts in to the elbow and then out to the corner. The inbounder runs across the lane and inbounds to 5, who then makes the long pass to a guard breaking deep. But this only works with pressure on the ball.

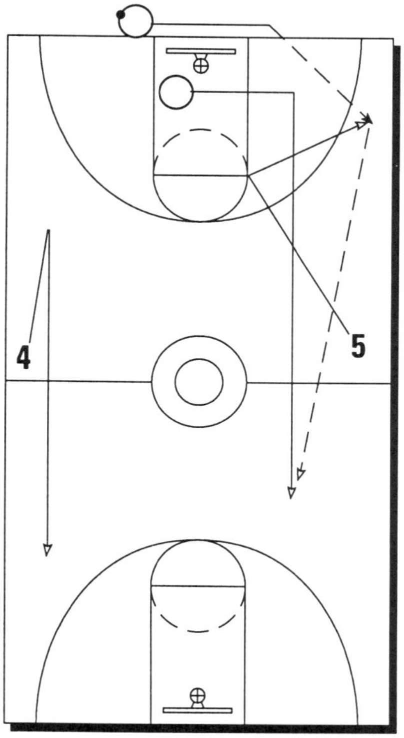

ball. Play 3-on-3 on a narrow floor. If they are dribbling down the sideline, chase them down. Don't run at the ball, run ahead of the ball. If you run at the ball, you will be too late. Run ahead to an interception point where you can cut the ball off. When we chase it down from behind, we call that "wolf."

Diagram 27

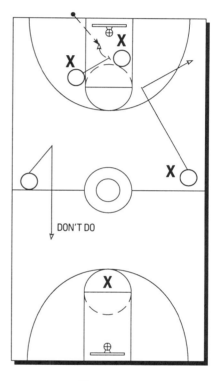

Diagram 28

(Diagram 28)   If there is no pressure on the ball and the defense has a safety, don't do it. Inbound to the guard. But, if the defense is playing the fifth man behind the guards, then you are all right.

(Diagram 29)   Run this on both sides of the floor. Keep the offense on one side of the floor. Face the guard on the inbounds pass. Don't let them catch the

Let me add one thing. Don't rotate up unless you can make the play.

Question: Where can you hide a weak defender?

(Diagram 30)   Answer: Hide her on the weakside at half-court. My second choice is to hide her deep.

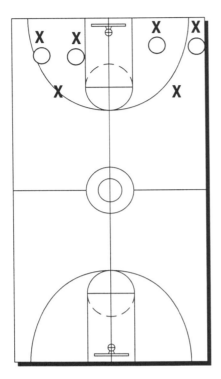

Diagram 29

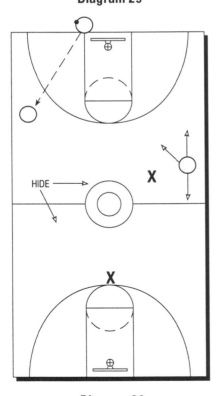

Diagram 30

ATTACKING ZONE DEFENSES

We get a lot of offense from our defense and in your eyes it might not be organized. In our eyes it is organized because that is what we practice every day. If you have a good shot when you get to the other end, shoot it. If not, back it out. As you back it out, look for the secondary break. If it is not there, usually we will run motion.

(Diagram 1)   I want to give you thoughts about zone offenses rather than giving you a zone offense. We set up the way you don't. If you are in a 2-guard front, we are in a point-guard set.

(Diagram 2)   When the ball is in the corner, all zone defenses are 2-3. It doesn't matter how they start. It seems to me that is something to attack, something good to know.

Diagram 1

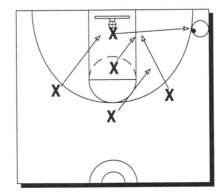

Diagram 2

(Diagram 3)   We must attack gaps and the baseline. Do you teach driving into the gap and drawing two defenders and then kick out to the wing? This makes the back man come up and leave the baseline open. Can you manipulate the zone? Can you make certain people go to certain spots and defend like you want them to do? If we can do that, then we can attack the way that we want to.

Diagram 4

Diagram 3

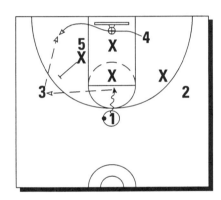

Diagram 5

(Diagram 4)   The point guard, 1, passes to the wing, 2, and the defensive guard moves over to guard him. The ball is passed back to 1, and 1 does not attack the gap. 1 attacks X1. X1 must defend 1, who then passes to 3 and makes the back man come out to guard him. Does he have to shoot every time? No. But if he never shoots, the zone will not come out to guard him. You will play the player who is weak defensively if she can score. You will devise an offense for her. If you don't have shooters, start a program to develop them. High school coaches don't have enough time to make shooters of players. They must be taught before you get them.

(Diagram 5)   Anytime the offside post, 4, sees the baseline man going out to defend the wing, that is an automatic short corner cut.

(Diagram 6)   If the baseline man goes out to guard the short corner, then we pass low-high, 4 to 5. We want 5 to step up the lane away from the ball.

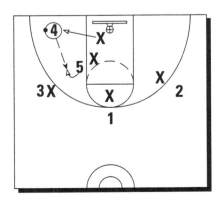

Diagram 6

(Diagram 7)   Teach your post players to read the defense. If the ball is on the wing, the post man can make an automatic flash.

(Diagram 8)   Do your guards know this? Do they know that they can use a wag dribble to distort the defense? How far will the defense go with the guard? Will she go all the way to the corner? Or will the back man step out and play her? Anytime our guard wags down, the top guard rotates over and the wing rotates up.

(Diagram 9)   Reverse the ball to the wing and you know that the back defender doesn't want to come high, but they will. If they don't, we shoot it. If they do, we pass in to the post.

(Diagram 10)   You can also wag dribble out of the corner. How far will the back man come? The weakside post, 4, goes to the short corner and 5 moves up the lane as the ball is passed to the short corner.

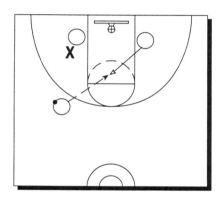

Diagram 7

Diagram 9

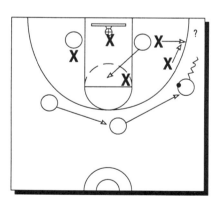

Diagram 8

Diagram 10

(Diagram 11)   We don't have a lot of schemes against a zone, we have reads. We can also use the wag dribble out of the corner and if we are in a four out set, we can send a perimeter player to the short corner. Anytime the ball is passed to the corner, we cut through. But if the ball is dribbled, we come back to the short corner.

(Diagram 12)   Anytime that the ball drives baseline, the weakside wing goes to the baseline for the skip-pass.

(Diagram 13)   Let's put it all together. 1 dribbles into the gap and passes to 2. X5 comes out to guard 2. 4 automatically breaks to the short corner. If the ball is passed to the short corner, 5 moves up the lane.

(Diagram 14)   If the ball is not shot from the short corner and cannot be passed directly to 5, the ball is passed to 1 and then back to 5, who has sealed.

Diagram 13

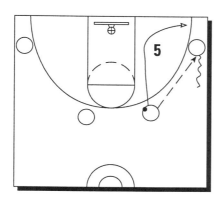

Diagram 11

Diagram 14

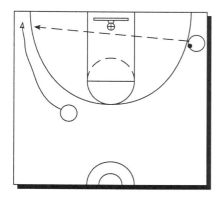

Diagram 12

(Diagram 15)   If the ball is not passed directly to 5, 1 attacks the guard and then passes to 3 on the weakside. 5 steps in and 4 follows.

Diagram 15

Inbound Plays

What do your inbound plays look like when you line up? Are you scouted? Can they tell what you are running just by the way that you set up? We want everything to look the same.

(Diagram 16)   2 is the shooter. 4 runs at this player and 3 replaces 4.

Diagram 16

(Diagram 17)   3 breaks all the way to the baseline. 2 to 3 to 1, who broke straight out. 4 continued across the lane and sets a doublescreen with 5. 3 will skip-pass to 2.

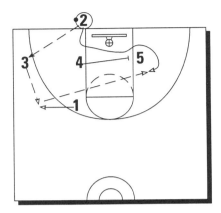

Diagram 17

(Diagram 18)   After you run this, the defense will try to slip a man over or under the screen. If this happens, 1 does not pass to 2. 5 will screen in, and 4 will get the pass from 1.

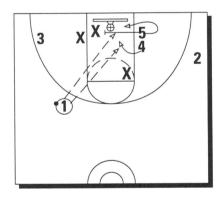

Diagram 18

(Diagram 19)   Starts out the same way, 4 runs in, 3 bananas to the baseline, but 4 stays at the block. 1 breaks out and the ball goes from 2 to 3 to 1.

(Diagram 20)   4 screens inside man, 3 screens outside player and 1 passes to 2. But before the pass to 2, 1 wags back as if she is going somewhere. 2 must first fake the same move as in the previous play. 4 steps up the lane. This is important because that holds the middle man in the zone.

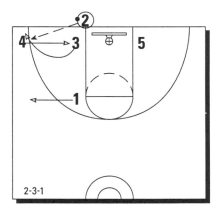

Diagram 19

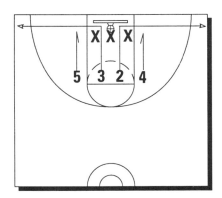

Diagram 21

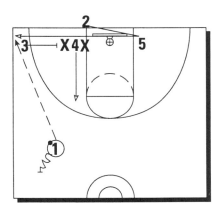

Diagram 20

Diagram 22

(Diagram 21)   Here is another set. 4 and 5 cut first and can screen. 2 will be the best option.

(Diagram 22)   "Orange." Against a man defense. Most people will guard in the lane.

(Diagram 23)   What do you do if 2 breaks off 3? If you don't switch, you trail. 1 passes to 2, who either goes to the corner or curls.

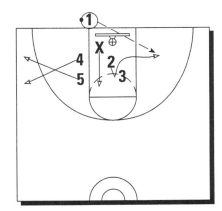

Diagram 23

(Diagram 24)   If you switch, 2 goes to the corner and 1 passes to 3. 4 and 5 get out of the way.

(Diagram 25)   "Blue" 2 screens for 3. The ball goes from 1 to 3.

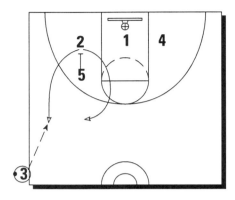

Diagram 26

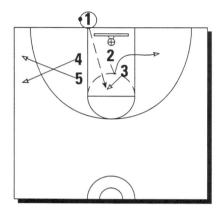

Diagram 24

Diagram 27

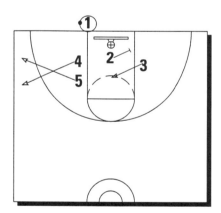

Diagram 25

(Diagram 28)   For the three-point shot, 2 is the shooter. 2 breaks high off of 4. 1 dribbles to the wing and then dribbles back. 2 sets a screen for 1. 4 backscreens for 2, who goes to the wing. Screen the screener and pass against the grain.

(Diagram 26)   Side-out. 2 is the best one-on-one player. 5 screens down and 2 comes up. 3 passes to 2.

(Diagram 27)   1 screens the inbounder, who breaks to the corner. 4 screens across for 5. As soon as 2 got the ball she started to drive. She has the entire side to go one-on-one. If we get cut off on the drive, 5 will come off of 4's screen. 2 can pass to 5 or to 3 for the three-point shot.

Diagram 28

Setting An Example As A Coach

When you coach, you are always learning. This entire theme of learning and continuing to learn, and setting an example as a coach, is important. Obviously you have to incorporate the things you have learned into your system, it must fit under your umbrella. It must fit into your own philosophy, your own personality, things that you are comfortable with in terms of teaching. When you come to a clinic you can't throw out your whole philosophy, but you can find a new wrinkle, a new drill, etc. This openness is very important in coaching. You can't get set in your ways because of changes in your talent, personnel, and rule changes. That's what Pete Newell always talks about, you must be flexible. Even if you aren't changing, you want to be on top of what your opponents are doing so that you know how to attack those things.

We all have someone in our life who had a major impact on us. In my life it was my dad. He was a teacher for over 45 years at both the high school and the college levels and also a great basketball player at the University of San Francisco. He played for two Hall of Fame coaches, Pete Newell and Phil Wolpert. I'm the youngest of six, and by the time I got here, there weren't any brains left over. What I did share with my dad was a passion for teaching. He reminds me a lot of Coach Wooden (UCLA retired). He was more than a coach, he was a teacher of life. One of the highs in the past six years was being around Coach Wooden.

My family had two passions, basketball and teaching. We all played. We have a basketball camp in the summer with over 2,000 players. My dad keeps his hand in coaching through the camp. He discouraged me at first from going into coaching, but what he was really doing was challenging me. He wanted to be sure that I was going into coaching to

make an impact on people's lives. He didn't want me to go into coaching because it was the natural thing to do after being with sports all my life. He wanted me to go into coaching to impact young people's lives, to become a teacher, to make a change and to bring something new and original to the game. Not that I was going to reinvent the wheel. It's not that complicated.

Coach Keady always said not to forget that when Dr. Naismith invented the game there was a peach basket at each end with five players going in each direction trying to put a ball in the basket, always hustling. He said, "That's basketball." The beauty of the game is that it is simple. There are different styles depending on your style, but it really is a very simple game. We sometimes over-complicate it. We get what we call paralysis from analysis. The more you think, the slower your feet become. If your kids are scared to make a move, scared to take a shot, or scared to be aggressive, the slower they become and the less effective they are. They rely less on their instincts.

While I was in college I knew I wanted to teach and coach and so I started writing to outstanding coaches. I chose five I knew were great defensive coaches because when I played that was one thing that I could always do. I wrote Bob Knight, Mike Krzyzewski, Gene Keady, Jerry Tarkanian, and Tim Grgurich (who is now with the Sonics). He was Tark's right-hand man at Vegas. The one thread through all of them, with their different styles, was that they were all tremendous defensive coaches. I told them I was in college, was an aspiring young coach, and asked what I should be doing at this stage of my career. I asked them for philosophy and literature from their programs, handouts, etc.

I had four folders in my room at college, one for each coach. I saved all the letters. I'll never forget that first letter from Coach Knight; it gave me inspiration. Then, they sent reading lists, book lists, etc. I spent time with each of those programs. I spent a month with Indiana in the middle of the season. I was on the bench for home games, broke down game film, and shadowed Coach Knight. It was during the January break, so they had two practice sessions a day. It was an unbelievable experience, a crash course in college basketball. Then I went to Purdue and did the same thing with Coach Keady. Different style, both intense, both great teachers, very valuable experience. Then I went back and spent time at Duke with Coach Krzyzewski, and eventually, over a four-year span, with Coach Tarkanian.

What I was looking for was to be able to evaluate the talent and tell kids where their strengths and weaknesses were, both individually and collectively. You want to stay away from your weaknesses, and play to your strengths. At the same time continue to work on your weaknesses. What you need to do is to surround yourself, and learn from, the best people, no matter what field you go into.

Listening is the most important skill my dad passed on to me. You had eye contact, the proper body language, etc. So, listening is a skill. That is a key. You can become a better teacher and a better coach if you can listen. I was hired at Purdue after spending a couple of weeks with Coach Keady and came back in the summer to work camps at Indiana, Duke, and Las Vegas. I worked all the camps. Coach Keady hired me and I was an assistant coach with him for three years, and it was a great experience. Then Coach Harrick gave me the opportunity to come back and I was an assistant with him for six years. I got the head position this year when Coach Harrick left. I learned a lot this year, in a hurry. That is what you must do when you are thrown into a tough situation.

You learn what pressure is when you lose by 48 at Stanford and are down 28 against Kansas on your own floor and are being booed by your own fans, that's pressure, and a reason to perspire. It's a normal human response. When I first got hired, I was concerned about whether we could win games, whether I could improve, and whether I could make in-game adjustments. All the media would ask about was my perspiration and my hair gel.

Los Angeles was a little different. I was the first coach who didn't have a rolled-up game program in my hand during a game. I was the first coach to wear gel in my hair, the first coach to take my jacket off, and the first coach to sweat profusely. So I broke all the UCLA traditions. The great thing is that they were so concerned about the sweat and the hair that it distracted them. Anyway, this was an amazing experience. I will need to distance myself from it, to put it into perspective and know what actually happened. I was thrown into the fire and I learned a lot more from failing this year than I did from the success.

The smartest thing I did this year was that I was going to learn on the job and they could expect me to work hard and learn through this process. Fortunately, we just kept improving. I told the team that they could expect from me what I expected from them, which was a great effort, keep working hard, have a positive attitude and bring a positive attitude to the table every day during practice and games. We ended up winning 12 games in a row, going to the Final Eight, and winning the toughest conference in America by three games, sweeping Arizona who won the National Championship. We beat the best in the ACC in Duke, and finished 15-3 in our league and finished 6th in the nation. But, we had gone to the bottom of the Grand Canyon and we slowly, inch by inch, day by day, climbed out of the valley.

One of the things I want to talk about, and I think it is the most important thing, is what we call the "Big A"—attitude. We call it our attitude umbrella. It is the Bruin Attitude. I don't like to call it rules. If you call it rules today it has a negative connotation. Kids don't like it. It is the attitude of Cal Ripken, Michael Jordan, Michael Johnson, Jackie Joyner, Tiger Woods, name any great athlete. Great athletes, great teams, possess a certain attitude, a certain approach. Under attitude there are a lot of things you can talk about. There are things that you learned from your parents and your family: say thank you, be on time, make no excuses, sharing, etc. I think it is important today that you make reference to other athletes in all sports who are successful and are great role models. It doesn't work today to say just do it, because I said so. You need to point out great role models in all sports and try to reinforce the things that we want done, because the reason those people have been successful is universal in terms of work ethic, listening skills, attitude, their whole approach. I'm always making reference to that type of person. Don't just do it because Coach Lavin says to do it. That's limited, and some kids take that as an ego thing or a power thing.

Coach Pete Newell always talked about teaching the "why." That's what coaches do. That's what parents do, teach the "why." When you teach the "why," then they embrace it and it becomes their own. They are not just doing it because you said so, like a robot. Why do you set a good screen and shape up after the ball? Because you will get yourself open and come back to the ball with your hands up. Now they understand. Why are we going to do everything lower to the ground? Why does our stance come from this power base? Because we are quicker, faster, stronger, and more explosive. Why is every great athlete, in the history of any sport, always down here in a power stance? Because they are quicker, faster, stronger, and more explosive! Do you want to make yourself a better athlete, maximize your athletic ability? If you can get five players to do that, you are that much better as a team. You are better individually, and five of you in this stance are better collectively as a team. So, teach the "why," it's very important.

Coaching is teaching. A great coach is a great teacher. Our classroom is different, we have backboards instead of chalkboards. But we are still teaching. We get to teach kids about life through basketball. I have eleven national banners hanging above my head in my classroom to remind me that winning is important too, but the reason that I got into this profession was to impact the lives of young people. So, if I allow the national championship banners to dictate the way that I teach then I'm not doing a very good job. I'm not leading by example in terms of enjoying the process, understanding the process, and realizing that those championship banners were won with great talent, but also by doing things right. That is what Coach Wooden's Pyramid of Success is all about. He was a teacher first, a coach second. His players were students first and athletes second.

This year we talked about "Brick by brick to the brickyard." Indianapolis was our goal. How were we going to get there? Every day is a workday, brick by brick, inch by inch. Sounds simple, sounds corny, sounds cliché, but there are reasons those clichés, those corny platitudes, are around. They have worked for hundreds of years. What you put into your game, you get to take out down the road. Just like a bank account. Collect down the road in the regional finals or a state championship. Input equals output. Those are the types of things that I have taken away from the great coaches. There are no short cuts. You must work. Work is a skill. Just like listening is a skill. To me, listening is a huge skill.

We do something every day in practice to wake our players up, get the blood flowing. It's called rally clap. We are also working on hand speed. The quicker your hands are, the quicker your feet are, the better career you can have as an athlete. Let me demonstrate. (Note—Coach Lavin did a staccato clap, clapping as fast as possible.)

When I get up in the morning, I do a rally clap. It's like starting the engine to a car, gets my heart started, gets my blood flowing. What does that have to do with basketball? The quicker my hands are as I trace the ball, that's one more deflection which leads to a loose ball, a steal, a pass ahead which results in a basket. We see the end result, but it came from ball pressure, stance, foot work, quick hands, quick feet, just trying to get one little deflection, a fraction of an inch. You get the key stop or the key basket and that's how you win big.

In basketball, you have to be mentally alert when the coach is setting an example. If I am slow and lethargic mentally, chances are my body movements will reflect that. But, if I am ready, down in my stance, I will be quicker to react. When I start, we will all start, when I extend my hands, palms down, you should be able to hear a pin drop. Quick starts, quick stops mentally leads to quick starts and quick stops physically. We add this to our stance drill every day. Pete Newell did this in the '40s and '50s. For 20 minutes his team would be in a stance with the hands up because basketball is played with the hands up. You must be able to keep the hands high in all aspects of basketball; in making the post moves, when pressuring the ball, one hand is high to stop the pass in to the post.

Now, back to the attitude, we call it the **Big A.** We do an attitude jack. After the rally clap. It's like a jumping jack, but when your hands go up, you yell "attitude." Sometimes I'll do this in the morning to get myself fired up because I have to set a good example. I think that what we are fighting more than anything else is the "too cool to care" syndrome. Right now it is the worst epidemic in America. As teachers, coaches, parents, that is what we are fighting. We are in a war with the "too cool to care" syndrome. We face it every day in the classroom. That's what gangs are about, that's what drugs are about, tattoos, crack, you name it, that's what we are fighting every day. So, we must lead by example. The kids don't like corny stuff because it's not cool. So I'm a gung ho, fired up, guy. Every person is different. Some people do it in a quiet way. They communicate their excitement in a different way. The important thing is that the kids see that example. I don't like it when a kid saunters out of a game when he is replaced. That is the type of thing I attack. That is not a good Bruin Attitude. When I coach, the most important thing to me, more than a

ball going in the basket, is the proper attitude.

We had seven starting lineups in the first two months of the season. When you make a shot or miss a shot, I watch to see how you react because that's attitude. If you miss a shot and drop your head, you're out of there. That's not Michael Jordan, Cal Ripken, etc. I don't care what sport it is, the great athletes possess a certain attitude and approach. That's what I am interested in. No matter what the caliber of athlete you have, you can teach the proper attitude. You are going to maximize their ability. That's going to be a by-product of teaching the proper attitude. If something goes against you, do something positive. Take all that frustrated energy and channel it in such a way to make you a more effective basketball player and now you help your team.

If you lose, don't hang your head, because when you hang your head, it means that you are defeated. You must be aware of the group dynamics of the team and make sure that you are always building the proper attitude of a champion. Whether you win a championship or not, you are always building toward the proper attitude of a champion. That's why the great athletes maintain a high level of excellence; they have a certain approach with the right attitude. And that's what I am interested in.

We have 23 rules for our program under the Attitude Umbrella. As a coach you are always adjusting the thermostat of your program in terms of how much to turn up the heat, when to cool it down. You are always aware of the climate of your classroom, and aware of the pulse of your team. Are they tired emotionally, do you need to do something that is fun? We went bowling at times. It sounds crazy, but if you have done your job throughout the season, now you can give them a little latitude, cut a little slack and get a lot more mileage out of that. Late in the year, do a lot less, because we want fresh legs. It becomes more mental late in the season. You aren't going to get a lot of conditioning the night before a game. It's either in or it isn't. You either have the level you need or you don't. An aggressive, attacking, confident team is going to have fun. That's what Arizona had. They were a 5th place conference team. They were a bunch of young guns having fun throughout the tournament. That confidence is more important than anything else. I learned how mental this game is, and how much of it is attitude, your preparation, your aggressiveness, your outlook toward life.

Stance. This, like attitude, is the umbrella over our program. It is the foundation to our program. Low, flexed, coiled, like sitting in a chair and then taking the chair away. We stay in this position offensively and defensively. Offensively, it starts with the rebound. We bring the ball down, tuck it under the chin, on the chest, with the elbows out. We turn and are thinking of making the 90' pass for the breakaway. If it is not there, we pivot and look for the outlet. The rebounder comes down with a wide base, a real wide base. He is solid, turns, and looks for the outlet. The outlet man comes back to meet the pass. Then he does the same thing. He catches and tucks and looks up the floor. Whether the dribbler is slow and takes 30 seconds to get to mid-court or is fast and streaks down the floor, either way he must be in a stance.

When you cross half-court, you must be in a stance with your arm-guard out. If you penetrate into a seam, you better be balanced so you can come to a jump stop, take the jumper, dump it off, or kick it out for a three. You better be on balance in your stance. The wings are in their stances, faking, etc. He is looking in. Can you hit the post? The post is in his stance, looking for the ball. Maybe he must take one big power dribble to the baseline to create a better angle. Post man, call for the ball. Everybody is the same. The post man has a wide stance, one arm is the target the other is the arm bar, helping to seal the defense. If the pass isn't good, but I am in a good stance, I can still short hop and scoop it. But, if I am straight legged and stiff, forget it. If you want the ball, get your hands up high.

If you don't work on this, late in the game you get tired and the hands drop, just like a boxer's. Late in the game with your defensive close out, the hands must be up. When a team is using an offensive jump shot late in the game, you must go after it with the defensive jump shot. Hands high. Everything we do is predicated with the hands up, and in a stance, sealing, screening, etc. That's our point of emphasis.

In a timeout, I don't want to call a timeout and diagram plays. I want my team coming out of a timeout aggressive, confident, thinking attack, attack, attack. I don't want them trying to remember a new play when they break the huddle. So, keep it simple, pass and catch the ball, ball movement, man movement, screening, we are going to get a good look and if we get a good look, we will shoot a high percentage.

Defensively, ball pressure, helpside, finish with a rebound, contest every shot and they will shoot a low percentage. Then, sprint in between and be in good condition. Beat them down for some easy baskets, and if we sprint down to the other end, we will prevent them from getting easy baskets. That's percentage basketball. You must make adjustments during the game, but as a coach your real work is done in practice in terms of conditioning, your fundamentals and your team play. If you have those three things you will have an aggressive, confident team, not cocky and arrogant, but aggressive and confident. Then they will have fun. If they aren't having fun, this game is a nightmare. Keep the fun in fundamentals. Discipline is not about ego and power. Discipline is about having fun, teaching them to stretch their ability. Discipline means deflections, loose balls, dunks.

Lets get back to stance. Everything we do is in stance. You are quicker when you are down in your stance. If you can make yourself quicker, you are a better athlete. Coach Keady used to say, "In a stance, we have a chance." No stance, no chance. He also said, no stance, sit on the bench. Its amazing what I learned from these coaches. I went to

STEVE LAVIN

Indiana, Duke, Vegas, and Purdue looking for side out-of-bounds plays, press breakers, etc. But it wasn't that. It was conditioning, fundamentals, and team play. If you master those three things every year you will maximize your team's talent. Each coach does that in a different way. I don't have a lot of patience with those players who drop their head when something goes wrong, or those who don't give maximum effort. As long as he is working, he knows that I am going to stay with him when he misses several shots. He will have confidence and won't be looking over his shoulder every time he misses.

You must take all of your experiences and integrate them into your own personality, your own philosophy, and do what is comfortable with you. I can't be anyone else. I've got to be Steve Lavin because that's who I am. You have to see your job as a challenge, enjoy it, lead by example, and not be concentrating on the pressure, but enjoy the process.

Recruit good players and winning will take care of itself. We have one of the better recruiting classes in the country this year. Coach Wooden left me a message the other day, a classic. He said, "Coach, we are so excited. The alumni and I are so excited about your recruiting class. We just can't wait. Look what you did this year with the talent that you had. And now you are even better. We know that we will not be disappointed." That's his way of needling me and letting me know what it is like to coach at UCLA, and what he had to deal with for 12 years when he coached and had 10 championships in 12 years. In other words, win the whole thing or we are going to hang you. There was a headline last week, and it said "They'll hang a banner, or they will hang Lavin." That shows you the mentality. I had to do some more rally claps that morning.

Conditioning. You must have conditioning. Sounds simple. We work a lot on mental conditioning, which is that attitude thing again. Have that self-control. There is always another play coming. You can't allow the next play to be affected by the last play.

You must always teach your team to play through. There will always be highs and lows. It's not if you fall down, but how you get up. You've got to lead with a positive attitude. We call it the Joe Frazier attitude. We want Joe Frazier basketball players. Joe Frazier was a great boxer, was tough, was a hard worker, and he was always there at the end. He might not win, but he was always there trying for the knockout punch. That's what I want. I want fighters with high tops. I want my team coming out of a timeout the way fighters come out of their corners for the next round. I don't want them coming out with paralysis from analysis. You don't want that. You want them fired up, bouncing out when the bell rings. That's where mental and physical conditioning comes in. Every day in practice all of our drills are competitive and repetitive. We compete and repeat. There is always going to be a consequence. The losers run. I present running as a positive thing. We do 17 sideline-to-sidelines in one minute. That's tough.

We do a thing called 60-point game. You just pass and catch, no dribbles and you can't screen. It teaches passing, catching, cutting and jumping to meet passes, V-cutting to get open. The defense is in all out deny because they know the offense can't dribble. If you get a layup, it is 5 points. If you get fouled, it is 5 points. Every pass is worth 1 point. There is no dribbling. Kansas does this and they start with no dribbles. Later they add one dribble, then two, and eventually it becomes motion. So, everything we do is competitive and we repeat it over and over again.

Basic footwork. We talk about our feet being like wheels of a car. Stop, start, change of direction, and change of speed, are some of the most important things in basketball. Offensively and defensively it comes down to those four things. These are the basics. You are like a driving instructor, showing the difference between driving downtown and on the freeway; instead of having a wheel in their hands, they have a ball.

(Diagram 1)   We want freeway speed from foul line to foul line. When we get below the foul line, this is downtown. Now there is a different mentality. You are in traffic. That's when you need to stop, start, and make some decisions. You can't be out of control in that area. That will get you out of the game. You must be able to see.

In the stance, the back leg is the drive leg, the push leg. This is the foundation of our program, we really break it down. The front leg is the reach leg. The foot on the reach leg is turned, toes pointed in the direction that you are going. The power leg pushes off. We want our stance very wide. In that way, if they do go around us, it must be a banana type of cut, and not in a straight line. You can't give them a straight line to the basket.

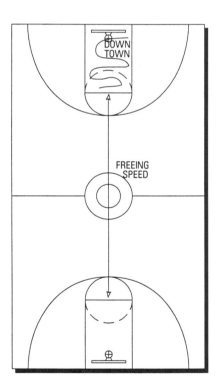

Diagram 1

Fifteen years ago the stance was taught with the feet as wide as the shoulders. Look at the old books. What is changed? The feet are much wider now. The wider you are, the harder it is to get around you. If we get beat, we go to a sprinter's stance. Now we run, glide, run. We must catch up with the ball. Do not stand up and become straight-legged. Turn, stay low, and go and get in front of the ball. We sprint. Point your toe in the direction you want to go. When you take the step, make it heel-toe. It keeps you low. The flexing of your knees keeps you low. If you go toe first, there is a tendency to raise up.

When we close out, you are going to run, shuffle and break down on the ball. We have made some subtle adjustments. We get wider and wider as we close. We skip-in with the wider base. What happened before was that as we closed down, the offensive man went around us. With our unusually wide base and skipping action, we are more effective. We want active hands, active feet, active lips, and in a stance. In practice, we run all of our verbal commands for 10 minutes. If you are not as strong, you must be smart. So, mental conditioning, and toughness, with the slides and hands up is a great reference point.

In the game timeouts, instead of drawing up a play, what I'm going to talk about is Joe . That is why we did the stance drill. We are the best conditioned team in America and we deserve to win this game. That's where we throw the knockout punch.

(Diagram 2)   Every practice and every game is an opportunity to make progress and you must see it like that. We have this hanging in the locker room. We list the season, 1-0, 3-3 etc. We finished 24-8, one brick short of our goal, Indianapolis. But also each practice was a chance to improve.

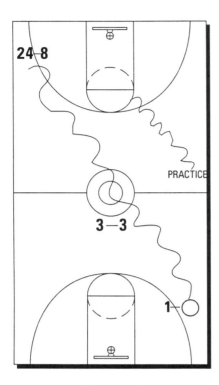

24-8

PRACTICE

3—3

1—

Diagram 2

Sports are like life, you do it day by day, inch by inch, brick by brick. There is no short cut. It is important to have a long-term dream or a goal, but how you get there is a micro. The big scene is the macro. That's great, but how you get there, that's micro. Day by day, and you need to talk about that with your team. You don't do it by looking ahead. Don't have one foot in yesterday and one foot in tomorrow. You want both feet in today, and that's how you get to tomorrow!

1-2-1-1 Match-Up Zone

When I first went to the University of Memphis, we had no one who could score. So, we had to run the press. We spent at least an hour every day on the press, sometimes two hours. The only way we could score was to shoot short jumpers and layups. We not only pressed and trapped, but we trapped on missed shots. We were trapping every trip down the floor. Our kids did not really understand the work ethic that it takes if you are going to press. You must sell them on the press. We want to go get it. Not only in basketball, but in life. In today's society, this is important. To be able to press effectively, you must have an aggressive attitude. The players must believe in it, and you must be able to communicate. The press makes it a 94' game, it changes the momentum of the game, and it exposes weak ball handlers. We know that we are going to give up some layups, but as long as we are hustling, we are going to cause more turnovers and cause more rushed shots than we are going to give up layups.

Here are some keys for a successful press. You must set up quickly. You must communicate. In our press several different people play several different positions. You can't come up from the back unless someone is coming behind. You must stay low, form triangles and anticipate. You must trap hard. The officials watch hands. Don't use your hands in the trap. Use your lower body. Make contact with the lower body and you will find out early in the game whether or not the official will call it.

Always keep the ball in front of you. Don't allow the ball to go over your head. If it does, sprint to the line of the ball. The back people in the press must always form triangles. Keep the ball out of the middle of the floor. Push the ball sideline. 90% of all inbound passes are to the right side of the floor, so we cheat to that side of the floor. When the ball

goes through the net, we have someone looking for their point guard. She doesn't look for the ball, she looks for the point guard. And remember, you only rotate up if you have back coverage.

(Diagram 1) X5 is the least athletic player. The best athletes are X2 and X4.

(Diagram 2) If the offense is a 1-4, we will bring our people up. Our back people match-up wherever they are. In order for us to be successful in the press, we cannot play 2-on-2 in the back. We must defend your two offensive players with one defensive player. We must equalize that with pressure on the front of our press, 4-on-3.

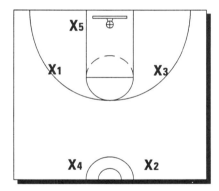

Diagram 1

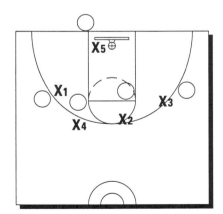

Diagram 2

(Diagram 3)   Drills. Three days a week we run the front drills of the press and three days a week we run the back drills of the press. Every player plays every position in the drills. This is a front drill. X5 is on the ball. The manager is at the top of the key. X1 and X3 are wing players. We allow the ball to go in. X1 attacks and pushes the ball sideline, get ahead of her and stop her. X5 completes the trap. X3 is off the right shoulder of the manager. We believe that you can move forward quicker than you can move laterally. X3 is about a half-step behind. When you trap, we want the hands up, but the rear end down.

going. Get a little behind the manager and then find the ball. We limit the offensive players in this drill. They can't dribble. We are working on the trapping. Then we allow the dribble.

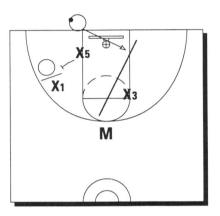

Diagram 4

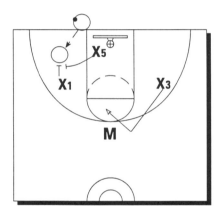

Diagram 3

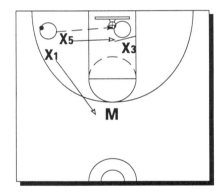

Diagram 5

(Diagram 4)   Now the ball is passed back to the inbounder. X3 must guard two people. We still want her behind this line (see diagram). If she has to give up a pass, we want it to be the one to the inbounder.

(Diagram 5)   X3 will attack the inbounder and as the ball goes over the head of X5, she will turn and follow the pass and trap the inbounder. X1 will immediately leave and the hands are up and they point the toes toward half-court.

(Diagram 6)   We don't want them to run directly toward the ball. X1 must head for the half-court jump circle. Forget the ball and find where you are

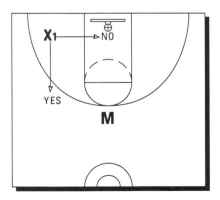

Diagram 6

(Diagram 7)   When the ball is passed back, the movements are reversed.

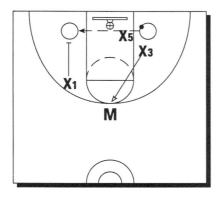

Diagram 7

(Diagram 8)   When the ball is passed back, X1 attacks the inside shoulder and pushes her sideline until X5 arrives. X1 cannot attack head on or she will be beaten by the dribbler. We don't limit the movement of the inbounder. She may break straight to the middle of the floor. We want X3 to be alert.

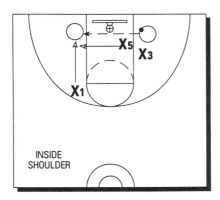

Diagram 8

(Diagram 9)   Another drill starts with all five players in the lane and the manager at the top of the key. Someone shoots the ball and X1 immediately looks for the point guard. X5 gets into the trap.

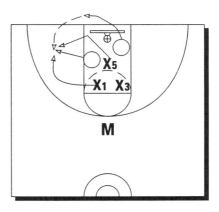

Diagram 9

(Diagram 10)   A back of the press drill. Run this drill on both sides of the floor at the same time. You need someone with a strong arm, so usually we use a coach to throw the pass. Each player lined up has a ball. X4 forms a triangle with the two offensive players. The sideline player can move anywhere she wants up and down the sideline as far as half-court. X2 is doing the same thing on the other side of the floor. The next player in line throws her ball to the coach and gets in the drill as the middle court player. The middle court player becomes the defensive player and the defensive player becomes the sideline player. The sideline player will go to the end of the line. We want to move the ball very quickly.

(Diagram 11)   The second back of the press drill. X2 and X4 set up in triangles. X4 defends 3 and 2. If the ball is on your side of the floor, you are up. The other person is back. Thus, X4 is up, X2 is back. They must communicate. X2 will call "back" even if she isn't very deep at this time.

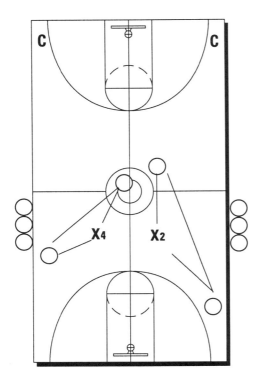

Diagram 10

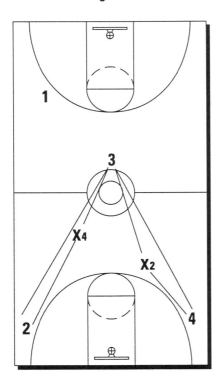

Diagram 11

(Diagram 12)   If the ball comes back to the inbounder, X2 steps up, X4 drops deeper and in the middle. The offensive players can move anywhere in the back court up to the baseline.

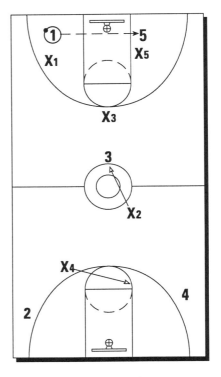

Diagram 12

(Diagram 13)   A breakdown drill which makes X2 and X3 call "up" or "back." The ball is passed back and forth between 1 and 5. You can't break up until your teammate calls "back."

(Diagram 14)   Let's put everything together. The ball is inbounded to 1. X1 and X5 are in the trap. X3 is covering 2. X2 is in the triangle, off the line. She is guarding two people. X4 is the back person because the ball is on the other side of the floor. She has deep responsibility even though she is almost even with X2.

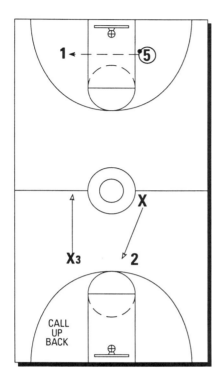

Diagram 13

(Diagram 15)   If 4 is very deep, X4 is deeper and to the middle of the floor.

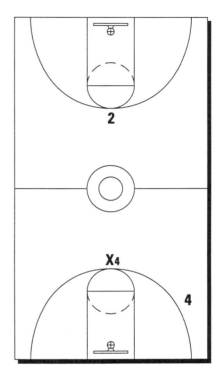

Diagram 15

(Diagram 16)   Sometimes a team puts two players deep. X2 stays near mid-court and X4 is in a triangle deep. This is the only time that she will be that far back. We will guard two offensive players with X4.

(Diagram 17)   If the ball goes back to the inbounder, X3 comes up to trap and X5 goes over because the ball was passed over her head. X1 breaks toward the mid-court center circle. X4 comes up, X2 drops back.

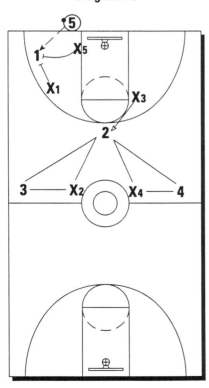

Diagram 14

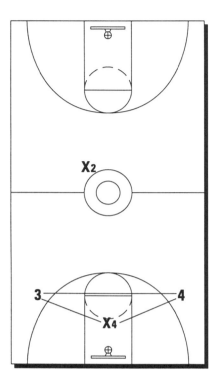

Diagram 16

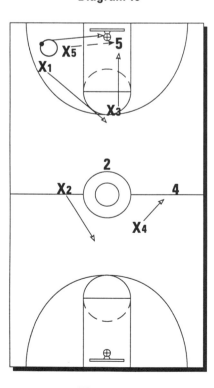

Diagram 17

(Diagram 18)   Suppose that we get beat on the sideline. 1 dribbles down the sideline. X1 stays on her shoulder. As she approaches, X2 is cheating a little more toward 2, knowing that she is going to stop the dribble. X4 is rotating up where X2 is. X3 rotates all the way back, X5 goes to the middle. X4 cannot go until X3 is sprinting by her or the offensive team will shoot a layup. In reality, X4 will leave a little sooner as she becomes comfortable with her teammates. The pass that the offense will most likely make is from 1 to 2. You will be surprised at how many passes X5 gets coming down the middle of the floor.

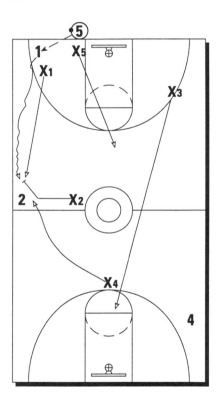

Diagram 18

(Diagram 19)   Keep the ball out of the middle. If X4 must give up a pass either to 2 or 4, the pass should go to 2. X1 should be putting pressure on 1 immediately. 1 should not be allowed to turn and look down court. X3 can also cheat down the floor to help.

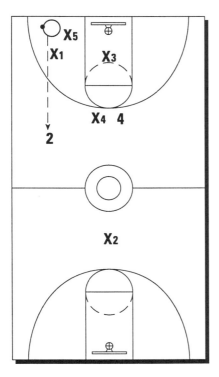

Diagram 19

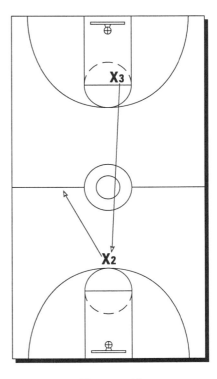

Diagram 20

(Diagram 20)   When X2 comes up to trap, X3 must rotate and take X2's spot. X3 must sprint. We press until we quit pressing. We don't have a rule. We get into a man defense.

(Diagram 21)   Drill, 1-on-1. X must sprint to them, break down, and control the dribbler.

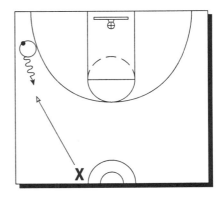

Diagram 21

(Diagram 22)   "Hold." We do not attack the inbounder if she receives a return pass. We wait. We let the inbounder come to us or else reverse the ball. Then we go get it.

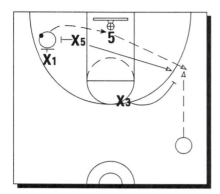

Diagram 22

(Diagram 23)   "Diagonal." This is used when the offense throws deep. The difference is that they do not put a person in the middle of the floor. We change the front of the press. When the ball comes out of the trap back to the inbounder, X1 does not point her toes to the middle of the floor, but comes back sideline.

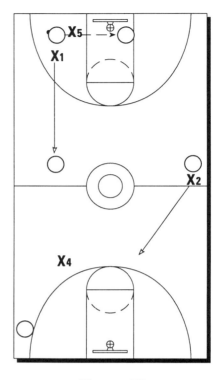

Diagram 23

Practice Drills and Organization

Note—*Coach Martelli's presentation was made in a gymnasium with players to demonstrate.*

I'm big on practice. I love practice. This is the teaching part of coaching. Once the ball is thrown up in a game, we lose control. I always feel as if this comes back to the teaching part of coaching. That is why we are at this clinic. You must understand that I coached in high school in a situation that was less than perfect. In fact, for three weeks at the start of the season I couldn't go past the foul line at the other end of the floor because the gym was set up for the school play. So, if you ask me, "Do you really know what we are doing?" the answer is yes. I've been there.

Let me ask you some questions about your practices:

1. How do you use your assistant coaches? And if you are an assistant, are you used during practice? I was an assistant coach for ten years. The first college practice I attended as an assistant coach I stood on the side and watched the team take layups for six minutes. Then, we scrimmaged. We practiced like that every day of the year. I had nothing at all to do with the actual practice.

2. Are you too involved in the logistics of the drill? Get someone to help you so that you are coaching the drills, not running the drills. If you are running a shooting drill you should not be the one feeding the ball. You are running the drill, you are not coaching the team. Are you too involved?

3. Can the oldest players on your team run your practice? In other words, do they know what is important to you?

4. Do you write it down? You must be prepared ahead of time. We were in the NCAA and other responsibilities kept me away from the team, so I wrote down the last practice of the year on the bus ride to the gym. It took me the entire ride to do it. But, because my practices fit a pattern, I could easily do it. I think that the biggest crime in coaching is wasting the time of the players and the coaches.

5. Do you use a whistle? If your answer is yes, I would ask you why? When in a game, they must hear your voice, so why not practice them hearing your voice?

6. How much extra running does your team do? And I ask you again, why? You do not coach track, you coach basketball. In 12 years of coaching, the suicides run by my teams is zero. I don't believe in them. I don't believe in excessive running. I can use drills with a basketball and call it conditioning.

Practice Plan

I spend a lot of time trying to formulate a plan. Here's what I try to do.

1. How do we want to play? What does that mean? I do that in September. You know who is coming back, what your players are going to be like. So, how do you want to play? Once you decide how you want to play, you must have an overview of the skills that the team needs.

2. From the overview, then I make a weekly plan. I will list general areas of offense, defense, and special. Then I break it down into individual and team. For example, under special, how many of

us have given up a field goal on a missed free-throw? I ask you, did you practice blocking out on a free-throw? It's amazing to me how much better you feel when you have it all written down.

3. Daily plan. Again, offense, defense and special. I will include pre-practice.

4. Practice. Start with stretch and warm-up, and rope jumping. Then our first drill will be a team drill from 4 to 6 minutes. Name your drills after someone famous. When they go home and tell their parents that they were doing Rick Pitino's drill, they are impressed. When you name your drills they know what they are going to do and it is more efficient.

(Diagram 1)   Delaware. Make the pass and follow the pass to the next line. The ball goes from 1-3-5-2-4. 4 takes the layup. These are all chest passes except the last pass to the shooter. The last pass is a bounce pass.

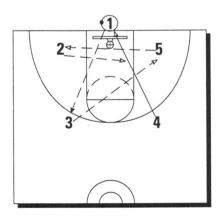

Diagram 1

(Diagram 2)   "Max Good." Each player at half-court has a ball. 4 breaks out to the wing, receives a pass from 1. 1 makes a fake away and then cuts to

the basket. 4 passes to 1, who takes the layup. 4 rebounds and passes back to 1, who is in the outlet area. 1 dribbles to half-court. The drill is then run on the left side of the court and this time 4 keeps the ball and goes to mid-court, which means that the players have switched lines.

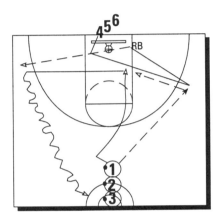

Diagram 2

(Diagram 3)   Backdoor cut. 4 breaks out to the wing, then makes a backdoor cut and gets the pass from 1. 1 rebounds and takes ball to mid-court on the left. This drill is run on both sides.

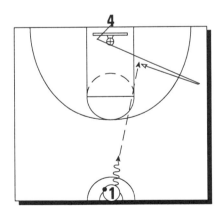

Diagram 3

(Diagram 4)   Screen a ball. 1 dribbles across mid-court, 4 breaks out to the wing and then sets a rear screen for 1. 1 and 4 run the screen and roll. Screener rolls off his inside foot.

Diagram 4

(Diagram 5)   Middle Jumper. 4 breaks out to the wing and gets a pass from 1. 1 cuts to the basket and 4 cuts off of the back of 1 to the foul line for the shot.

Diagram 5

(Diagram 6)   UCLA. Catch and Go. The ball is on the baseline. 2 passes to 1 and flashes to the ball. 2 gets the return pass, and drives to the basket.

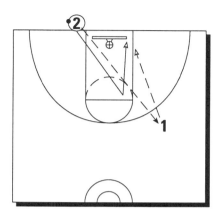

Diagram 6

(Diagram 7)   Catch and Sweep. Same as Diagram 6, except when 2 catches the pass from 1, 2 brings the ball across low, and then makes the left-handed dribble to the basket.

Diagram 7

(Diagram 8)   Catch, Fake and Go. It is exactly that. 2 receives the pass back from 1, turns, fakes the shot and drives to the basket. Be sure that you do these on both sides of the floor. I ask you this about your practice. The drills that you do with your right hand, do you also do with the left?

Diagram 8

(Diagram 9)   Vanderbilt. Use two balls and run this from both ends at the same time. The rebounders are non-players, like managers. The rebounder passes to 2, who starts to dribble to half-court. 2 makes the pass to 6, who makes a return bounce pass to 2 for the layup. Another rebounder takes the ball out of the basket and makes the pass to 3, who starts the dribble in the other direction and makes the pass to 5, who makes the return pass to 3 for the shot. 2 goes to the end of 3's line, 3 goes to the end of 2's line. We run this for four minutes.

(Diagram 10)   Celtics. Coach stands on the sideline, 1 makes a speed dribble to half-court. Once 1 is over half-court, the coach will call out a dribble move, such as "behind the back, opposite hand." 1 does that and continues in for the shot. 3 rebounds and passes out to 4, who goes the other way.

Once we finish our team warm-up, we will do individual defense. If you do this drill, please don't do it any more. (Drill has players spread out looking at the coach, they slide as he points right, left, front, back.) This sliding stuff has nothing to do with the game. Let me show you how to do it.

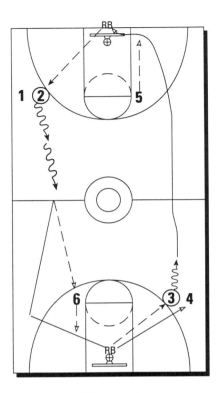

Diagram 9

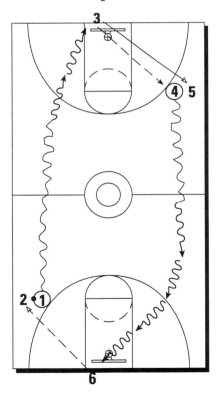

Diagram 10

(Diagram 11)   Put your players in a straight line looking at the shot clock. We run this drill for 35 seconds. We ask them to slide three steps to the left as quickly as they can, and then slide three steps back to the right. They do this for 35 seconds.

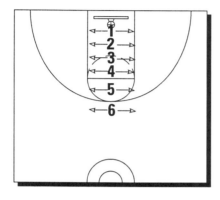

Diagram 11

(Diagram 12)   We now make a three-step slide to the baseline to cut off the dribbler.

Diagram 12

Practice Organization

We don't practice longer than two hours and ten minutes. As the season gets longer we will decrease this. We can work 20 hours a week, 6 days a week.

10-13 minutes	stretching and jumping rope
4-6 minutes	team warm-up
4 minutes	individual defense (slide drills, etc.)
10 minutes	defensive stations
10 minutes	shell defense
6-8 minutes	shooting
5 minutes	foul shooting
Half-time	
6 minutes	team competitive drill
6 minutes	individual offense
10 minutes	offensive stations
10 minutes	team offense, shooting and foul shooting

We do about 26-minutes a day shooting, including foul shooting. Every practice is mapped out the same way so I can plug in what I want to do in any individual practice.

Shell Defense. We do shell defense every single day. We have many varieties. Take the team that you play against, take their offense, and that's your shell defense. Whatever it is the teams in your league run, that is your shell defense.

(Diagram 13)   This is the shell that I know. Now, we never do this. We always adjust it to the offense we are going to face.

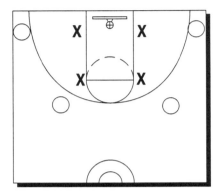

Diagram 13

(Diagram 14)   If you are going to play against the flex, practice this. Whatever your shell rules are, apply them. What you have done is, you have started to scout your opponents. You can come up with as many varieties of shell defense as there are offenses.

Diagram 14

(Diagram 15)   This is what we did the day before we played Kentucky. Mercer is on the right, Epps on the left. Coach has the ball at the top of the key.

Two big men, 4 and 5 are at the high posts. Epps comes under the basket and 5 comes down. As Epps starts, Mercer starts and comes off of the screen set by 4. And they clear the side for Mercer. That was our team defensive practice the day before we played Kentucky. Shell defense every day based on what the other team is going to do.

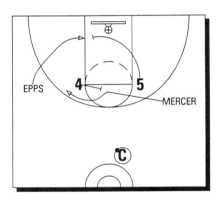

Diagram 15

(Diagram 16)   Shell vs. UMass. They always put Camby (C) on this block. 4 would clear from the other block and they would go wide. That's what we did in shell defense.

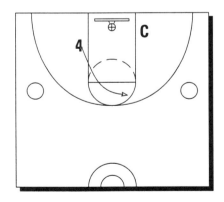

Diagram 16

We do shell defense every day for 10 minutes in October and November so that when we face a particular team we make the adjustments. The only way that you can get off the floor is if you get 3 stops.

(Diagram 17)   A team defensive drill. "Change" 4-on-4 or 3-on-3. When I say the word "change," drop the ball. The offense becomes defense and the defense becomes offense and we will go to the other end of the floor. The coach will pass another ball to the offense.

Diagram 17

Philosophy. This is our first defensive rule. No layups. This is what it entails. First, guard your man. You must break down while guarding the dribbler. Second, five players must run all of the time. Third, five players must break their backs to block out. How do you give up a layup—off the dribble, off transition, off the glass. In the "change" drill, they change ends. Now, "switch." This is the same drill except that we don't go full-court. You must talk in this drill. When I yell "switch" drop the ball and switch from offense to defense. You not only switch from offense to defense, you switch men. You are not allow to guard the person who was guarding you. You must talk.

Someone said that they tried a drill and it didn't work. They stayed with it and it still didn't work. My suggestion, get out of it. Sometimes I have a drill or a play that works with one group and doesn't work with another. It just happens. Don't stay with it and frustrate yourself and the team. Get away from it.

Now for some shooting drills. There are hundreds of good shooting drills. You don't need an expert to put a stamp on it, you have a shooting drill within your offense. Whatever it is you do in your offense, that is what your shooting drill should do. I challenge you to make your shooting drills to fit your offense. We do a lot off of screens, so we do each of these for two minutes, pop, curl, and fade.

(Diagram 18)   "Pop." 1 passes to 2 as 2 comes out, catches, turns, and shoots. That's all. Do on both sides of the floor.

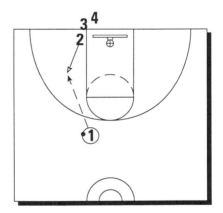

Diagram 18

(Diagram 19)   "Curl." 1 passes to 2, who has curled. 2 turns and shoots.

(Diagram 20)   "Fade." 1 passes to 2, who has faded to the corner. 2 shoots.

Diagram 19

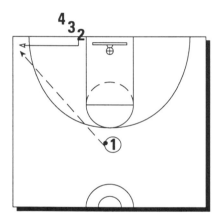

Diagram 20

What about position shooting? If you have bigger players that you limit the areas of their shooting, take them to the other end of the floor and let them shoot differently than this.

(Diagram 21) "Pitch, fade, fill." We must dribble the ball to get our teammate a shot. We don't dribble to get ourselves a shot. We penetrate, pitch, fill, or fade. 1 dribbles to the elbow. We tell the shooter whether he is going to fade, fill, or pitch. On fill, he goes behind the dribbler. On pitch, he goes away from the defense.

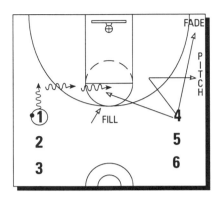

Diagram 21

(Diagram 22) Post play drills. Penetrate to the elbow on the dribble. The post moves away from the defense. Some coaches tell their post players to go to the front of the rim when the ball is penetrated. But, then one man can guard both players.

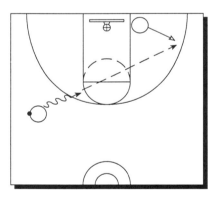

Diagram 22

(Diagram 23) Penetrate to the baseline. Post comes to high post area. Why? Because the defense goes to the ball. The post will step away and be open. This is a good shooting drill, a part of your offense.

Foul shooting. "Win the game." On the scoreboard, or with your managers, the score is 70 to 70. Each man will shoot a foul shot. If they make a foul shot, we get one point. If they miss the foul shot, the opponent gets two points. If you lose the game, then the team will do pushups or sit-ups.

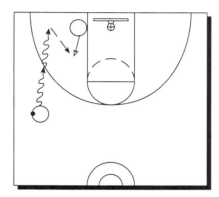

Diagram 23

Here's another thing we do. Split your team into two groups. This game is called "33." Each player shoots two shots in a row, the team will shoot 33. This occurs at both ends. They are competing against each other. The second part of the contest is this. Who is the best foul shooting team in your league and what is their percentage? Now, each end is not only shooting against each other, but also competing against the best team in the league.

Notice we have a half-time built into our practice. We will take two or three minutes and sit on the side. As coaches, we always talk to them before a game, at half-time, and after the game. But, in practice we only talk to them before practice. So, we discuss several things to emphasize such things as spacing, etc. and then send them back out onto the court. Go over what is important to you for the remainder of practice. We had years that this was a great idea. This last year it wasn't any good. We got away from it. It was a waste of time and an

irritant we didn't need. I think it's a terrific idea and we will try it again next year.

Now, we have some competitive team drills.

(Diagram 24)   "4-4-4." Team A has the ball. Team B is on defense. If Team A scores, it is Team B's ball and Team A presses to mid-court. Team C guards the other half of the court. It is total chaos.

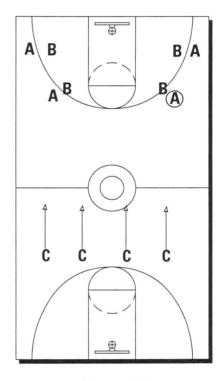

Diagram 24

(Diagram 25)   Once the ball gets to half-court, Team B attacks Team C and Team A steps off.

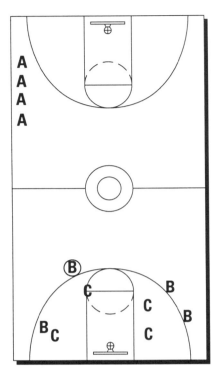

Diagram 25

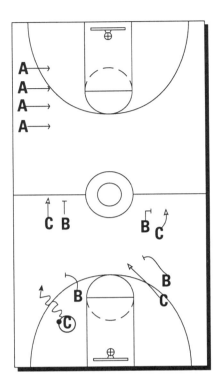

Diagram 26

(Diagram 26)　Whatever happens at this end, Team C will have the ball and Team B will defend until half-court and then Team A will be the defensive team.

(Diagram 27)　"Score and Stop." This is a full-court drill. Team A vs. Team B. Team A scores and it is now Team B's ball. But in order for it to count, Team A must stop Team B coming back. If Team A doesn't get a stop then Team B is trying to score at the other end. If Team B scores, then Team B must stop Team A to get a point.

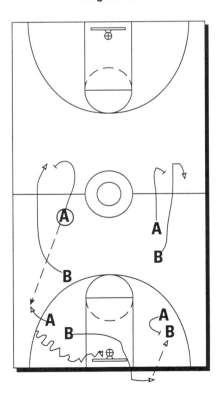

Diagram 27

(Diagram 28) "Girls' Basketball." Old time girls' team basketball had a two-dribble limit and you could not cross half-court. 12 players on the court, 6 players per team. Every time a player touched the ball, she had two dribbles.

Remember, name the drills so that your players know what you want. In this way you are not always stopping practice to explain. After we do competitive drills, we do individual offense and team offense. Then we rotate back into shooting and foul shooting.

Here is another foul shooting drill. "Partner Foul Shooting." Two players to a basket. Shoot 20 times, two at a time. Alternate shooters. If one of the two players doesn't get the percentage you have set, make the player who made the shots do the punishment. This puts more pressure on the shooter. They won't let each other down often.

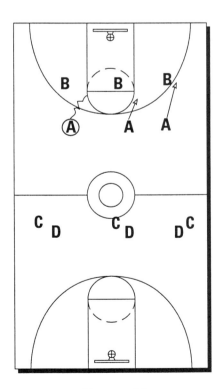

Diagram 28

This is just a matter of opinion, but I seldom scrimmage. I don't like it, I've never liked it. We do it about once a week. If you are a high school coach or a grade school coach and you scrimmage your first team against your second team, the only thing that is going to happen is that you are going to leave that segment of practice miserable because if your first team loses, we are mad. If our first team beats our second team, we say they are supposed to. Now, if you mix and match, i.e. starting point guard with second team other guard, then OK. But if you play first team against second, the second team will leave very disheartened.

Here's an alternative. I have 35 index cards on my cards. They say things like, "down 7, our ball, 1:50 on the clock, other team shooting a two-shot foul, one time out left." Anything that you can think of. We do situations every day in practice. Here's how we do them. The first time we do them, we let the team do them without coaches. Then we do it again and coach them. Here's one for you. Down, 4-5 seconds left. In our game the clock stops when the score is made. What do most teams do? They take a three-point shot and try to get fouled. What you should do is take the ball out and throw it to the front of the rim. You must know who the best player on your team is to throw the ball the length of the floor. You must practice this. The other team won't foul. Catch it and lay it in. The clock stops again and we are down two with 2.8 seconds left. If you practice these, your chances of success are better.

We end our practice with foul shooting. We will put half at each basket and maybe make five in a row so they can't just depend on the best shooter. When you finish practice, do you feel good about it? If you don't, it's not always them. Some of the time it is us. It all comes back to teaching and coaching.

Blocker/Mover Offense

Philosophy

Coaching is about leadership. Leaders are learners and learners are leaders. You can't lead if you don't learn. And you can't learn if you don't feel. You must get involved emotionally if you want to learn something.

Keep an open mind, take what you need and put it into your system. The principles are the same, but there are a lot of different methods of doing things. You must develop a philosophy. Ninety-five percent of communication isn't verbal. It's not what you say, it's what they see.

Coaching is such an emotional job that you have a tendency to become satisfied. That's something that can't be allowed to happen. You can't let it happen to your players and you can't let it happen to yourself. A coach must be creative in what he does. And you can't dwell on a win or a loss. You've got to learn from that and move on. Sometimes a win is harder to live with than a loss.

You must be a motivator. You must create a need in a person. You can't be a good coach if you can't motivate. Motivation takes a lot out of you emotionally as a coach. Motivation causes a person to act. Our challenge as a coach, as far as motivation is concerned, is to turn a person into a self-starter. How do you do that? You must create a need in that person. There are different ways of doing that. We try to focus on the intangibles. You must find whatever there is that will make them give their best effort. Players respond to sincerity. You must develop responsibility at the college level. I don't believe you can work them too hard. The

greater the investment the greater the interest. You must develop responsibility to the program, to the group, the teammates. You need to structure their experiences. You have to teach them. They have to hear it and you need to show them on the board, they must see it. Then you must set up controls and practice and make it realistic. So you must have a structure.

If you want to motivate you must have strong inner relationship skills. You must be able to build relationships. This is a good time in the off season to do it. You must have strong recognition, and strong approval. As a coach, you must keep evaluating what your philosophy is, what your attitude toward coaching is, how you are going to handle your players and what the relationships are. Remember, to motivate someone, you must create a need in them and they must be held accountable. Your practices must be well structured and you must have good relationships with your players. Finally, you must give strong recognition and approval.

Ways to Score

- Off the defense.
- Transition and secondary break.
- Out-of-bound plays.
- Half-court offense.
- Half-pattern, entries into motion, motion.

Blocker/Mover Offense

There are two schools of thought about motion. One is the Indiana school of thought where there is 5-man motion with everyone screening for everyone else. Then there is the one created by Coach Bennett of Wisconsin which is the blocker/mover. In this, you have designated screeners. With this offense there are some principles that should be listed. What are our objectives? You must get a shot. You must get a good shot. We talk about that all the time.

- The first thing you must do to get a good shot is that you must take care of the ball.

- You must have ball movement.

- You must have spacing. That's a hard concept to teach.

- There must be player movement.

- You must get your teammates open.

- You must get second shots.

  Blockers must: be intelligent, see the floor, be selfless, be tough with a thick set build, be excellent screeners, and they must be able to find the ball.

  Movers must: create offense, be assertive, be relentless, be good shooters, be smart, be able to read screens, be able to cut and have good footwork.

Rule: Blockers never screen for other blockers but movers can screen for other movers. Blockers screen for movers. A blocker can be a post player or a perimeter player. A mover can be a post player or a perimeter player.

(Diagram 1) Lane/lane. Both blockers are post players. They screen movers as they come through. All offenses are the same in that they put people in position to handle the ball so they can score. These blockers stay close to the lane, one high and one low.

(Diagram 2) They can down-screen and can also set skip-screens.

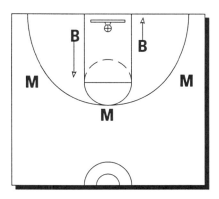

Diagram 1

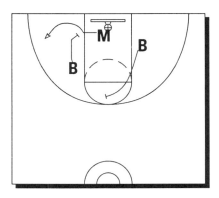

Diagram 2

(Diagram 3) Movers can screen for movers. The blocker sets a cross-screen and then the mover comes off of a down-screen set by another mover for the shot.

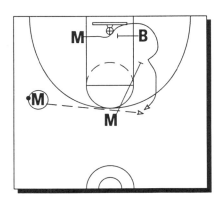

Diagram 3

(Diagram 4)   Wide/wide. Both blockers stay wide.

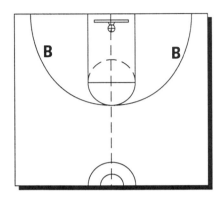

Diagram 4

(Diagram 5)   Top/bottom.

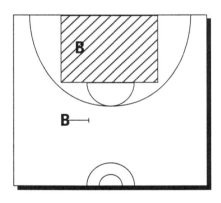

Diagram 5

(Diagram 6)   Free blockers. The blockers are not limited in their movement. We use this alignment when we have strong perimeter players. They are setting screens on the perimeter. If they can shoot, they can step back and shoot.

(Diagram 7)   One free/one bottom. If you have a point guard who can't score, then make him a blocker.

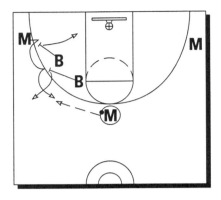

Diagram 6

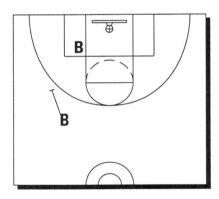

Diagram 7

(Diagram 8)   Lane mover. Give him a certain area in which to operate.

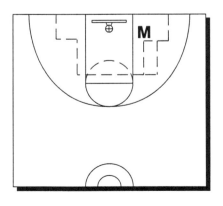

Diagram 8

(Diagram 9)   A free mover and a post mover. The blocker can screen down for the post mover. Your alignment will be determined by where you place the blockers.

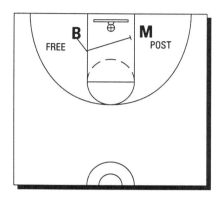

Diagram 9

Teaching this. You teach this like you teach motion. Once you determine who will be the movers and who will be the blockers, then you use the breakdown drills. You don't drill blockers coming off of screens because blockers don't get screens.

(Diagram 10)   We do 5/5 in the mid-court area. No switching, no dribbles. Catch and square up. Do ten passes.

Diagram 10

(Diagram 11)   We do 3/3 in this area. Five passes.

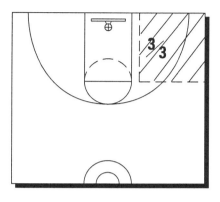

Diagram 11

(Diagram 12)   Shooting drills. Obviously you do the moves that you will get in the offense. Screen down and shoot. Screen laterally on the other side.

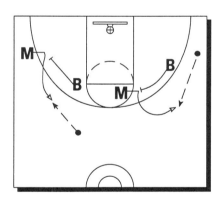

Diagram 12

(Diagram 13)   Screen, step back and shoot. Shoot the shots that you will get in your offense.

(Diagram 14)   With blocker/mover, you can do 2/0, 2/1 and 2/2 with the coach as the passer. The blocker can down-screen and then reverse and do a backscreen.

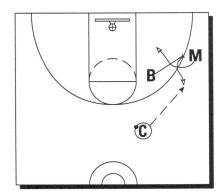

Diagram 13

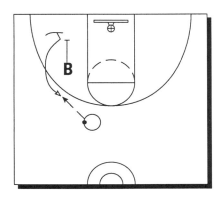

Diagram 14

(Diagram 15)   Three on one side of the floor.

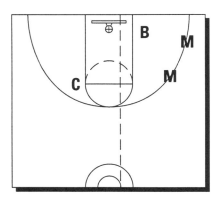

Diagram 15

(Diagram 16)   4/4 with no dribble. You must work 5/0 to get the spacing and timing. Then go 5/5 half-court. We then go 5/5 convert on the miss. We stay structured. Next is 5/5 for three possessions, and finally 5/5 scrimmage.

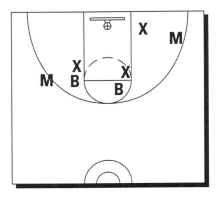

Diagram 16

This can become a good jumpshot offense, but you still need to get the ball inside. The point guard who can't score, make him a point blocker. It is a topside offense, keep the ball off of the baseline. Patience plus execution equals production.

Team Concepts

Philosophy

Any team playing an opponent of comparable ability should not be bothered by a full-court pressure defense. It's important for teams to keep proper spacing, play with poise and confidence, and to attack the basket. The teams that have trouble are the ones who don't keep the court balanced, panic and make hurried decisions, or are afraid to look to score in an advantage break situation.

A team's guards should be skilled enough to dribble the ball up court, one-on-one, against anyone they play. By keeping good spacing, the defense is unable to double-team a guard without leaving an opening somewhere on the court.

It is important for a team to practice against a full-court press every day. Players will not only get sharper at their execution, but will learn to feel more comfortable against pressure and seldom panic in a game situation.

Teams cannot afford to be too conservative either. They should look to attack the basket. If a team doesn't look to score when they have a numbers advantage on the break, they run into several problems. One: it is easy to turn the ball over if a team tries to pull the ball back out while the defense is still recovering. Two: by telling players not to attack the basket it makes them feel as though they aren't as good as their opponent and will hurt their confidence. Three: if a team has trouble scoring in an advantage break situation, they will have even more difficulty in a 5-on-5 situation. Also, it is important to look to score quickly because teams are very vulnerable when they are in transition from their press to half-court defense.

Presses can be used effectively to pick up the pace of a game, tire another team down or to get the defense playing aggressively, but with proper offensive execution, turnovers should not be a problem.

Terminology

Positions:	Diagrams:
1 - Point Guard	Pass
2 - Shooting Guard	Drive
3 - Small Forward	Screen
4 - Power Forward	Cut
5 - Center	Defender

Lag Man–The player who is behind the level of the ball making himself available for a release pass if the man with the ball gets into trouble.

Middle Man–The player who looks to receive the ball or at least keep the defense occupied near the center of the floor.

Deep Man–The players who runs the floor and makes himself available for the long pass.

Wings–The shooting guard and small forward who play up and down the sidelines.

Rules

1. Never catch the ball on the stand still. Be breaking toward the basket or coming back to meet the ball. This will help prevent interceptions.

2. The deep man should always stay in line with the ball. If the ball is on the sideline, he should be on the same sideline, etc.

3. The middle man should always break to the basket when the deep man catches the ball on the sideline. The "safety" or deep defender will often follow the deep man, leaving the basket area uncovered.

4. 4 and 5 should not dribble the ball when they catch it in the middle. It is usually in traffic and 4 and 5 are generally not good dribblers. They should catch the ball, pivot toward the basket and make the appropriate pass.

5. Players should never pick up their dribble in a corner or behind the basket where they can easily be trapped.

6. The point guard should remain in the center third of the court and 2 and 3 should stay in the outside third. This helps in keeping good spacing.

7. 2 and 3 should always sprint to near mid-court then come back, making themselves available for the inbounds pass.

8. The inbounder should not line up behind the goal because it eliminates the long pass option.

Alignments, Options and Diagrams

(Diagram 1)   It is important to be cautious of traps when the ball is near the sideline, but the corner areas and the area under the basket are extremely dangerous. They should be avoided whenever possible and players should never pick up their dribble in these areas.

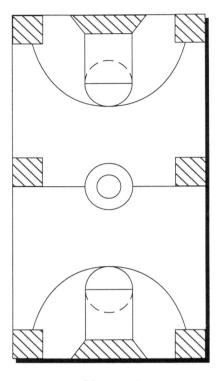

Diagram 1

(Diagram 2)   The best passer between 4 and 5 inbounds the ball, and the other man should sprint down the court. The point guard breaks to the top of the key and works to get open in the center of the floor, outside of the trapping area. 2 and 3 break to near mid-court and make themselves available by the sidelines above the corner. The inbounder always looks for the deep man as the first option.

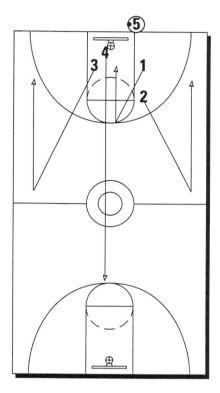

Diagram 2

Man-to-Pressure

(Diagram 3)   Against a man-to-man press, everybody should empty and let the point guard dribble the ball up the court 1-on-1.

(Diagram 4)   If the defense tries to run a man up to double-team the ball, the player whose man goes to double should receive the ball.

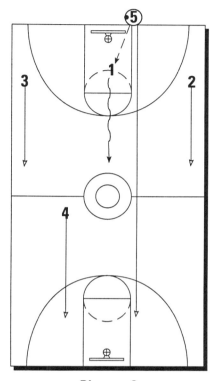

Diagram 3

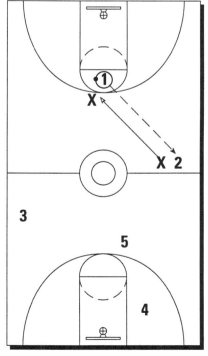

Diagram 4

(Diagram 5)   It is critical in receiving the pass that the player go back to meet the ball because the other defenders may be rotating up.

(Diagram 6)   Once the pass has been made, the point guard should empty and give the other player room to drive the ball up court.

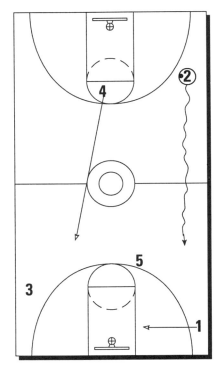

Diagram 6

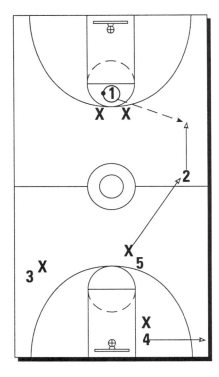

Diagram 5

Zone

Point Guard Entry:

(Diagram 7)   The point guard should receive the ball outside of the trap area. 5 should sprint to the middle of the court and make himself available. The wings come back to create openings for the pass.

(Diagram 8)   If the point guard hits the middle man, he pivots around looking for the deep man at the top of the key or for the wings running the floor.

(Diagram 9)   If the middle man hits the wing, they look for a 2-on-1 break with 4 as a trailer.

(Diagram 10)   If the middle man hits 4, they look for a 3-on-2 break.

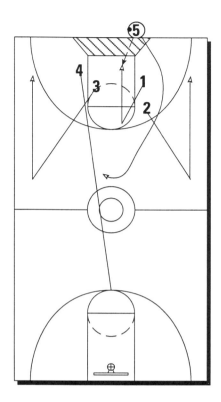

Diagram 7

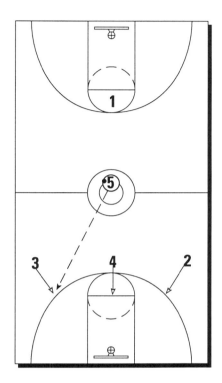

Diagram 9

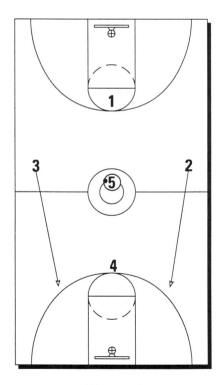

Diagram 8

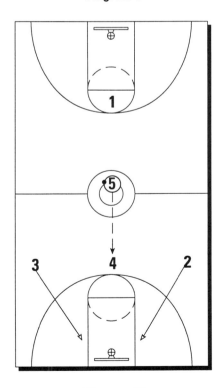

Diagram 10

(Diagram 11)   If the point guard hits the wing, he remains as the lag man. 5 looks for the opening in the middle, the opposite wing looks to receive the ball breaking toward the basket and 4 makes himself available on the sideline.

(Diagram 12)   2 now has several options.

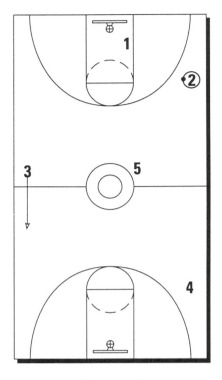

Diagram 12

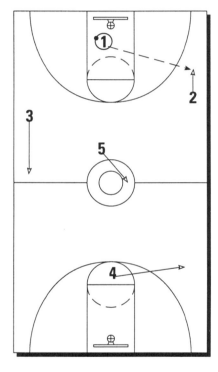

Diagram 11

(Diagram 13)   If he passes to 5, 4 cuts back to the middle and the wings sprint their lanes. 1 remains as a lag man. 5 would then have the same options as he had when he caught the pass directly from the point (see Diagram 1).

(Diagram 14)   If he hits 4, 4 looks for 5 cutting to the basket.

(Diagram 15)   If the 5 man isn't open, 4 passes the ball back to 2 and gets into the offense.

(Diagram 16)   If he hits 3, 3 and 4 look for a 2-on-1 break with 5 as a trailer. Note: the wing to wing pass is very good against a 1-2-1-1 press.

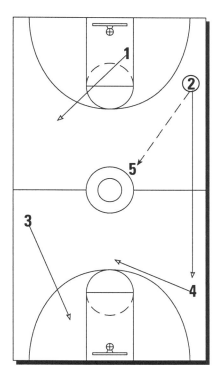

Diagram 13

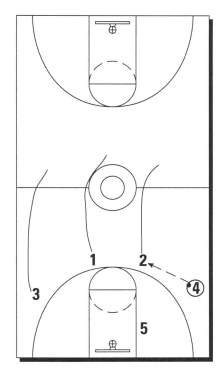

Diagram 15

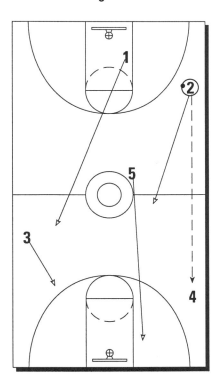

Diagram 14

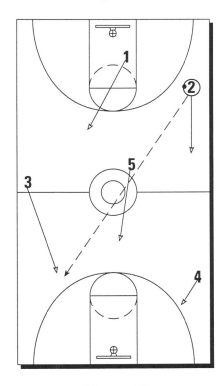

Diagram 16

(Diagram 17)   Another option for 2 is to drive the ball to the wing. 4 goes to the block to post-up. 5 comes as a trailer and the point guard makes himself available for a lag pass.

(Diagram 18)   If 2 is unable to do any of the previous options, he reverses the ball back to the point guard. 3 comes back toward the ball and the point guard has the same options as he had initially (see Diagram 7).

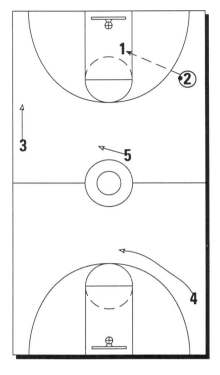

Diagram 18

Wing Entry

(Diagram 19)   The pass to the wing man is thrown when the deep man isn't open and the point guard is being denied the ball. 5 should run the baseline to improve the angle and shorten the pass.

(Diagram 20)   Since the point guard was denied the ball, his defender will be behind him and he will usually be open for a quick pass, cutting to the middle.

(Diagram 21)   From here, the point guard looks to drive the ball hard down the center of the floor for a 3-on-2 break.

(Diagram 22)   If the point guard is unable to receive an immediate pass from 2, the point guard becomes the middle man. 5 stays back as a lag man and 4 remains the deep man. From here the options are the same as when the wing receives the ball from the point guard in the point guard entry (see Diagram 11).

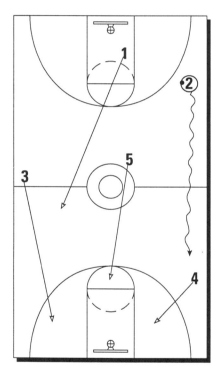

Diagram 17

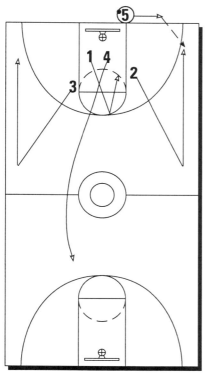

Diagram 19

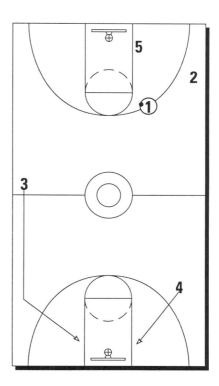

Diagram 21

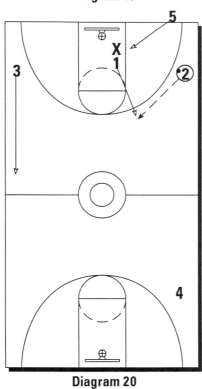

Diagram 20

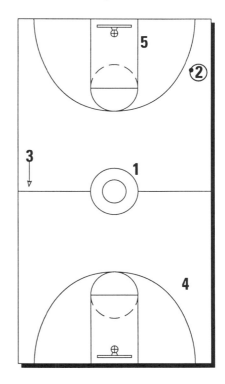

Diagram 22

Deadball

(Diagram 23)   In a dead ball situation (when the inbounder isn't allowed to run the baseline) it helps to bring the other big man back to set a pick for the point guard. After setting the pick, 4 rolls back to the ball. It is important for the offside wing to come all the way to the baseline between the trapping areas to make himself available for the pass.

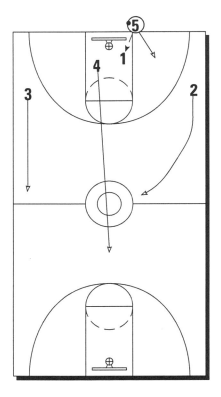

Diagram 24

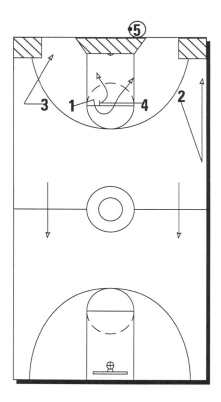

Diagram 23

(Diagram 24)   If the point guard or the wings receive the ball, 4 runs the floor to become the deep man and the press break is run the same as normal.

(Diagram 25)   If 4 receives the ball, the point becomes the middle man and 5 runs the floor to become the deep man, and the point guard becomes the middle man. The options are then the same as normal.

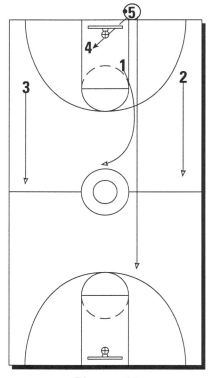

Diagram 25

Running a Great Practice Everyday

Planning a practice is very important. At the University of Texas we spend two hours every day planning the next practice. We have goals we want to accomplish each time we step on the floor. The time spent organizing our practice is putting down what we want to accomplish on paper and discussing what we did the day before that we need to improve or expand on.

For a preseason workout, try to make it as fun as possible. Let the players scrimmage so they can get some conditioning without them realizing it. Do not do wind sprints this early in the season.

From October 15 to November 15 we film every practice and zero in on different segments of each practice. Practice does not last longer than two hours.

Goals for our practices:

1. Conditioning

2. Fundamentals

3. Building Individual & Team Defense

4. Transition Offense

Always assume that your players do not know what you are talking about, so start at square one. I personally plan the practice the night before at home, then some more in the morning, then finally meet with my staff.

Typical Practice Plan

Every practice is on a computer so that coaches can have a copy and the players know what they will be doing.

3:30 - 3:45	Individual or Free Play
3:45 - 3:55	Stretching
3:55 - 3:59	3-Line Drill Straight Passing
	2-minutes—Bounce pass with last pass finishing with a power lay-up
	2-minutes—Figure 8's (If they miss a lay-up in practice, we will extend a minute)
4:00 - 4:08	Guards—Routine shooting, dribbling and passing
	Forwards—4-minutes—Post moves 4-minutes—3-on-3
4:08 - 4:13	4-Man Drill (Diagram 1)
4:14 - 4:19	Zig-Zag Drill—Defense has to put head on the ball. If the offense scores, they keep it coming back (Diagram 2).
4:20 - 4:28	Orange/White—3-on-2 (Diagram 3).
4:28 - 4:34	Transition Drill
4:35 - 4:50	Transition Full-Court—Call traveling closely. Make them pivot on the off foot.
	For a right-handed player, pivot on the left foot. Praise goes much farther than negativism. Make a rule for games that the coach talks to the referee, not the players.
4:50 - 4:57	Free-Throws—Forwards must make 20 out of 25 and the guards must make 22 out of 25 or better.
4:57 - 4:58	Water Break

4:58 - 5:06	Position Work—Guards—Shots in a minute.
	Forwards—4 minutes—Jump Hooks and 4 minutes—2-on-2 Post Play
5:07 - 5:22	Transition Emphasis on Defense
5:22 - 5:30	Free-Throws
5:30 - 5:38	Position Work
5:38 - 5:45	Orange & White

Try to teach in practice game situations so your players will be prepared and thus you do not have to waste any time outs.

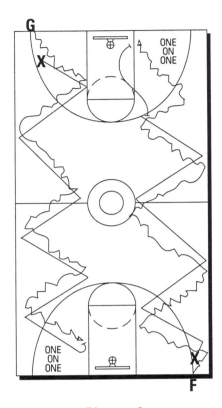

Diagram 2

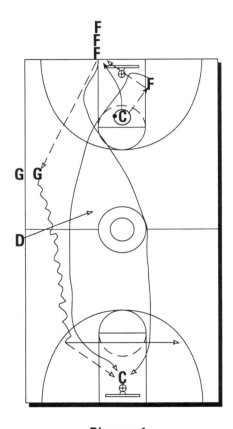

Diagram 1

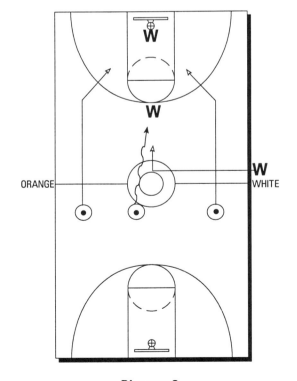

Diagram 3

Texas Swarm Defense

Zone Presses are determined by letters:

A = Full court

B = 3/4 court

C = 1/2 court

Man Pressure is determined by numbers:

100 = Full court

75 = 3/4 court

50 = 1/2 court

Defense dictates the tempo of the game, not the offense. Teams that attack pressure to score give us more trouble than those that just want to set up their offense.

Here are two looks of where we want to trap and where the players rotate. (Diagrams 4 and 5)

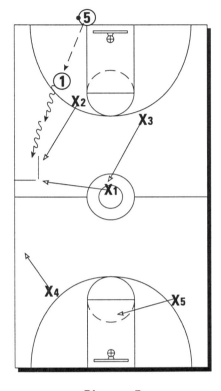

Diagram 5

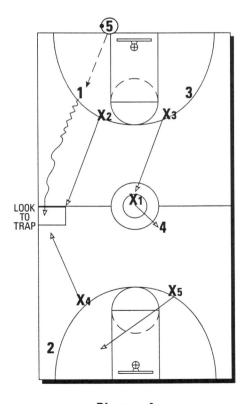

Diagram 4

"ROVER"

A Match-Up Zone

Why we use the match-up:

TALENT: If you play superior teams with inferior players, you need an unorthodox approach to defense. If your opponents have better skilled individuals, it is my belief that you cannot play these teams with a conventional defense. It does not matter whether your approach is man-to-man or a traditional zone alignment, the skilled players will be able to isolate the weak player into a one-on-one situation.

IT CREATES CONFUSION: Your opponents will be confused with what you are doing.

TEAMS MUST PREPARE: Teams will have to spend extra time preparing on how to attack the match-up.

IT IS NOT DIFFICULT TO LEARN: Introduce the defense in the first week of practice and it will fall into place quickly.

CONSISTENT: It is consistent with our philosophy of man-to-man defense.

HIDES A WEAK PLAYER: Teams with less talent usually have players with poor defensive skills.

FLEXIBLE: It allows for different setups to help disguise what defense you are using.

NULLIFIES OVERLOADS: Makes it difficult to use the overload principle in attacking zone defense.

COMPLEMENTS OUR MATERIAL: It allows for placing your best defensive players where their talents can best be utilized.

ALLOWS OPPORTUNITIES FOR PRESSING: Can press/trap either full-court, 3/4 court or half-court situations out of the match-up.

TEAM RULES
FOR THE "ROVER" MATCH-UP ZONE:

- Keep the ball on the perimeter [Deny the ball from going inside to the post area]

- Reception of all passes to the wing and baseline to be received outside the offensive threat area [Normally the 15' to 18' marks depending on the level of competition]

- Deny straight line cuts to the basket from the strongside

- Force the weakside cutter to the ball to go through an obstacle course. No straight line cuts to the ball

- Cut off penetration drives to the basket

- Increase the angle for all passes to the wing and on the turnover

- Front the low post

- The weakside player is responsible for lob passes to the post

- Guards [Key and Guard] are responsible for high-post entry passes

- All players are responsible for communication [When there are Cutters-Screens-Lobs]

INDIVIDUAL SKILLS TO BE TAUGHT

- Teach—how to read, to control, to anticipate and then how to react to the offense

- Teach—how to pressure and to deny passes to the perimeter

- Teach—the aggressive/physical game

- Teach—low post defense [slides/switches]

- Teach—how to contest cutters [strongside and weakside cuts]

- Teach—defensive rebounding responsibility

- Teach—transition to the offensive end of the court

INDIVIDUAL RESPONSIBILITIES FOR THE "ROVER" MATCH-UP DEFENSE

KEY: "K" Point—Position is with the back to the basket
- Responsible for designating match-up coverage

- In a One-Guard Front—Key has point responsibility

- In a One-Guard Front—Key pushes the ball to the right or left of center court

- In a Two-Guard Front—Key has the responsibility for the offensive player to the right

- In a Two-Guard Front—Key has high post responsibility when the strongside guard has the ball responsibility

- In a One or Two-Guard Front—Key provides helpside defense for the guard and for the forward

IDEALLY: Key should be tall with long arms and quick
REALISTICALLY: Key will be your smallest player

GUARD: "G" [Second Guard]
- Responsible for first man to the left of Key

- In a One-Guard Front—Guard has wing coverage

- In a Two-Guard Front—Guard has high-post responsibility when Key is responsibility for the ball

- Has help responsibility for penetration from the right or left of his position

- Has weakside rebound responsibility when on the weakside

IDEALLY: The guard is quick, agile, tough and an excellent weakside rebounder with size
REALISTICALLY: The guard is our second guard or small forward

FORWARD: "F"
- Responsible for the first man to the right of Key

- In a One-Guard Front—forward has wing coverage

- In a One or Two-Guard Front—forward pressures wing when the ball is covered by Key

- Has help responsibility for penetration from the right or left of his position

- Has lob responsibility to help the post when on the weakside

IDEALLY: The forward is the best rebounder and tallest player
REALISTICALLY: The forward is the worst defensive player and a good rebounder

CENTER: "C"

- Responsible for the coverage in the middle of the court

- Usually plays on a line between the ball and the basket

- Fronts low post player

- Plays behind and to the ballside when post is high

- Controls the lane line from the free-throw to the baseline

- Prevents high post cuts to the low post area

- Main communicator on all cuts

- Plays ballside most of the time

IDEALLY: Toughest and quickest of the big men
REALISTICALLY: Biggest forward and most aggressive big man

ROVER: "R"

- Responsible for the second man to the right or left of Key

- In a One-Guard Front—usually covers ballside baseline

- Usually responsible for all strongside/weakside cutters

- Has most baseline responsibilities when the ball is at the wing

- Must anticipate the flow of the ball

IDEALLY: Quickest player with size and ability to recognize the offense
REALISTICALLY: The small forward or biggest guard

BASIC DEFENSE:

- Weakside defense must always sink to the middle for help purposes

- Weakside/strongside defense must communicate with each other

- When the ball is on the baseline, the defense must sink to the middle and weakside defense will be inside the free-throw line

- Be able to recognize double-team situations

- Recognize rebounding responsibilities

STEPS FOR TEACHING THE MATCH-UP

- Introduce the match-up the first week of practice

- Control all offensive moves

- Start with the basic coverage and then move to the complex

- Teach the slides with basic ball movement on the perimeter

- Teach cuts from the top of the circle [strongside-weakside]

- Teach cuts from the wings [strongside-weakside]

- Teach reaction and help to the ball

- Teach the slides for the turnover

- Teach double-teaming/trap

- Teach how to pressure/control the ball on the point

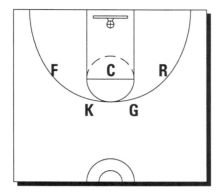

Diagram 1
Basic 2-3 set (Right)

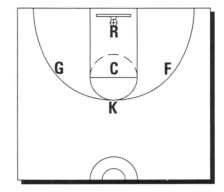

Diagram 4
Basic 1-3-1 set (Left)

Diagram 2
Basic 2-3 set (Left)

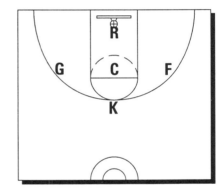

Diagram 5
Basic 1-2-2 set (Right)

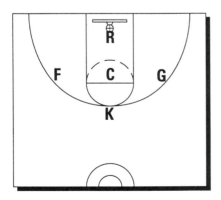

Diagram 3
Basic 1-3-1 set (Right)

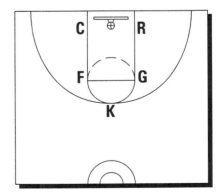

Diagram 6
Basic 1-2-2 set (Left)

Diagram 7
Ball coverage 2-3 set

Diagram 10
Ball coverage 2-3 set

Diagram 8
Ball coverage 2-3 set

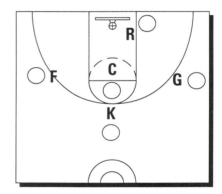

Diagram 11
Basic coverage 1-3-1 set

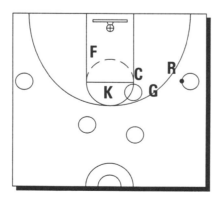

Diagram 9
Ball coverage 1-3-1 set

Diagram 12
Basic coverage 1-2-2 set

Diagram 13
Strong Side Cut to Baseline

Diagram 16
Coverage

Diagram 14
Coverage

Diagram 17
Strong Side Wing Cut to the Baseline

Diagram 15
Weak Side Cut to Baseline

Diagram 18
Coverage

Diagram 19
Weak Side Wing Cut to the Baseline

Diagram 22
Coverage

Diagram 20
Coverage

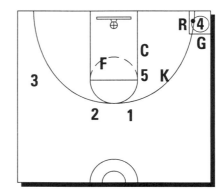

Diagram 23
Baseline Trap

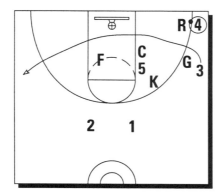

Diagram 21
Wing Cut to Wing from Overload

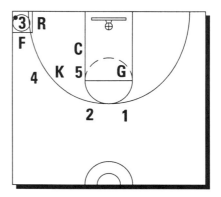

Diagram 24
Baseline Trap

Turning It Around

What I'd like to talk about first doesn't have anything to do with X's and O's. It is about some things that relate to what I call "turning it around." I inherited several situations where the team hadn't won, the program was down. I'd like to share some of the things that I have used.

I. Introduction:

This year we went to the tournament, we beat Vanderbilt and lost to UCLA. A couple of days after we lost to UCLA, ESPN flew me to Chicago, picked me up in a limo, and I was on ESPN. It really hit me how fortunate I am. I can remember that it wasn't that long ago that I was working in a Catholic school, trying to raise money to buy shoes for our team. I spent 13 years as a classroom teacher, from 5th grade geography to Advance Placement History. I was a ninth grade coach for four years, JV for one, then varsity coach for eight.

In my first game, at the end of the first quarter we were down 16-0, and it was 22-0 before we scored. I then became head coach at Wheeling Central Catholic High School in Wheeling, West Virginia, and my first year there was the worst record in the history of the school, 4 and 18. That's where I got into the idea of what are we going to do to turn this thing around. Two years later we were 25 and 2 and won the state championship. At Loyola it was the same thing. The previous year the record was 2 and 25. We were 17 and 13 the following year, the biggest turnaround in Division I, the first winning season in seven years. So, my whole career seems to be paradoxes.

In 1985 I sat in the last row of the University of Dayton Arena to see a former player of mine play for Navy in a NCAA Tournament game. I had never been

to a NCAA Tournament game. One year later, I was on the bench at the Charlotte Coliseum as an assistant coach with Xavier when we played against Alabama in the NCAA Tournament. Then, I get the head coaching job at Loyola, and here I am in a coaches meeting the day before we play. This is in Sacramento in the Arco Arena. There I am sitting around a big table with Lute Olson of Arizona, Denny Crum of Louisville, Clem Haskins of Minnesota and guys like that. It's like one of those pictures, "circle the one who doesn't belong."

I feel I have some perspective in what some of you are experiencing in terms of going through the various levels. In 1995 while at Xavier, we played Georgetown in the NCAA Tournament. Last year we were 13 and 15, our first losing year, then this year we were 23 and 6 and back to the Tournament. So, this has given me a good perspective.

Let me share some of the ideas I have found helpful in turning programs around. It doesn't have anything to do with X's and O's. The longer I'm in this, I am more and more convinced that it has less and less to do with X's and O's and more to do with motivating kids, to get them to play extremely hard and unselfishly.

II. The Team:

"The game begins and ends with the players."— Morgan Wootten. Nothing is more true. You must have fairly good players to win. The first thing I ask my assistants after they have scouted a prospect is "how tough is he?" The second question is "how fast?" But you can't recruit. If you can't recruit better players, you must make your players better. I have found that the team with the best players usually wins. At Loyola I told my assistants, don't tell me what they can't do, tell me what you are doing to make them better. Basketball teams are made from November to March, basketball players are made from March to November.

Your program must be year round. What are you doing right now to make them better? I believe the three most important months of the year are March, June and July. Digger Phelps said "The only games people remember are the ones you play in March." That's tournament time. June and July are the best times to improve as individuals. "You must inspire your players."—John Chaney. That's the responsibility of a coach, to inspire the players. You must put them in a basketball environment.

Here are some of the things we did back when I coached high school.

a. School library—get the librarian to order some basketball publications.

b. Calendars, posters, brochures, etc. in my classroom. Get them thinking about basketball.

c. Visit college practices. Let them see how hard they work.

d. Visit college games, especially your young players.

e. Visit All-Star games.

f. Get college coaches to write letters to your team.

g. Visit the site of the State Championship. We'd give our kids two 5 x 7 cards with Charleston written on it. We told them to put one card on the refrigerator and on your bedroom mirror. The first thing you see in the morning and the last thing that you see at night are these cards reminding you of the State Tournament. Get them thinking about basketball all year.

h. Motivation. Bart Starr said that Vince Lombardi used to find a different way to motivate the team every single day. That's a heck of a challenge for a coach.

i. Have them to your home.

j. Have a countdown in the classroom. Everyday I would have written on the board the amount of days until the start of practice. I wanted our kids thinking about basketball in one way or another every single day. When John Calipari was at UMass, I asked him for advice. He said, "You need to make visible changes." When the players return in the fall, they must see some changes. We repainted the court, we repainted the locker room. We changed shoe styles. We changed the home team bench. We got new practice gear and T-shirts, especially for the feeder programs.

From March to November:

a. Meet individually with your returning players, and anyone who wants to be a player. What do you think we need to do to be better as a team and for you to be better as a player? Questionnaire.

b. Senior exit interviews. What did they like or dislike about the program? Questionnaire.

c. Summer workout program with a daily checklist.

d. You write two letters to them, the first letter yelling at them and the second letter praising them.

e. They write two letters to you with their workout sheet.

f. Summer leagues— if you attend they will know it's important.

g. Open gym: Rules: Played games to 7 straight, all man-to-man defense. Everyone must pass mid-court before a basket counted. Tip-ins counted two points, and play 4-on-4.

h. Summer camps.

III. **Support Groups**:

a. Your staff. The most important people are your assistant coaches. They must be loyal and conscientious.

b. The administration. You must be a great teacher in your school.

c. The teachers. You must have the other teachers on your side. Take no shortcuts and expect no favors. I sent a letter to the faculty at the beginning of each academic year. I listed the potential players and said that I wanted to know if their conduct or their effort academically wasn't up to the standards.

d. The parents. The team is like a big triangle. As the coach you are the base of the triangle. You must consider what is best for the team. As a parent, it's opposite. They have the triangle reversed. They want to know what is best for their kid first, then the team. It is important that you get the parents on your side. I used to give players and parents contracts. This listed the rules for the team. I asked for support of these rules. Both the players and parents signed them.

e. Other coaches. You may have to share kids. You must help each other.

f. Boosters. You need banquets and awards, they can help.

g. Feeder schools. We had clinics, open practices, grade school nights, all-star games.

h. Student body. I took out a half page ad in the school newspaper last week. "Thanks for your great support this year."

IV. **Your Role As a Teacher and Coach**.

You must appreciate how important your role is. "Our chief want in life is someone who will make us do what we can."—Ralph Waldo Emerson. I push our guys to be as good as they can be. To turn a program around, you must be a self-starter, have a high energy level and you must be aggressive. You can only eat an elephant one bite at a time. Every day we take one bite out of an elephant. "You must never blame the kids."—Eudie Joseph. If he doesn't play hard, don't play him. It's your fault if you play him. Be very demanding, have a high level of expectations. We want them to play hard, and to play together. We tell the players that their concept of hard play is totally meaningless. The only one that counts is mine.

V. **Conclusion**.

John Adams said, "The Revolution was affected before the war commenced. The Revolution was in the minds and hearts of the people." The people had already broken away from the British before Lexington and Concord. You need to get your kids to the point where they expect to win. Once it gets going, they will believe and it will happen. Once you get it turned around, it is a beautiful thing. And one last thing, William Shakespeare said, "This above all else...to thine own self be true." We have a great responsibility with these kids. But remember, the motivation part is the most important.

The Pressing Game

I told our team I want two things from them. First, I want them to be great. They must listen, work hard in the weight room, on the court and in the classroom. The second thing I wanted was for our team to be a pain in the neck to play against. I want teams to dread playing against Xavier. That's why we press.

Let's talk about our mental approach to the pressing game. We press every game. When the ball is taken out, we are pressing endline to endline. If you are going to be a pressing team, you must be committed to that. If you half believe in it, your pressure isn't going to be what you want it to be. I hate to give up one floor board. We press every game. If you can handle our pressure, then we will change it a little. But, we are going to find out early whether you can handle pressure. Our players know the word "attack." We believe in pressure defense, we believe in pressure offense. We press to equalize our lack of size. We attack. When we are on defense, we are really on offense. We are attacking. **Attack! Score! Press!** The tendency is for your team to lean back and get into transition. When we score, we are leaning forward, we are coming to get you. Will you give up some layups? Yes, you will. One of the reasons we press is that we are not a good shooting team. Our press is an offensive concept for us.

(Diagram 1)   Initial alignment. X4 is on the ball, X1 is on the ballside, X5 is opposite. As soon as we score, we sprint to those areas. Those are their general areas of responsibility. They pick up whoever shows up in that area. It's a zone alignment, but it is a man press. You don't defend a specific player. You go to your area and pick up whoever shows up.

(Diagram 2)   If 1 runs to the opposite corner, X3 stays with him. If 2 goes deep, X2 goes with him. If they screen, you can switch, but you are still responsible for a man. We tell our players. "What we are about to ask you to do is impossible, but to make our press work, you must do it. Once you match up to that player in your area, you cannot allow him to catch the ball." That doesn't mean to face guard, because you can't be beat deep either. You can't stay behind him either. We make it as hard as we can for the other team to get the ball inbounds. This takes a real commitment on your part. We will change our alignment by taking X4 off the ball, but the other four players are always in those spots. If the man runs the baseline, X4 runs with him. Remember, it is a zone alignment, but it is a man press.

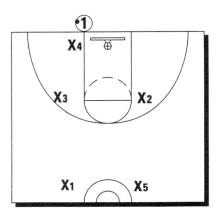

Diagram 1

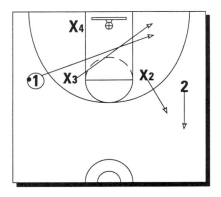

Diagram 2

(Diagram 3)   We line up this way against a 1-4. We love this. The more players they put in the backcourt, the more players can screw it up. The teams who are the hardest to press are the ones that spread you out.

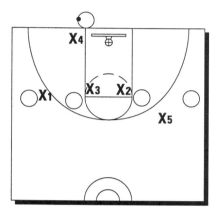

Diagram 3

(Diagram 4)   Decisions! This is the most important part of the press. The first decision is what do you do when the ball is successfully inbounded. Do you trap or don't you? We only trap players who can dribble. Never trap a bad player. We want the bad dribbler to have the ball.

(Diagram 5)   The second decision is don't allow the pass up court. Make them dribble the ball up court. If someone passes the ball to your player, you are coming out.

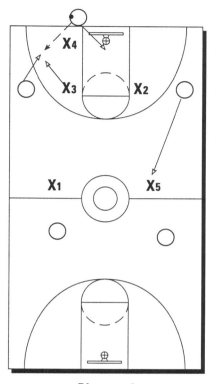

Diagram 4

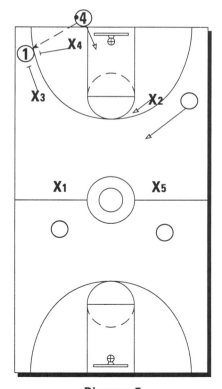

Diagram 5

(Diagram 6)   If the ball comes out of the trap back to 4, we do not trap 4. 4 is a bad ballhandler. X2 does not go up to trap.

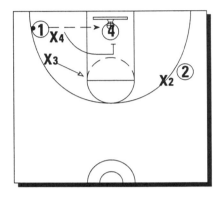

Diagram 6

(Diagram 7)   We want 4 to dribble with X4 on his hip. Now we may trap near half-court because X5 has 2. You must practice what the other three players do when the ball is trapped. You players must know who you want to dribble the ball and who you don't want to dribble. Remind your players that it is a man press. They can't pass the ball up the court.

We practice the way that we play. We practice up and down the court. We recruit fast players. We want to be faster every single year. But, when I coached in high school, we also pressed. We want to give the other players a chance to screw up.

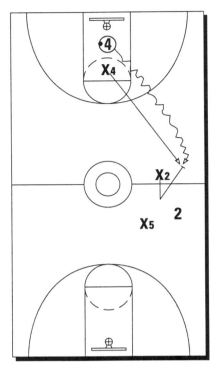

Diagram 7

(Diagram 8)   One of the things in the press is the concept of quick pickup. You must practice this. One of the drills we use is the circle drill. We start them in a circle. The coach will call either "blue" or white" and when he does, that team immediately takes it out-of-bounds. The other team must sprint to their areas. Quick pickup is crucial. And the players must talk. We also start this drill from the free-throw alignment.

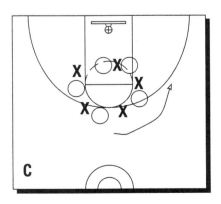

Diagram 8

(Diagram 9)   Greyhound Drill. Three teams, blue, white, grey. This is 4-on-4-on-4. Blue steps off the floor.

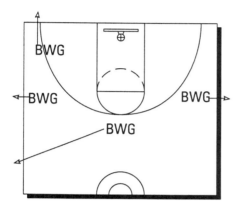

Diagram 9

(Diagram 10)   The white team inbounds the ball and the grey team presses.

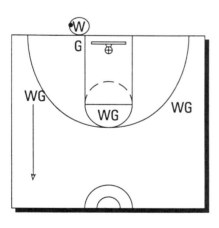

Diagram 10

(Diagram 11)   When the white team scores, or there is a turnover, the white team goes the other way 4-on-0 and the blue team does not defend.

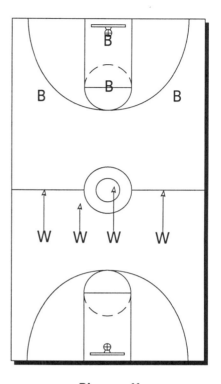

Diagram 11

(Diagram 12)   As soon as white scores 4-on-0, then the blue team takes the ball out-of-bounds and the white team must get into the press. The blue takes the ball up the floor, and then after a make or a turnover, they come the other way 4-on-0 with the grey team waiting as the blue team did before. When they score, the grey team takes the ball out-of-bounds and the blue team presses. Quick pickup is paramount.

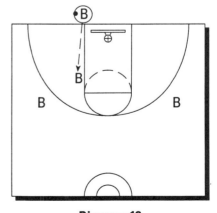

Diagram 12

(Diagram 13)   Minnesota. This is another 4/4/4 drill. Grey team starts on offense against the white team. After they score, they press until mid-court where blue enters the picture and the grey team leaves the floor.

(Diagram 14)   Breakdown drills. The best way to do this press is 4-on-4 and 5-on-5 because decision-making is such a big part of it. We work on back-tapping. A big part of our press is pursuit. 1 is on offense and starts the drill by dribbling toward the other basket. 2 runs behind and tips the ball to 3. 2 and 3 then go 2/1 against 1. Don't run directly behind him, don't lunge for the ball. Run along side and run through the ball.

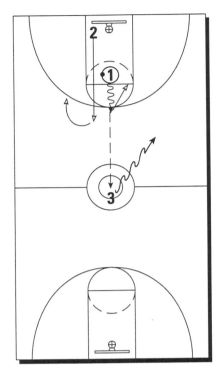

Diagram 14

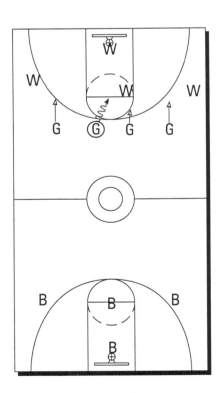

Diagram 13

(Diagram 15)   3/3 or 4/4 pursuit. The coach is in the middle. Coach will pass the ball to the offense. Two defensive men play defense while the third man tries to tap from behind. We also do this 4-on-4.

The biggest thing is that you must practice this way every day. The way we press means that there will never be a static situation. I will never know what will happen. The players must be drilled and conditioned to make the decisions on the fly. It gives our team great spurt ability. If you press this way, you must believe in it. Our kids like to play this way.

Question: How do you crash the offensive boards?

Answer: We send three players to the board, the two guards drop back. When I coached in high school, I sent four to the board, and we practice this. We hit and spin, etc. It is hard to get to your spot in the press if you are hitting the board and we score.

Question: Do you always have three line up on the same side in the press?

Answer: Yes, I heard Jerry Tarkanian say "The more they think, the slower they get."

When you play this way and your kids believe in it, it becomes part of their personality. This is an equalizer for lack of size.

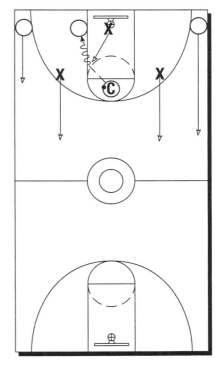

Diagram 15

Building an Offense

In the process of building an offense, let us mainly be concerned with the **Fast Break**. There are two types of fast break:

Primary—If only two players are back on defense and the offense can get a good shot with only two passes or less.

Secondary—When the offense cannot beat the defense down the court.

Fast Break Drills

In the practices set up some drills and use these as warm up drills for the team. Fast Break Drill #1— (Diagram 1) Here are some teaching points for this drill. Have the players run full speed. Three lines passing back and forth then finishing with a layup. The middle player jump stops at the coach, then bounce passes to the runner on the left and immediately runs to the wing for an outlet with this player's back to the sideline, calling for the ball. The player running the right wing goes and gets the rebound out of the net, takes the ball out-of-bounds and throws to the outlet. Have the players run down the sideline after the layup.

Fast Break Drill #2 (Diagram 2) Have the players rebound out from their forehead, so that defenders can not go over their back and get the rebound. Turn to the outside of the defense and take one bust out dribble. This is when the wing takes off and the rebounder throws the pass for the wing to run down and score. Do this drill on both sides simultaneously.

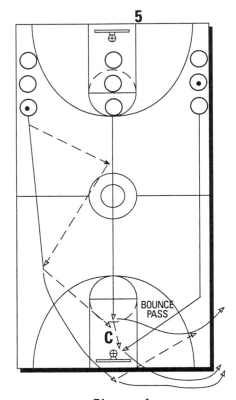

Diagram 1

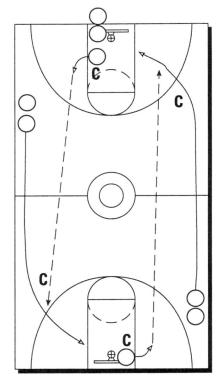

Diagram 2

Fast Break Drill #3 (Diagrams 3 - 4) Once the shot is taken, all three must block out. The two players on defense must stop penetration and cover the basket. The offense needs to look for a layup then try to get a shot in two passes or less. The point guard can step in the direction of the pass either for a 2-point shot or a 3. The middle player is always the one back on defense for the 2-on-1.

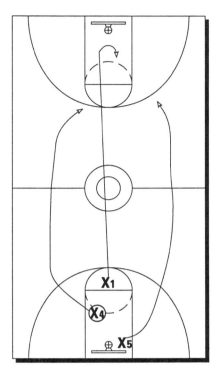

Diagram 4

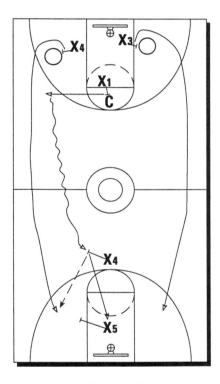

Diagram 3

Fast Break Drill #4 (Diagram 5) In this drill the offense has to recognize how many players are back on defense. The coach can send three, which would be a triangle defense, or four, which would play a box defense, or five, which would play man-to-man defense. In this figure the coach sends three players back on defense. Therefore, the offense must run a secondary break filling the five spots that are circles, making a strongside. If the coach wants to have the offense run the primary break, then only send one defender and the offense only sends two players, not all five.

A question may be, what if the guard only sees two defenders back? The answer to this question is to do it just like Drill #3 (3-on-2).

Things to look for from your personnel. The big players (4 or 5) need to compete to get the ball out of the net and compete to get down the floor. The runners (2 or 3) have to be able to run the sidelines hard. The outlet (1 or 2) have to be good ballhandlers.

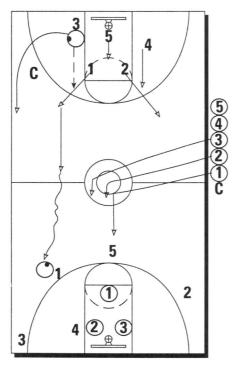

Diagram 5

Secondary Break

In the secondary break (Diagram 6) the players need to fill these spots. 4 is following the ball by going from block to block trying to get it inside. 3 goes below the block and straight up the lane, making sure not to be lazy or weak on the screen for 5. Secondary break teaches one basic principle and that is ball reversal. (Diagram 7) The defense is strong at the beginning of the break, but a ball

reversal breaks all of that down. If the defense tries to stop the reversal, then look opposite or down low (Diagram 8).

Spacing is not a problem for the secondary break as long as the five spots are filled with either big or little. Motion offense can flow into progress because of where the players are at the end of secondary break.

Diagram 6

Diagram 7

Diagram 8

DEFENSE

Defense—Try to battle everything the opposition does.

The first question to ask is how to teach close-outs?

The defense must shoot over the hand. We have a lot of three-minute drills where we break the players up into different groups and mix up the positions. We will have the players play sideline defense so they close out and keep the offense on the sideline. The defense has to put pressure on the ball and pressure on the pass.

How much room does the defense give the offense?

That is an individual thing. If a player is extremely quick, get way up into the offense. If a player is not as quick, take a step back so the player can still contain the offense. Early in the season we will do one-on-one from mid-court where the offense can not go outside the width of the key. (Diagram 9) Watch out for the buddy system so that everyone is working hard.

Where do you want your players for Post Defense?

During the pre-practice period we teach our post players that if the ball is below the free-throw line

extended, then full-front with a hand up and sitting on the offense's thigh. (Diagram 10) When the pass goes to the top of the key get around on the bottom side.

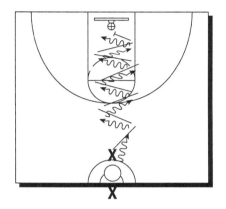

Diagram 9

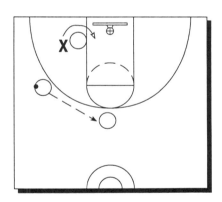

Diagram 10

How do you get through screens?

We try to do different things. First try to steal the pass. (Diagram 11) The next thing is to get there when the pass gets there and finally avoid the screen. (Diagram 12) X2 says "room" so X4 automatically gives the player the room to get through. X4 needs to extend the downscreen.

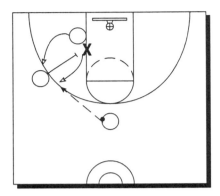

Diagram 11

Diagram 13

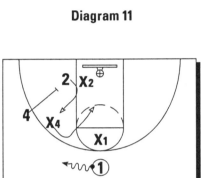

Diagram 12

Diagram 14

Ball screens, X1 steps over the top of the screen and X5 must step up. X1 and X5 will double 1 on the ballscreen. Be the aggressor on defense (Diagram 13).

Stagger screens, with single screens the defender needs to avoid high or avoid the screen low. But against a stagger screen the defender needs to shadow the offense. (Diagram 14) If the offense slips X3 then X4 will be up to slow that cutter down. When X2 shadows, try to ride the offense with a forearm.

Lateral screens, X5 must force the offense high because there will be help from X4. If X5 forces the offense low there will be no help and X5 will be on his own (Diagram 15.)

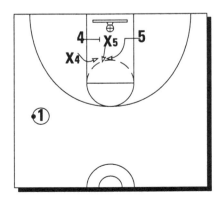

Diagram 15

2-2-1 Press

We like for X5 to stay home. As the ball begins to approach half-court, X1 needs to start cheating to the sideline. X2 and X4 look to trap in the designated areas (Diagram 16). When the trap has been made, the press will look like this (Diagram 17).

How do you teach transition out of 2-2-1 into man-to-man?

First of all stop the ball. Then practice it so that the defense just naturally picks up the closest person. The defense must communicate to make the transition the most effective for this type of press.

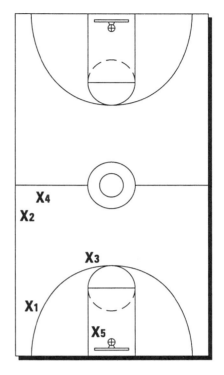

Diagram 17

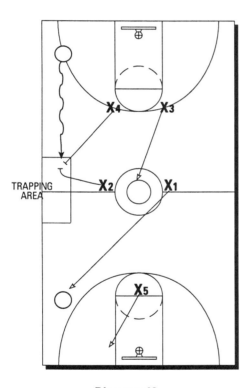

Diagram 16

POST PLAY

Offensive Development

"Basketball Games Are Won at the Post."

The Big Man must now be able to rebound, shoot, block shots, pass, dribble, screen, run full-court, and most importantly, protect the basket (play defense).

In our philosophy, the first aspect of developing a post man is positioning. It is, by far, the most important phase of the pivot attack and is the primary area of attention before feeding the post and teaching moves and shots.

We break the fundamentals of the low post attack into the following phases in this order:

1. Positioning
2. The Target
3. The Pass
4. The Catch
5. The Move
6. The Shot

Positioning:

This phase of the game is vital! Each square inch of the floor area in the pivot (post) is vital territory and takes a pretty good man to hold it. Our post men must realize the fact that the battle for position in the pivot is a rugged operation. Physical and mental toughness is the prime prerequisite to play here.

Basic Post Position:

The post man should position himself above the block—normally he should face inward.

As the ball is brought to his side, he should:

a. Pivot into the defensive man
b. Form a big base (legs/arms spread wide)
c. Favor the side of the lane where you are strongest so you will be moving toward the center of the lane to your strength. (Some posts can play both sides, but most can't.)

Principles of Pivot Play:

1. Be active—move your feet—fight for position.

2. Bend the knees—make yourself a big target. Never stand up straight.

3. Vary your position. Leave and come back. Walk your man up the lane. Keep the defense honest.

4. Leverage is vital. Control the defensive man—he must not control you. Leverage is gained through contact, foot and body movement. Remember, the feet and legs only move your body, just as on defense, so move your feet.

5. Get the defensive man to improperly position himself. Once he does, don't let him correct himself!

6. Create as much room for the pass as you can. Examples:

    a. If he fronts, force him away from the basket as far as possible to create more room for the lob pass (go higher or out further).

    b. If he plays you on the top (high side), walk him up the lane to create space for a baseline pass.

    c. If he plays you on the bottom (low side), walk lower and keep him on your rear.

d. If he plays behind you, feel for him by setting up as close to the lane without getting a three-second violation.

7. Prevent or inhibit movement by the defensive man.

8. Give a target with the hand away from the defensive man. Protect the target area with good use of the body.

9. Don't release the man from your rear too soon. Normally after ball has been passed and is nearly to you.

10. On the lob, use the hip to nudge him. Hold him off with the hip until the ball reaches your nose. Stay close to the defense and roll to the ball. You have one step to the bucket—no dribble—don't push off—hands should both be above your shoulders.

11. Never take your eyes off the ball!

The Target:

1. The post man should establish the target with the off-hand away from the defensive man and protect with the body and forearm (backside).

2. The passer should read the hand and pass away from the defense.

3. Don't feed the post if the defensive man is more than two feet off of you. Make your man play you.

The Catch:

1. In most cases, two-handed.

2. Bring the ball under the chin area—Chin it.

3. Look baseline side first—look for the foot.

The Move:

1. You may use one dribble only from the low post —baseline power move! It's a two-handed dribble (one) to power inside. Lower your center of gravity. It gives you balance (shoulders square to backboard, unless dunking the ball) and explosion.

2. Drop-step with authority. You must own the post when you have the ball. "You are the King!"

3. You have three basic options:
   • Shoot
   • Pass
   • Power Dribble Baseline

4. Turn around jumpshot (10').

5. Hook shot—conventional and jump hook.

It is vital that you perfect your passing skills.

Don't make a difficult shot out of an easy one. Don't force a shot. You know if you are in control or not.

To be a constant scoring threat you only need three basic shots:
   • Turn-around jumper
   • Hook
   • Power Mover (Layup)

From the low-post your rule is "Shoot first, pass second."

From the high-post your rule is: "Pass first, shoot second."

Close-Out, Help, Cover Down

(Diagram 1)   The drill begins with the ball on the point and the defender in help position at the foul line. When the ball is passed to the wing, the defender closes out on the ball. When the ball is returned to the point, the defender sprints back to help position.

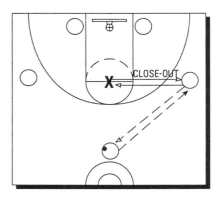

Diagram 1

(Diagram 2)   With the ball on the wing and the defender in a ball pressure situation, should the ball go in to the post, the defender will now cover down (back to the baseline) and dig at the ball.

Diagram 2

(Diagram 3)   The ball is passed back out to the wing and the defender closes out on the ball. This drill is continuous for 30 seconds—technique and effort are emphasized.

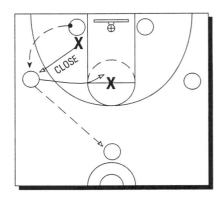

Diagram 3

Full-Court Triangle

Defend, Block Out, Rebound, Transition

(Diagram 1)   Play begins with the coach (C) shooting a perimeter jump shot. The X-team must block out and secure the rebound. If they fail to do so and the offense (O-team) gains possession of the ball, these two teams play four-on-four at that basket.

Once the X-team gains the possession, the O-team then transitions down the floor to defense the D-team. While in transition, it is imperative that the O-team communicates with one another and establishes match-ups.

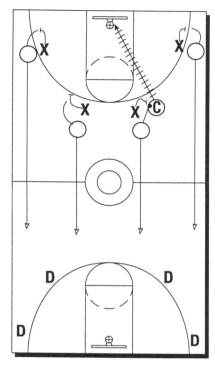

Diagram 1

If the D-team establishes possession, the drill repeats itself.

The goal of Full-Court Triangle is to work on and improve our defensive transition. Incorporated in this drill will be extensive work on our defensive and offensive rebounding. It is critical that the offensive team crashes the glass hard and at a game pace. If they do not, the purpose of the drill is lost.

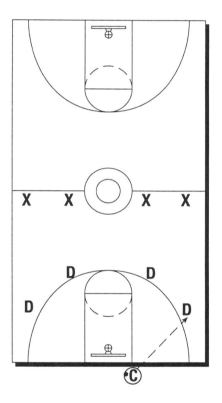

Diagram 2

The X-team resets to half-court.

(Diagram 2)   As the O-team approaches the D-team, the (C) at that end will inbound the ball to the D-team. The D-team must make at least one pass before they attack the basket to score. The O-team's objective is to transition, communicate, defend and prevent the D-team from scoring.

If this objective is met and the O-team secures the rebound, the D-team will now transition to the other end to defend and block off the X-team.

(Diagram 3)   As the D-team is in transition, the X-team leaves from half-court to spot up offensively. Again, the emphasis placed upon the D-team is to transition and communicate. (C) will shoot a perimeter jump shot once the D-team has matched up in transition. The D-team must then work to secure the defensive rebound.

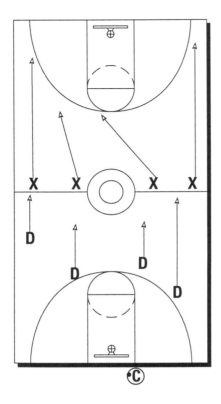

Diagram 3

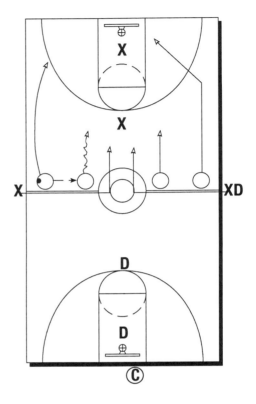

Diagram 1

Fast Break

Transition, Condition, Finish the Play

(Diagram 1)   The drill initiates by the O-team attacking the two X defenders. Once the ball is advanced across half-court, they will sprint to the center circle and then work to get into the play defensively. Once the O-team crosses half-court, they have five seconds to shoot the ball.

The X-team works to establish possession of the ball (rebound, steal or advance after a make by the offensive team, after which they attack the D-team at the other end of the floor. The O-team resets.

(Diagram 2)   Fast break league is continuous non-stop action. Generally, we will compete for 4 three-minute quarters. One member of each team will keep their respective scores. A coach will be stationed under each basket to call fouls. All fouls are one point as are all baskets.

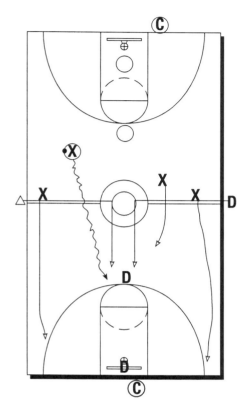

Diagram 2

3-on-3/4-on-4 Transition

(Diagram 1)   The offense and defense line up across the free-throw line. Coach will pass the ball to one offensive player, his defender will have to sprint to the baseline as the other players transition to other basket. Coach can designate whether play is continuous or one possession.

Emphasis for the offense is to take advantage of 3-on-2 or 4-on-3 situations, scoring as quickly as possible. Finish the play.

The emphasis for defense is to bluff and recover, containing the ball. Do not give up an easy basket. Block out and rebound.

(Diagram 2)   Drill will continue at other basket.

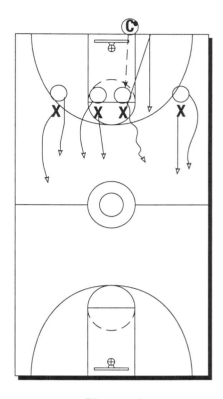

Diagram 1

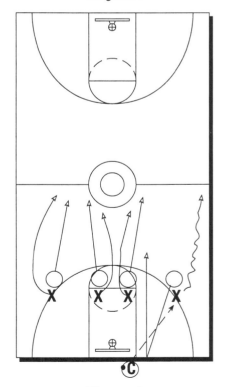

Diagram 2

"21" Shooting Drill

(Diagram 1)   Teams are divided at opposite ends of the court. The team which makes 21 baskets at the respective spot wins and the teams then move to the second spot. The team which wins the best of four spots, wins the drill and the losing team must run. The four spots are designated 1-4. In case of a tie, a shoot-off is conducted from spot 2.

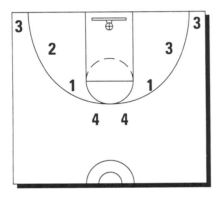

Diagram 1

Intensity Shooting

(Diagram 1)   The player begins under the basket and on the whistle, initiates the drill by shooting a layup. The player then rebounds his shot and takes two hard dribbles away from the basket, squares his body to the basket and shoots.

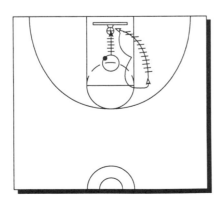

Diagram 1

(Diagram 2)   He rebounds his shot (make or miss) and takes another two hard dribbles to another spot on the floor. This is continuous for one minute. The player must make a minimum of ten baskets.

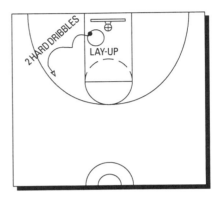

Diagram 2

Block-Out Shooting Drill

(Diagram 1)   The drill begins with two lines of perimeter players at half-court and four post players in the lane area. Coach under basket determines who is on offense and who is on defense. Coach at half-court passes to either perimeter line. The player dribbles hard to the middle of the court. The opposite line offense runs the lane. The guard makes a pass to the wing for a jump shot.

Emphasis for perimeter offense is hard dribble penetration, good wing or baseline jump shot, then crashing offensive boards.

Emphasis for post offense is to move around and go to the boards hard, making the defense block out.

(Diagram 2)   Emphasis for post defense is to block out, rebound and throw outlet pass to managers on the wing.

Emphasis on perimeter defense is to help and recover, close out, contest shot, block-out and rebound.

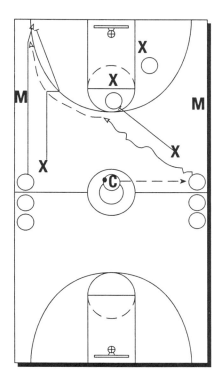

Diagram 1

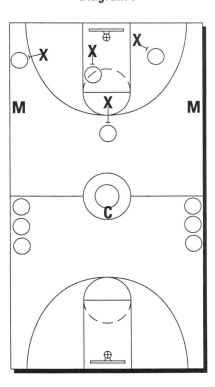

Diagram 2

Circle Transition Drill

(Diagram 1)   Players line up around jump circle, alternating crimson and white. Players jog around the circle until the coach throws the ball to a player or puts the ball in play (i.e. loose ball). The offense then attacks the basket, trying to score as quickly as possible. The defense is containing the ball, not allowing an easy basket and forcing the offense to run half-court offense. The drill is continuous until the coach blows his whistle. When the whistle blows, players circle up and the drill starts over.

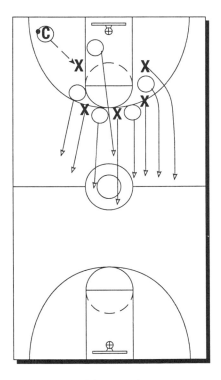

Diagram 1

Perimeter Shooting Drills

Short Jumpers in Transition
(Diagram 1)   Purpose: Develop the short range jumper in transition. We must become adept at not only the long range transition jumper, but the 10'-12' short jumper as well. Two passers, players must run at full speed, line 1 shoots the angle jumper while line 2 shoots the baseline jumper.

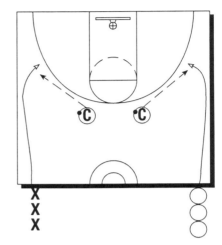

Diagram 2

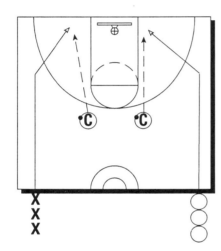

Diagram 1

Diagram 3

3's in Transition
(Diagram 2)   Purpose: To develop confidence, comfort and consistency in our 3-point shooting. Two passers, players again must run at full speed.

Slide Shots
(Diagram 3)   Purpose: Practice the jump shot created by our "slide" play. Two passers at the elbow, the shooter will cross at the top of the key and set up for the jump shot on the wing opposite the passer. Emphasis is placed upon making sure the shooter's feet are set properly and he squares himself with the basket.

"Box" Jumpers
(Diagram 4)   Run to simulate our "box" play. The shooter sets the imaginary backscreen at the elbow and then breaks to the top of the key for the jump shot. Work to set a good screen and utilizing proper footwork to set up for the jump shot.

KELVIN SAMPSON

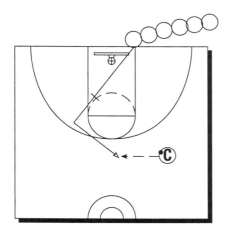

Diagram 4

"Post" Jumpers

(Diagram 5)   Simulation of the perimeter players' cuts when we run post out of our 1-4 set. Players take the defender down and then break for the passer at the elbow. The passer will hand the ball off to the shooter, who then takes the 15'-17' jumper. Variations can be used with the shooter using one or two dribbles.

Diagram 5

Finish the Play

(Diagram 6)   Players will cut in from the hash mark, receive the pass from the coach and score by taking it hard to the glass. A manager will be stationed beneath the basket with pads to simulate contact. Nothing pretty here—just concentration on finishing the play, no matter what the circumstances.

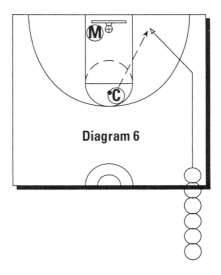

Diagram 6

Shooter Series

(Diagram 7)   Here we are working on shots which develop out of our "shooter series." Players will cross beneath the basket and then fade, curl or "pop-out" off of the chairs stationed on the baseline depending upon which cut is being emphasized at that particular time. Emphasis on setting up the defender and utilizing proper footwork to ready yourself for the jump-shot.

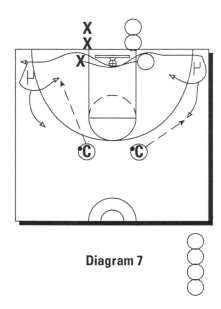

Diagram 7

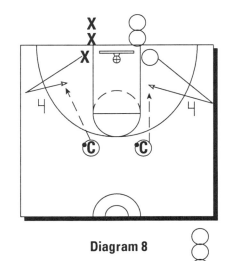

Diagram 8

Back-Cut Jumpers
(Diagram 8)   Here the shooter begins on the block and takes his imaginary defender out to the wing (designated by the chair). When the shooter reaches the chair, he will then back-cut hard, receive the pass and finish off the play with the 10'-15' jumper. Emphasis is placed upon resetting and back-cutting hard as is done in our 1-4 offense.

Black/White Press

Press establishes identity—Rick Pitino way of playing.
Attracts players and fans.
Makes system be up tempo, press, and fast scoring.
System is considered organized chaos.
Opposing coaches have hard time scouting these presses.
No set rules on when to go trap.

Objectives:

1. The purpose of defense is to distort the offense.
2. To fatigue your opponent.
3. Get players to play at a tempo they are not used to playing.
4. Makes opponent's best players play beyond what they are capable of or used to doing.
5. Can easily double team opponent's best players.
6. The aggressor wins offensively and defensively.

White

White is a 1-2-1-1 press. The players' hands must be up and their knees bent. This is very important. (Diagram 1) This press is used when your team scores a two-point field goal.

4 man—Does jumping jacks trying to get a piece of the ball or for the opponent to throw the ball higher. After inbounds pass, drop to the level of the ball.

3 man—Force the opponent to the middle, taking away the easiest pass. If you intercept the pass, you are right at the basket for a layup.

2 man—Force the opponent to the opposite sideline.

1 man—At half-court with the defense on the outside.

5 man—On the opposite side with the defense. Go up far enough to intercept the line of the ball.

- Switch on all screens.
- Go with any cutter.
- Try to always be backside to baseline.

Box principle (Diagram 2)

Used when the player is not in a trap situation, and the basketball is on the sideline. 3 puts pressure on the ball.

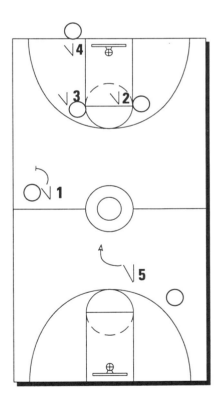

Diagram 1

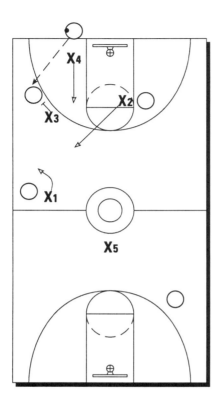

Diagram 2

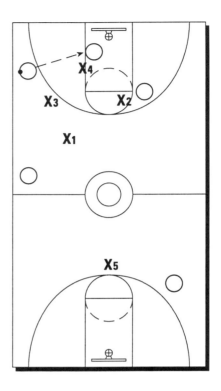

Diagram 3

Diamond principle (Diagram 3)

Used when the player is not in a trap situation, and the basketball is in the middle of the court. Match-up man-to-man, trying to get the person 4 is guarding to dribble. If the person gets out of control, then trap. Do not trap if the player is in control. This may make players play positions they are not used to playing.

Trapping Opportunities

1. The out-of-control dribble.
2. When the ball is facing the cheerleaders.
3. Trap sideline, backup middle.
4. Trap to get the ball out of excellent point guards' hands. Once the point guard passes the basketball, then the point guard is denied.
5. Double a great player or scorer to get the ball out of their hands.
6. Trap when team is in a chaotic, panic position.

Black

Black used to be a 2-2-1 but is now a 1-2-1-1 press. (Diagram 4) This press is used when your team scores a three-point field goal.

- Deflections are the biggest statistic in the system.

- System gives you more shots.

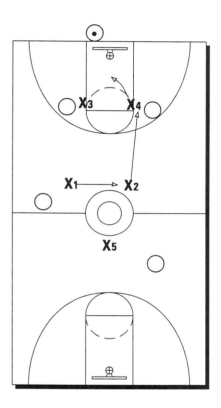

Diagram 4

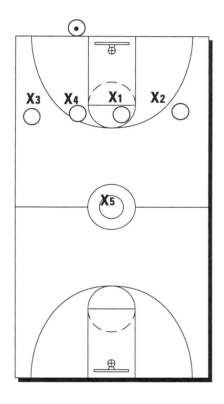

Diagram 5

4 man—Try to help on the opponent's best player.

3 man—On the left wing.

2 man—On the right wing.

1 man—In the middle or ballside deep.

5 man—Is deep or weakside deep.

- Can be used against 4-across sets in dead ball situations (Diagram 5).

Scouting for the Press

What is the opponent's press alignment?

Who inbounds?

Can the inbounder handle the basketball?

Who catches the first pass?

Do they diagonal—cut (Diagram 6)?

Should we deny their point guard?

Will they attack at the end, or will they reset offense?

Who are their shooters?

Who are their out-of-control players?

Who are their high-turnover players?

Can we get their best players or big men away from the basket, or in a non-scoring position?

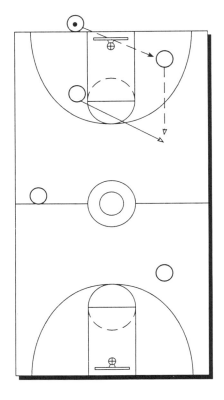

Diagram 6

Defensive Breakdown Drills

Defensive situations covered in every practice:

- Defending the ball in open court situations
- Defending the ball in half-court situations
- Wing denial
- Post defense
- Helpside defense
- Help and recovery
- Affecting the shot
- Block-out and rebounding (with outlets)
- Transition defense (*)
- Penetration rotation (*)
- Screens on and off the ball (*)
- Choke-down and recovery

(*) After the first week of practice, continued throughout the season, we switch all players in all positions in our drills.

(*) All drills used follow the same procedure of no fouls, no out-of-bounds, always play until the whistle blows. Drill ends with block-out and rebound.

1-on-1 Contest (Diagram 1)

Diagram 1

- Defender follows his pass to the player underneath the basket.
- As the player under the basket fakes passing high and low to both of his teammates, the defender must trace the ball in order to cause deflections.
- On the coach's command, the player passes to either one of the players out at the three-point line.
- The defender must hustle out to the perimeter and properly close out on the offensive player.

Points of emphasis:
- Keeping the ball out of the middle.
- Forcing the dribbler to the short corner then cutting him off.
- Proper close-out footwork.
- Leave feet only when shooter does.

Options:
- First time, offense must catch and shoot.
- Second time, offense has one or two dribble limit.

Double Contest (Diagram 2)

Diagram 2

- Coach hits wing whenever he can.
- Defender one pass away is two steps away from his man in a deny position.

- Weakside defender is in the middle of the floor in an open stance help position seeing both.
- Coach can drive it to work on stopping splits.
- Coach passes to defender in middle of the floor who passes right back to the coach. This is done to make sure the defender sees the ball and is in proper help position.
- Ends with box-out—rebound—outlet.

Points of emphasis:
- Communication.
- Defensive positioning.

Helpside Exchange (Diagram 3)

Diagram 3

- Working on denying ball reversal and helpside defense.
- Cuts made at full speed like false motion.
- Give offense the ball if open and let them play.
- If the coach shoots, player must block-out.
- Stress communication.

Points of emphasis:
- Downscreen, backscreen, exchanges.
- Penetration by the coach for helpside position.

Seal Down (Diagram 4)

- The coach passes to the third offensive player, who drives the baseline.
- Low defender must cut off penetration two steps outside the lane.
- High defender must drop down underneath the basket in help position, looking to break up a pass along the baseline.

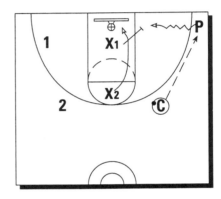

Diagram 4

Flash Help Recover
(Diagram 5a) (Diagram 5b) (Diagram 5c)

- The coach hits the wing, the defender must stop him 1-on-1.
- Once stopped, the offense reverses the ball to the coach.
- Defender jumps to the ball.
- Offense V-cuts for flash, defender must bat down the flash feed.
- Wing player (who has the ball) drives.
- Defender must get over outside the lane to take the charge.

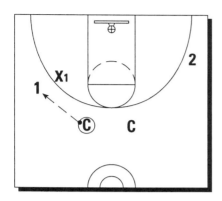

Diagram 5a

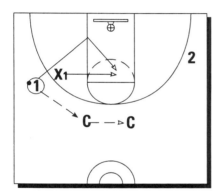

Diagram 5b

Diagram 5c

Post Defense (Diagram 6)

Diagram 6

- Defensive player starts facing the ball and both block players must remain stationary.
- Post defender steps around top side in a closed stance when the ball is above the foul line.
- When the wing takes the ball below the offensive player at the block, the defensive player takes a fronting position (closed).
- After the ball is passed back through the coach, the offense may skip to direct feed.
- If the offensive player receives the ball, the defense must work on walking up under the offensive player. (Offense must shoot turn-around jumpshot.)

4-3 Scramble (Diagram 7a) (Diagram 7b)

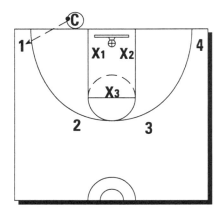

Diagram 7a

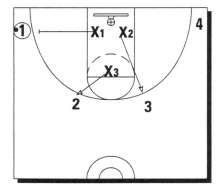

Diagram 7b

- Defensive drill.
- Three defensive players must defend four stationary offensive players beyond the three-point line and try to close-out and counter.
- One defender on the ball with the other two defenders learning how to leave furthest offensive player open by using angles.
- All four offensive players must crash the boards and all three defensive players must block-out.

Choke-Down (Diagram 8)

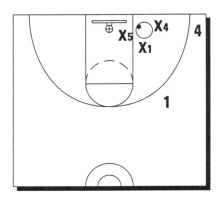

Diagram 8

- Defensive breakdown.
- Three offensive players against three defensive players.
- The ball starts in offensive post player's hands with both perimeter defenders starting in choke-down position.
- The ball is passed back out and fed as often as possible (play is live).

Points of emphasis:
- Choke-down position, defenders must take away post man pivot moves and see their men at same time.
- Close out to shooter and contest, keeping ball out of the middle of the floor.

1-on-1 Driving Line (Diagram 9)

Diagram 9

- Players form a line on the wing outside three-point line, the coach has the ball further up the wing.
- Player 1 starts on defense and player 2 starts on offense.
- The coach passes to offense. The offense has a one dribble limit and tries to score. He has one chance to score or put it back on the offensive board.
- The defense goes to end of the line and offense goes to defense.

Points of emphasis:
Offense:
- Catch the ball in a triple threat position.
- Work on offensive moves (shot fake, jab series, hip-to-hip).
- Make all moves toward the rim, not away from the rim.
- Create space between yourself and the defender with your one dribble.
- Offensive rebound after shot.

Defense:
- Low stance (feet parallel to the sideline).
- Keep the ball out of the middle.
- Force offense to the baseline.
- Make offense take a contested jumpshot.
- Box-out.

Options:
- One dribble limit.
- Two dribble limit.
- Start at NBA three-point line.
- Start off the dribble using dribble moves.

TEAM DEFENSIVE DRILLS
3-on-2 Back 3-on-3 (Diagram 1)

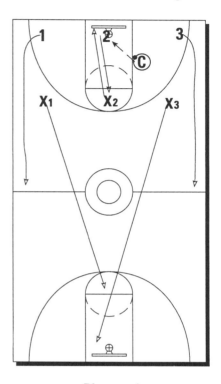

Diagram 1

- Coach passes to 1, 2 or 3.
- The defender of the man who catches the ball must touch the baseline before getting back into play.
- The other two defenders sprint back on defense as 1, 2 and 3 come down 3-on-2.
- X2 sprints back into play, trying to make it a 3-on-3 situation, communicating with his teammates as to who to take.
- The drill continues as X1, X2 and X3 rebound and bring it down 3-on-3.

4-on-3 Back 4-on-4

- Same rules apply here as in the 3-on-2 back 3-on-3 except you start out with four offensive and four defensive players.

1-on-1 (Diagram 2)

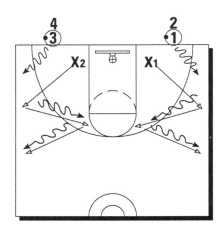

Diagram 2

- Offensive player dribbles back and forth from the sideline to the lane line on his way to half-court.
- Defensive player tries to force offensive player toward the sideline and then will cut him off.
- Defense player is trying to turn the dribbler.
  —Two turns is good.
  —Three turns is great.
- At half-court, the offensive player turns and throws a chest pass to the next player in line and then closes out and defends.

Points of emphasis:
- Play as if there is no help.
- Don't get beat down the middle of the floor.

Options:
- Run, slide, run.
- Add extra defensive player in back line to bluff help.

2-on-2 (Diagram 3)

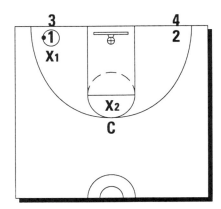

Diagram 3

- Man guarding the ball plays as if there is no help (X1).
- Man off the ball is bluffing trap (X2).
- When the pass is made to the coach, the defender chases him down (X2).
- When the offense gets the ball to half-court, they turn, drive to the basket and dunk the ball. They then quickly get ready to defend the next two players in line.

Points of emphasis:
- Help man sees both.
- No splits.

Options:
- Challenge defenders to work for a 10-second call.
- Run and jump, rather than help and recover.

4-on-4 (Diagram 4)

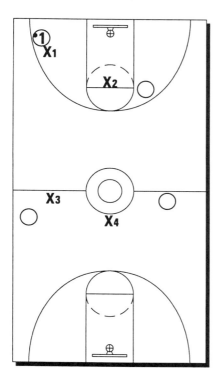

Diagram 4

- Same as 2-on-2 up front.
- Back players in open stance, ready to help or steal.

Points of emphasis:
- Good positioning of deep man.
- No splits.

5-on 5 Transition (Diagram 5)

- The coach throws to 3, 4, or 5.
- The two defenders whose men did not receive the ball must touch the baseline and then recover.
- The defender whose man gets the ball and the two guards recover immediately.

Points of emphasis:
- Communication of defense.
- Offense running lanes wide.

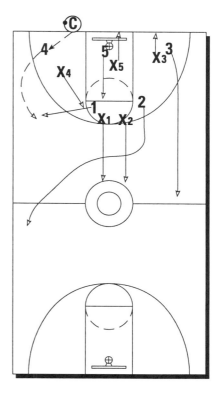

Diagram 5

Chase Drill (Diagram 6)

- Form two lines. One sideline, foul line extended, one under the basket.
- 1 throws the ball off the backboard, rebounds it and passes to 2, who is now sprinting toward the opposite basket (must receive ball before half-court).
- 2 dribbles full speed toward the opposite basket for a layup.
- After 1 passes the ball, he sprints toward 2, trying to deflect the ball from behind and "get in the play."
- 1 now sprints toward the sideline, foul line extended, and fills the lane.

- 2 rebounds his own shot and passes to 1, then chases him from behind, trying to deflect the shot and "get in the play."

offense lob the ball up. Their feet and lower body drawcontact.

Options:
- 4-on-4, 5-on-5.
- Set up 4-4 offensive sets and scramble by doubling on the pass or dribble. Example: UCLA cut, point defender doubles the first wing pass.

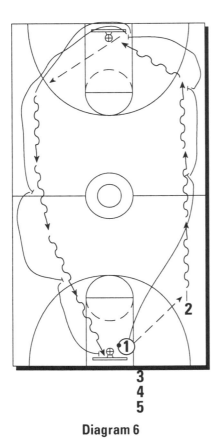

Diagram 6

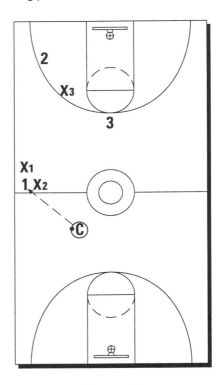

Diagram 7

Trap Drill (Diagram 7)

- Half-court trap drill.
- The coach passes to the player in the trap, or the player dribbles into the trap. From there it's live.
- Intercept or read the ball.
- When the ball is passed out of the trap toward the basket, the two trappers chase from behind, scramble, and defend.

Points of emphasis:
- Trappers are just trying to stay big with their hands up, trying to deflect and make the

One Minute Drill (5-on-5) (Diagram 8)

- Offense tries to hold the ball for 60 seconds.

Points of emphasis:
Offense:
- Spacing and constant movement with purpose.
- Protect the ball.

Defense:
- No helpside rules, deny everything and try to deflect.

Options:
- Offense can't dribble or one dribble.
- Offense tries for a certain number of passes.

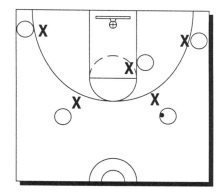

Diagram 8

4-on-4 Screen Down (Diagrams 9 and 10)

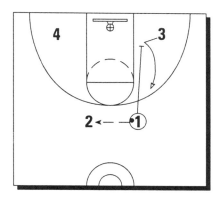

Diagram 9

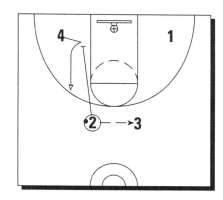

Diagram 10

- Guard passes to guard and then screens down.
- Repeat over and over and play live.

Points of emphasis:
Offense:
- Stay wide.
- Screen and pop.

.Defense:
- Jump to ball.
- Slide through ballside of screen.
- Deny guard to guard.
- Talk on screens.

Shell Defense (Box and Triangle)
(Diagrams 11a and 11b)

Diagram 11a

Diagram 11b

Defensive drills for fundamental positioning including:
- Ball defense.
- Deny defense.
- Helpside (splits).
- Post defense.
- Jumping to the ball.
- Weakside flash.
- Help and recover.
- Rotation.
- Choke the post.
- Contesting shots.
- Blocking out.

3-ON-3 DEFENSIVE SERIES

(Diagram 1)　　UCLA Cut:
a.　cut off post
b.　screen down
c.　post up

(Diagram 2)　　Flex Cut:
a.　backscreen
b.　downscreen

Diagram 1

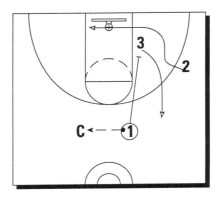

Diagram 2

(Diagram 3)　　Baseline Cut:
a.　backscreen
b.　duck-in
c.　same: other side

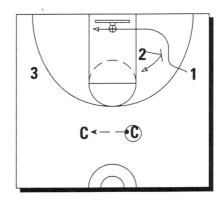

Diagram 3

(Diagram 4)   Double Screen:
a. screen on baseline

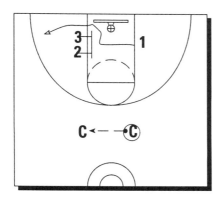

Diagram 4

(Diagram 5)   Staggered Double:
a. caboose
b. step out

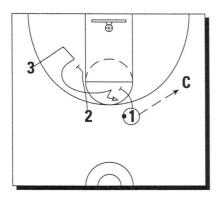

Diagram 5

(Diagram 6)   Triangle "Screen the Roller"
a. screen across
b. screen down

(Diagram 7)   Screen and Roll:
a. go either way

(Diagram 8)   Dribble Weave:
a. exchange

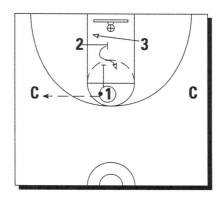

Diagram 6

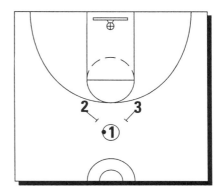

Diagram 7

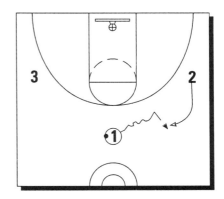

Diagram 8

(Diagram 9)   Dead Ball Set:
a. screen down
b. screen across

(Diagram 10)   Scissor Cut:
a.   cut off high post

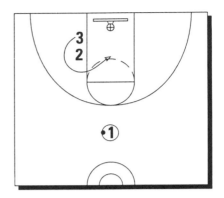

Diagram 11

Diagram 9

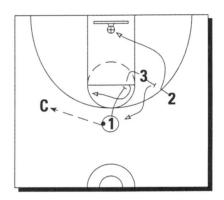

Diagram 12

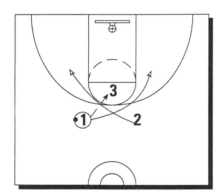

Diagram 10

(Diagram 11)   Curl from Stack:
a. curl
b. post up

(Diagram 12)   Shuffle Cut:
a. shuffle
b. screen down

(Diagram 13)   Post Feed from Wing:
a. feed from below

(Diagram 14)   Pull and Kick:
a. penetrate to draw "two"
b. kick it to shooter

(Diagram 15)   Pass and Go Behind:
a. pass and go behind
b. screen and roll

Diagram 13

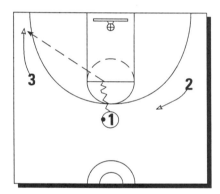

Diagram 14

Diagram 15

OFFENSIVE SETS TO DEFEND IN YOUR 4-ON-4 SHELL

Diagram 1
Screen away

Diagram 2
Dribble penetration

Diagram 3
Dribble penetration with screening

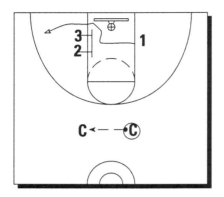

Diagram 4
Backscreen

Diagram 5
Double screening

Diagram 6
Doublescreen on wing

Diagram 7
UCLA cut

Diagram 8
Three-man weave

Diagram 9
Dribble, hand off

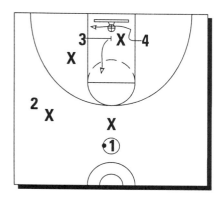

Diagram 10
Cross-screens flash high

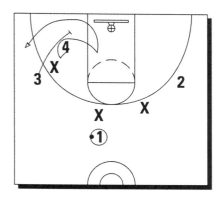

Diagram 11
Screen-Rescreen

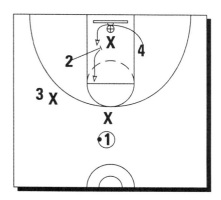

Diagram 12
Small on big cross-screen

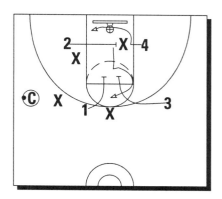

Diagram 13
America's play
(small for big cross screen and a double down)

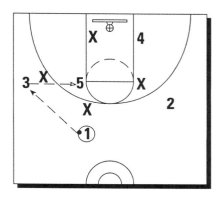

Diagram 14
Ball thrown to the post man

Diagram 15
Single screen on one side while there is a
doublescreen on the other side

Coaching Today's Athlete

There is no difference between the way I view basketball now and when I was a sixth grade coach. Someone recently asked me what I thought about the differences. I said that before I dealt with kids from 14 to 18 years of age who were immature and had no idea what they were going to do with their lives, and now I deal with kids who are 18 to 22 and are immature and have no idea what they are going to do with their lives.

One of the most interesting things about coaching is the people that you deal with. Yesterday I met with somebody in budgeting, I met with somebody in academics, I met with a vice-chancellor, and had a preliminary meeting about our new floor. At 3:30 there was a press conference where a high school player announced where he was going to go to school. I can't be there by NCAA rules. He announced that he was going to attend our school. He is conceivably the best recruit in our school's history. We all know what that means from the alumni.

There are only two good places to coach, an orphanage (no parents), and a prison (no alumni). A perfect season for alumni is when the team goes 29 - 0 and the coach gets fired. I have four guards, three of them can bench press over 300 pounds. I have a senior who bench presses 350, he was second team all-conference. Now, I have a young phenom who can barely bench press 185 who is going to turn this program around at the age of 18. Coaching a kid in the '90s is different because of the expectation level, not only put on by his family and alumni, but by the media. I rode out here on a plane next to a man who had a lap top computer with him. He told me he has made millions in business, starting in 1979, by teaching people, as a consultant, how to get along with each other. I said, "That's an incredible coincidence, because that's what coaching is all about, how to get along with kids and how to integrate them into your team."

I was eating breakfast this morning and there was a father with four young children sitting next to me. What was happening with those four young children was a bargaining session. "If you drink your milk, you can watch cartoons." "If you will sit still, we will buy that doll we saw in the gift shop." It was negotiation, parent and child. I told my sons one time that I worked until I was a sophomore in college and I had always given my paycheck to my father because that was done in Chicago. My sons asked "Grampa stole your money?" No, he didn't steal my money...that's what was done. My father didn't ask my opinion until I was about 25 years of age. And I looked at this man with his four beautiful children and he was negotiating by reward; you know in the coaching business we can't do that. But we are dealing with kids all the time who have been raised that way. They are not just used to negotiating, they are almost used to extortion. "I will be quiet if you buy me a toy." That's a natural human instinct. Giving in to that means buying a bigger toy the next time. We've all seen it sink into our culture. It is called self-gratification. I call it a pain in the neck. You are given charge of somebody else's children. You are held responsible for their play and their conduct and more than that, you are held responsible for their growth as adults. That's a hard job. But it's been pushed into coaching.

I picked up the paper this morning. The headline is "Super Coach or Cruel Taskmaster?" "A local high school pompon coach has many fans and many critics." To one girl she is a super teacher, a role model and friend, and a coaching genius. But to another, she is an evil taskmaster who pushes too hard and selectively picks on students. "She totally gets out of line the way that she yells at you," said this 17-year-old girl. The coach said she sent a letter to parents explaining that she was a tough taskmaster and that she demanded discipline. "They knew all of this going in. I cannot let them be less than the best they can be." I don't know much about that situation, but we are a profession under fire. People are misinformed about what we do, and the problem is that most of you are doing it for a deep love, not only for the sport, but for the involvement of the kids that you have the opportunity to work with. Except for the police, I often feel that coaches are the last bastion of discipline.

Many times we are looked upon in an unfair way. I think that rather than looking upon what we are doing wrong, we adapt, we don't adopt. Those are two different words. Good coaches adapt to situations. They don't change their principles. Most of you have spent your professional lives building, establishing, understanding what you are all about and what your philosophy is going to be. You must adapt it to certain situations, but you must never change the principles. There is a saying. "Potential loses games, performance wins games." Often when you hear that a kid has potential, that is just another way of calling a kid a dog. Unrealized potential will be the breakdown of our culture, not just coaching.

I often hear that my team is a bunch of over-achievers. How can you over achieve? I think they are getting the most out of the God-given talents they have. You get to a point where they play to their potential. I've seen coaches point out a player and say that he is really playing hard. Isn't that a sad comment? Because that means he stands out from other kids. You hear it more and more because there aren't a lot of kids who are playing hard. I have a rule with my staff. We never say "you are playing hard" because that needs to be an expectation. If you don't, you are not allowed in the gym. Playing is a privilege, not an expectation. The thing that has happened is we have started to recognize things as unusual that were basic ideas about competition.

Let's look at some of the things that influence kids. Certainly environment. When I was a high school teacher, I was initially just a teacher and then I became an entertainer. I originally was somebody who was to instruct, but then I was supposed to be part of the media explosion in our country. When I grew up we all worked, we played ball, we didn't have TV.

When I read a book about King Arthur, I pictured King Arthur. I didn't picture Richard Gere. That really translates to coaching. Did you ever do this with kids? You are working a ballhandling drill and he crosses the ball over in front of him as he starts left. You say "You can't do that. Imagine being guarded by Michael Jordan." First of all the kid is confused when you use the word imagine. They have no imagination. They have been victimized by all visual stimuli (TV, CD Rom, VCR). Everything has come in to the kids we are coaching now, visually. "Coach can I watch tape?" "Why?" "I want to see how I played. You don't know how you played...would you like to see clips of all of your missed jump shots?" "Then you can write down where you missed those shots and why you think you missed them." "But that's too much like an assignment." What they are really thinking is: I want you to fix me. I don't want to be part of the cure. Cure me! Coach me! Teach me! But I don't want to work that hard.

We have also been victimized by due process. I used to write out a referral and give it to the dean. One day I gave one to the dean and he said "Jerry, did you actually see the cigarette in the kid's hand?" "No, I just made that up for the hell of it." "We have to make sure of his rights." Due process is a tough, tough, process in the athletic arena. I don't really ask our players what they want to do. It is not a democracy. They have input, but I tell them, "It is your game but it is my job." I put a timeclock in the gym one time. They came in, they punched in. We went to work. In real life they are going to have to do that. I will do what is best for the team when they are on the floor. Off the floor, I will do what is best for the individual. Isn't that real life? We all have jobs. We don't set the rules where we work. But in our homes we have a chance for individual expression. We can't drive as fast as we want. We fit into institutional rules, values. There is due process in those rules and values. But they are built out of the democratic process.

But, you set the rules on your team. Permissiveness. Everything now has probation. There is no probation for our jobs, is there? And now they see pro basketball on TV. I went to Chicago stadium. I saw basketball up close. I saw it on the playgrounds, in high school gyms, in college gyms. Seeing Michael Jordan and others over and over again has distorted the view of those who have regular ability. What they see on TV is not what they have within them, yet that is the level that they are striving to be. It's incredible how many kids say that they will be in the NBA. They have been conditioned to believe that whatever Michael Jordan does, they can do. They are inundated by all of this stimuli and it gives them an unrealistic view of basketball.

The second thing that affects them is the parents. Expectations. And if they don't live up to expectations, then it is your fault. A terrorist group has started. By word of mouth, several parents can give you a bad rap. At the last high school where I coached, I had a section for parents of former players. I invited them back. I wanted to keep them around so that in case they were standing next to one of the terrorists in a gas station, they could say, "That's not true, we still go back to the games. The coach meant a lot to my son." Don't let the positive people become apathetic because you don't deal with them. One other rule that helped me was that I would never talk to parents unless their son had spoken to me first, and then our first conversation had to be with all of us together. Most of the time the kids were fine. Another thing I did with parents was that I contacted them once a week through the mail. I don't want a kid classified in any way. In college, I have banned all meetings of my staff about kids. There is a tendency to just talk about what a kid can't do.

Here's another big area of influence in their environment, their peers. This is the age of individualism. "Why would you want to be part of a group? Why would you go to practice?" Then, there's substance abuse. When I grew up, you pitied addicts. There were no recreational drugs. This is something that has to be dealt with. The key to all of this is communication, the art of communication.

Let me give you a brief example of what I did last year. I had a terrific senior. He was everything you wanted in a player, everything you wanted in a son. He loved life. I had a freshman who had the potential to do what my senior did. But I was worried about him. So, I held up two sheets of paper. I put my senior's name on one paper and listed his many pluses. I put my freshman's name on the other piece of paper. I said that being in our program is like having a bank account. You make deposits and you build up a balance. The senior has a good balance. He is going to be allowed to do some things because he has a good balance. I told the freshman that he wasn't here when I was yelling at the senior as he was learning. I don't need to yell at him anymore, but even if he makes a mistake one time I will look the other way because he has a track record, a balance. Now, as a freshman, you have two things going for you. One, you came. Two, you had a good pre-season. But you aren't on the same page. I hope that in two years I am holding up this paper and using it as an example for someone else. You are equal as a person with my senior, but not equal as a player in the program.

We have a lot of understandings in our program, not rules, understandings. For instance, our team sits in the front row of every class, the middle three seats. I tell them how they are going to wear their hair. "But, coach, this is the nineties!" I don't allow earrings. "But Michael Jordan wears an earring." I'm not coaching Michael Jordan. Are the kids different, or are we? I get a letter every week from the same lady. She asks me why I don't put the names of the players on the back of the uniforms. I write back very faithfully, they have the name on their uniforms, UNC Wilmington. We are a team. We have their names on their shooting shirts, their first names. Not nicknames because when they take out their shirts years from now, I don't want their kids to see a shirt with some silly name on it. I offer to buy this lady a program in each letter. The number of the shirts listed in the program corresponds to the name of the player. She hasn't quite grasped this concept.

Team. What's wrong with the team concept? We are trying to blend people, to be a part of something. If one of our players misses a class, our whole team runs at 4:30 AM, except that player. We don't run much. Peer pressure can also be developed by coaches. I tell them every year. The weakest member of your team will take you down. Get them up. Make him feel responsible to you. The day that our player drinks in public, he loses his scholarship. I tell them this when I recruit them. Some people don't want to be recruited by us.

Many of them do want guidelines, but they want them to be administered fairly. All they want to know is "what are the rules?" Don't change the rules, that's not fair, and I ask them to buy in. For instance, I have our kids sign contracts. We convert man-to-man on everything, make or miss, and you better be next to your man. When we rebound defensively, we run a dribble fast break and you better be running. We all block out and I have designated rebounders, they must take two steps to the board. I have designated safeties, and they better be back. I don't want to give up easy baskets, and I try and get easy baskets. I ask our kids, is it fair for you to do that?

Another thing is a mental thing. I ask them if they can keep the player off his right hand. They say yes. So, if he goes left that's not your responsibility, that's mine. I want you to keep him out of the lane, so play off of him. That means that he must shoot a jump shot. So, jump shots are on me, layups are on you. Fair? They agree. I put these things in a contract form and they come in and sign them. If you don't do these things, you are out of the game. These are simple things and you can hold kids accountable for them. We chart them. We build in standards that they buy into.

We try to talk about trust. I hold up a sheet of paper. I say this is our relationship. If you lie to me (I tear off a corner), that's where our relationship will be, and that corner will never grow back. It's amazing how many players come back and tell me that they have used that same thing with their children. You can crumple up the paper and the relationship is bruised, but you can always straighten the paper out. Honesty is hard. Honesty is not personal, it is a statement of how you feel. If a kid comes in and asks why he isn't playing, do you say "you aren't good enough, I made a mistake recruiting you."? It doesn't work that way. I told my staff, if anybody ever drinks in public, I will fire him the next day. Perception is reality in coaching. That one beer becomes three beers and on and on. I have never gotten a technical foul in 31 years. If one of our players does, I will dismiss him from his scholarship. I want to be able to go into the meeting at the end of the year concerning officials and say what I think. I haven't bitched all year, and I want the right to say who I think isn't doing a good job. I never complain and I don't want to be cheated either. High school is the worst. They get their checks and go home. The kids are looking at you and you must teach them that life is not fair. We must fight through it.

Let's talk about some coaching techniques. I play everybody on my team. After a win, I want everybody in the locker room to feel good. But when you lose, if you have some players who didn't play, they are really discontented. They band together and you get a rift on your team. I strive to get everybody in as early as possible. One of the things that has happened is we have only lost two games in February in three years. We have our legs. We practice hard because we have good team morale. Everybody can be successful. I have specialists. I put in my 8th, 9th or 10th kid for a certain out of bounds play. Its amazing how many times something good happens to that kid. His teammates are pulling for him. If you can build morale so that the kids really pull for each other you are going to have a good team. Statistics become meaningless. Feelings become important.

Every day I have a "thought for the day." I ask them what it is, and we talk about it. We give them things to read, slogans and mottos. I may have them write about their thoughts on a certain article in the paper. I give out questionnaires and I post the results. "Who do you feel is the best practice player?" It gives kids an appreciation for their teammates. We do this in the preseason. We assign teams for the pick up games. You get a point if you win the game. We mix up the team. It's amazing at the end of the preseason who your top five players are in terms of points. It tells you a lot about their competitiveness.

Here are four statements we hear a lot.

1. Kids today just aren't hungry enough.

2. Kids today have too many distractions, computers, video games, etc.

3. Kids today aren't as competitive.

4. If a kid today isn't a star he just gives up.

But those are our views. Those aren't the players' views. Those are our perceptions of players. Sometimes they just don't know that they aren't working hard. Tape one player for an entire practice and then view the film together. It's up to us to show them. Coach K at Duke told me he spends more time talking to his players than he does coaching them. Spend time listening to them. I want them to come in to see me all the time. Not to talk basketball. Then they will start to trust you. Never assume that what motivated you will motivated them. If you don't like their behavior, do a little probing before you pass judgment. Sometimes things are happening in their lives that you don't know about. Let your players know you are always readily accessible.

I think everybody wants us to be different. I think we are all pretty good. You are here to help kids, not to just win games. If you are allowed to help them, you will have a major impact on their life. I do think that you must have more than just a shoot from the hip plan. You must have a concrete organization that sets up the betterment of kids through proper communication and accountability.

Last Second Situations

There is a game within a game. It includes:

- The first possession of every quarter.

- All out-of-bound plays, endline and sideline.

- Every play after a time out.

Over the last 14 years, I have charted every game for the game within a game. For example, if we score on an out-of-bounds play, we get a point. If we are stopped from scoring, the other team gets a point. The correlation of winning the game within a game, and the game itself is over 90%. As a coach, you can control this because some things are consistent. There is a stoppage of play. You can set your defense and set your offense. We spend from 5 to 7 minutes in practice on special situations at the beginning of practice, always 5/0. I do it early because it indicates that it is important. At the end of practice, we do special situations live. If we really do our jobs as coaches, kids will never see anything in a game that they haven't seen in practice. In these late situations, you need a "go to" player.

(Diagram 1)   You can run this against man or zone and you can run it out of a lot of sets. 1 passes to 4 and cuts to the ballside block. 2 goes to the other block. 3 V-cuts and comes to the perimeter and gets the pass from 4.

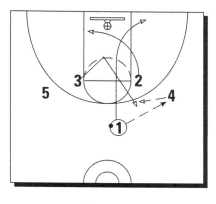

Diagram 1

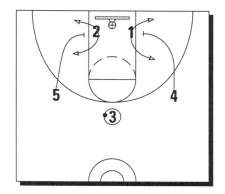

Diagram 3

(Diagram 2)   The big players now screen down for 1 and 2.

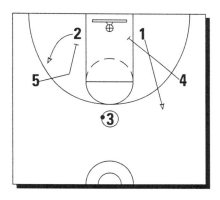

Diagram 2

Diagram 4

(Diagram 3)   If the defense is playing zone, we would run the same thing except we would screen the bottom of the zone.

(Diagram 4)   You can also run it from the stack. It ends up the same, 4 and 5 out, 2 and 1 on the block. 1 passes to 4 who passes to 3.

(Diagram 5)   1 and 2 can now backscreen. Or, we can downscreen on one side and backscreen on the other. This is a good catch-all play for late in the game because you don't know what the defense will be.

Diagram 5

Full court situation. At the beginning of the season, we put players on the endline and they have three seconds to go the length of the floor and shoot. We time them. They will always shoot too soon. Most players don't have a good clock in their head. You need to show them that. This has really helped us. You know that often a player is dribbling with momentum and he pulls the trigger way too soon. You should have a primary inbounder and you should find out who can throw the ball full court the best. Have them throw at least seven and always throw to a target, not to a player. Practice this. When a team scores against you late in the game, they will immediately relax. Practice taking the ball out-of-bounds and immediately throwing it down court to a target. We have a designated "fly man." Don't look for that man, throw to the target. The man will be there.

(Diagram 6)   There are two kinds of alignments that bother people. One is the direct line. There is no helpside, there is no ballside. You are forced to pick a side. The most difficult throw to defend is the one right over your head.

(Diagram 7)   This alignment bothers people. I saw a team have 2 and 3 pinch and 1 broke long and if you get the ball into the front court you can always call time out. The best out-of-bounds plays are run from half-court. There are two decisions you must make. Are you going to run a full-court play or are you going to get to half-court and call time out? The next decision is this. Are we going to call time out when we have a chance to win the game? That's a hard one. I have always felt better not calling time out because we practice this way. But, your kids must know that and they must practice it. They must get right into what you are going to do. Also, are you going to foul if you are up three? I change this game to game. It will depend on who we are playing. If you haven't made up your mind beforehand, there will be indecision. If it doesn't work out, you will lose your kids' trust.

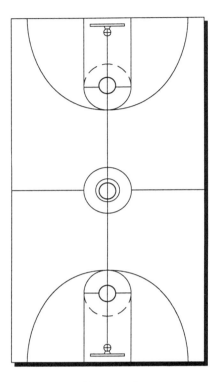

Diagram 6

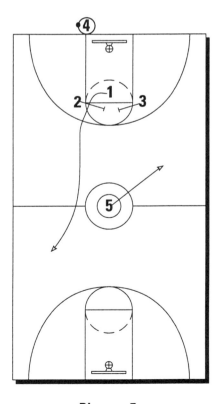

Diagram 7

(Diagram 8)   I've had a lot of luck with this alignment. 3 is my best player. If you know the defense isn't going to have someone on the ball, then you need to draw people closer to the endline. Usually X4 will float near mid-court. It is hard to guard 1 and 2 if they line up like this. Always take one of these players and run him directly at the floater, X4. You can eliminate the center fielder with a cutter.

(Diagram 9)   It's amazing how many times you can make this pass.

(Diagram 10)   Here is a play we used. If you put all five of your players ballside on a sideline out of bounds, all the defenders will be on the ballside. 4 and 5 doublescreen for 3. 5 then comes off of 4 and 4 breaks low.

(Diagram 11)   We have 3, a shooter, in the corner. 4 is at the rim. 2 will break to the ball and then away and there is no one on that side of the floor to defend 2. But we set that up by putting everyone on ballside.

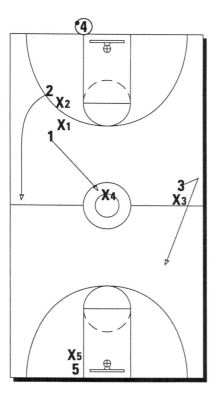

Diagram 8

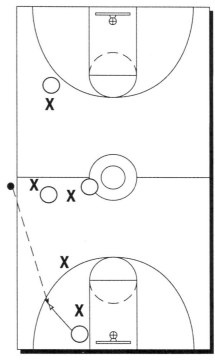

Diagram 9

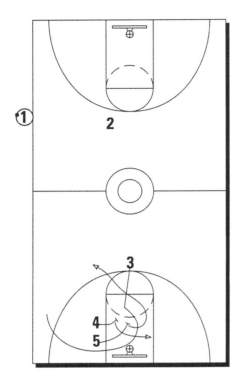

Diagram 10

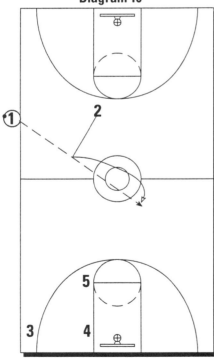

Diagram 11

(Diagram 12)   I bet I have about one hundred plays for three-point shots late in the game. This is a very simple one. Almost every coach in America says "Give up two" and they are guarding the perimeter. I say that human nature says that any pass you make to the inside, someone will turn their head. They have been conditioned to get to the level of the ball. If the perimeter man will move opposite of the turn of the head and get the return pass from inside, it will get you a better shot than any play you have ever drawn. We work on it every day. Practice this as a shooting drill.

Diagram 12

Let me finish by telling you, don't give up. Don't give in. Continue to do what you have been doing. The only way to be successful is to do it your way and do it consistently. All the discipline, all the rules must be administered fairly. Please don't believe coaches must give in to what the principles of coaching are. They are the same as the principles of teaching. You will give them something they can't get anywhere else so they can progressively become successful and, most of all, a happy adult.

Developing the Fast Break and Quick Hit Plays

This system has both a great risk for an advantage and a great risk for a disadvantage. If you are playing someone significantly better than you and both teams take the same number of shots, you will lose. If an average number of shots is 80, then to win you either have to play slow or fast by taking either 40 shots or 120 shots.

The team must be a great offensive rebounding team because there will be more offensive rebounding opportunities in this system. It is a speed game where you try to run the ball down court and shoot in three seconds every time. Why take shots with five players back ready to defend when you can shoot against three, two or even one?

Most players do not want to play fast. They say they do but they really do not. Once they slow it down, this system is done. A major problem is your own players, because they do not want to get this tired for a whole game. If they do this for a whole game however, they will win. If they do not do it the whole game you will lose. The enemy is your team.

Fast Break

When the ball goes through the net, every player knows exactly what their role is.

5 man—Takes the ball out of the net and the outlet must be done with perfection (Diagram 1). This position can not block out because this player has to get the ball out of the net. 1 and 5 have to do their role automatically. Go so fast that you do not recognize the defense.

Diagram 1

1 man—Catches the outlet and speed dribbles to the elbow faster than anything (Diagram 2). The faster the ball goes in the hands of 1, the faster everyone else will go. Then pass for a score.

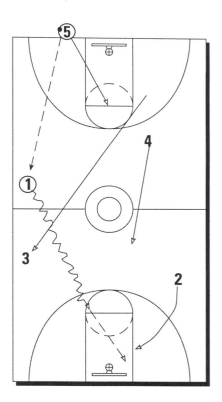

Diagram 2

3 man— Has to be the flat-out hardest working player (Diagram 3). Does not have to be a scorer, but just has to play hard all the time. There are two reasons for this: the first being to get open for a score and the other is to drag the defense for others to get open.

2 man—This role is the designated shooter. This position will get 20 open shots a game. The player must sprint, spot up, catch it and shoot it (Diagram 4). If the player catches it and turns it over, then that player is on the bench. Shooting the ball in three seconds makes for a very low turnover ratio. Encourage them to not worry about making mistakes. Then, they will make more shots.

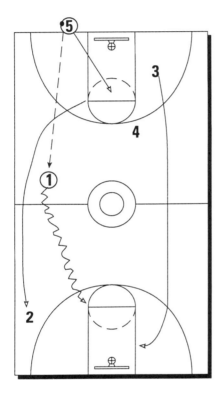

Diagram 3

5-1-3 Drill—1 catches the outlet and looks for 3. Fast players may not run hard 75 times like they need to. Finding players who will play fast is a problem. Officials will sabotage the system because they do not want to run this fast. Your opposition will try to sabotage this system. But the opponent will not run back 75 times so you will stop you, not the opposition.

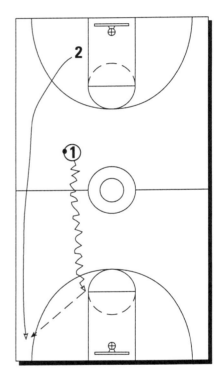

Diagram 4

4 man—This is your best offensive player. This position catches from 1 and can shoot or drive with live ball (Diagram 5).   Any time the ball is passed ahead 1 to 2, then 4 cuts to the block. This is where the best player is getting a second look. When 4 vacates top of the key, 5 takes that spot. 4 can use 2's shot as an opportunity to get the ball again. 2 does not have to pass to 4, but can.

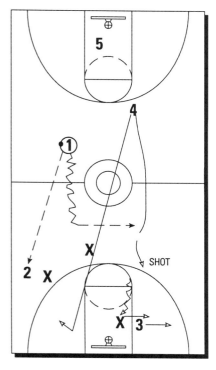

Diagram 5

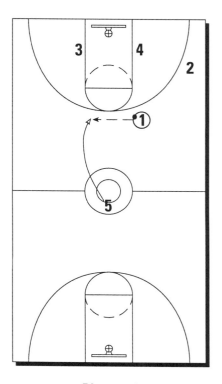

Diagram 6

5 shoots the ball on the reverse (Diagram 6). Or goes to rebound, which gives the offense triangle rebounding position (Diagram 7).

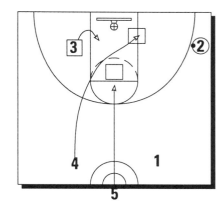

Diagram 7

2-H This is a handoff from 1 to 2 for a shot (Diagram 8).

Diagram 8

Pick and Role 1 comes off of 5's pick to score (Diagram 9).

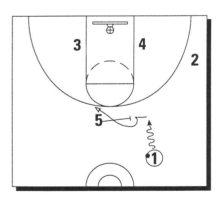

Diagram 9

4 Pick 5 down-screens for 4, who then sets a ball-screen for 1 for the shot (Diagram 10).

Diagram 10

3 Back 1 crosses half-court with the dribble and 3 cuts into lane, then darts back to the block for the ball (Diagram 11).

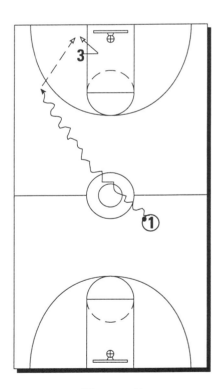

Diagram 11

Drills for Individual and Team Defense

I was a high school basketball coach for five years, an assistant football coach, coached the golf team, was the athletic director, and even sponsored the senior prom. So, I've done everything that you have had to do. I can assure you I understand your situation. I was a head coach the first year out of college. My principal said we had losing teams six straight years. I said that I would change that, and I did. I stretched it to seven. We went 2 and 19, and it was the most difficult thing I had to do in my life. We had a great bunch of kids, but we had nothing to fight with. The second year we went 6 and 16. Then we got 14, 16, and 18 wins and it was a lot of fun. Four years after I left, the kids we started in the 4th grade played for the state championship.

I'm going to tell you what we do at Kansas. What we do is not a secret. Come and watch us practice and you can see how we do it. Watching someone teach is a lot more important than hearing what they do. Think back to high school. Think of the meanest teacher you had and then think of the best teacher you had. I'll bet you that for over half of you it's the same person. It's the way you teach it. Our practice is always open to coaches.

I want to give you the overall view first, then break it down into drills we use. What do you want to do when you get on offense? You want to get the best shot you can possibly get, with the board covered. That must be part of it. That is the only way you can get extra possessions. The best shot you can get is the layup from the fast break. We are going to play as fast as we possibly can and try to get layups. On defense, we want to do the opposite. Our first goal in defense is to steal the ball. Our second goal is to make you take an outside shot over a hand, and for us to get the rebound. It has to be all three of those. The third goal is that we don't want you to run your offense. Have a defensive player of the week and get shirts. Printed on the front is "Defensive player of the week." On the back of the shirt is "When is the last time they ran their offense?" Kids took pride in their defense, and that is one of our goals. The fourth goal is that we want to speed up the tempo. If we are better than the other team, we want a faster tempo so we get more possessions. One way to do that is to trap. We used to run more full-court pressure. I've gotten to the point where I like to cover half-court situations as opposed to full-court. We still do some full-court stuff after a free-throw, but we do it less often and this makes it more of a surprise.

We also have some offensive goals. We want to get a layup, but if we don't get it, we want at least three passes in the offense. We want to change sides of the floor and we want to give the defense a chance to make a mistake. We must have patience offensively.

(Diagram 1)   One of the first things we do is to mark the floor. We use the volleyball court lines and add to them. On defense we don't want the ball in the middle of the court. When we get the ball on the sideline, we want to keep it there, and we call this "sideline." We don't want the ball to change sides of the court.

(Diagram 2)   If the ball is here, we are going to guard them toward the middle. If the ball is on the sideline, we don't believe in playing between the ball and the basket. We want the right foot of the defense to be just opposite from the left foot of the offensive man. The same with the left. If the boards of the court ran across, we would want your foot to be on the same board as the offensive foot.

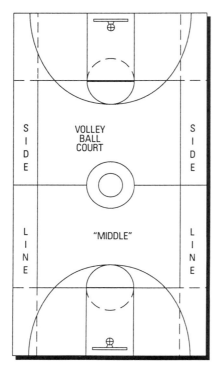

Diagram 1

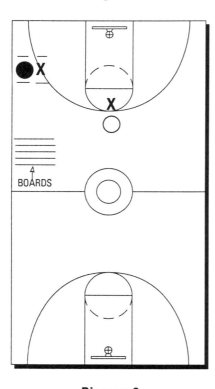

Diagram 2

If the ball is in the middle of the court, we are going to play you head up between the ball and the basket. We say to "guard your yard." We want you to keep the offensive man from going by you for one yard on either side. You cannot allow the offense to drive in that yard. That keeps the offense from making a straight line drive to the basket. We will be on you as tight as we possibly can, because we want you to do one thing—we want you to dribble as long as we can influence where you go with it. But, we don't want you to get a straight line drive.

(Diagram 3)   We don't allow you to drive the baseline. We try to influence you that way and try to stop you. X1 must beat his man to the corner of the backboard. We are playing a team defense, so hopefully we will have someone come across the lane and double-team outside the lane. Now this is like a temporary zone press, we will have two double-teamers, two interceptors and a roamer.

Diagram 3

(Diagram 4)   In the middle of the court we will play a little more conservatively. We tell the defense to keep the man in front of you. Get as close as you can, but you can't get beat. You must realize your limitations. Our wings will deny the pass to the sideline. We want our wing defensive men to know whether or not they are guarding a shooter. If the dribbler gets away down the middle and you are guarding a shooter, you must be able to fake hard at the dribbler and still be able to guard your man. If you are guarding a non-shooter, you can get all the way back and stop the dribbler. Hopefully, if you are guarding a shooter, you will be able to slow down the dribbler so the point defensive man can recover.

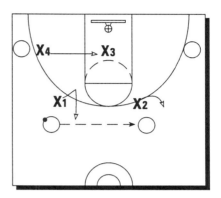

Diagram 5

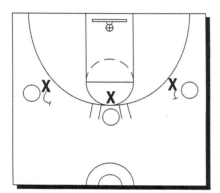

Diagram 4

(Diagram 5)   Four-man shell drill (we also do it with five men). We talk about guarding the ball, being one pass away and being in the help position. There are only three things to do, guard the ball, deny, and help. When the ball is passed from guard to guard, X1 drops in the direction of the pass and then denies the return pass. X2 guards the ball. X3 denies, and X4 goes from the deny position to the help position in the lane. The men are calling "ball," "deny," or "help." We do this throughout the entire season.

(Diagram 6)   Guarding the dribbler on the sideline. The coach makes a pass to the wing. The defense influences the dribbler to go baseline, or else toward mid-court, but not to the middle. We want the defense to be as close to the man as he can possibly be, especially when the dribble is used. Get almost underneath the offensive player when he raises the ball. If the dribbler goes baseline, turn and run and beat him to the corner of the board.

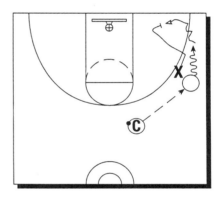

Diagram 6

(Diagram 7)   Guarding the dribbler in the middle. We don't do this on the same day as the sideline dribbler drill. The only change is that the defense must be more conservative. Guard your yard. We are really playing one-on-one. When the shot is taken, get your hand up.

(Diagram 8)   Form double. We are guarding on the sideline with another defensive player in help position in the lane. A manager is on the other side. We influence the dribbler into the double-team. Don't foul.

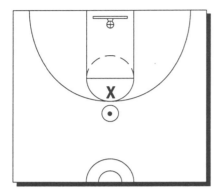

Diagram 7

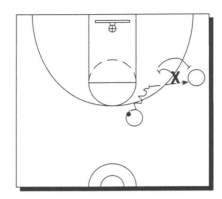

Diagram 9

Diagram 8

Diagram 10

(Diagram 9)   Help and close-out. Drop off the wing, make the dribbler pass and then close-out on the wing. Fake at the dribbler hard. When you go back to the wing, run at him hard but break down the last step and a half so that he does not go around you into the middle.

(Diagram 10)   Close-out and challenge shot. This is similar to the last drill. The ball is passed to either side and the defense works on the close-out. The offensive player has two dribbles. Get a hand up on the shot. The shooter goes for the rebound, so the defense must block-out.

(Diagram 11)   Vision. Defense starts in the help position in the lane. Offense goes up the line, and the defense must adjust. The offense then comes back to the block and the defensive player must go back. From there, the offense sprints to the top of the key and the defense must deny that pass. The offense then goes to the low post and the defense full fronts. The offense then goes to the corner and the defense denies.

(Diagram 12)   Vision continued. The offense cuts along the baseline. The defense goes as far as the help position and opens up. Sometimes the coach can dribble into the lane and the defense must be able to stop him. When the wing makes a cut, I do not have our defense open up to the ball; I want the defensive man to turn his head and follow the cutter.

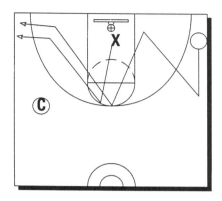

Diagram 11

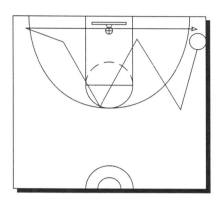

Diagram 13

Diagram 12

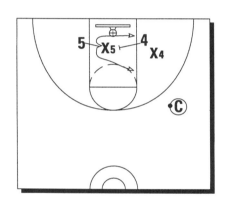

Diagram 14

(Diagram 13)   Vision continued. This is the move of the offensive man.

(Diagram 14)   Defend lateral screen. The coach has the ball. 4 sets the screen away. X4 is in full front position and has contact with the offensive player. X5 starts with his back to the baseline. X5 stops the screener with his forearm "flipper." If you are in a defensive stance you won't be screened.

(Diagram 15)   Defend lateral screen continued. X5 turns and rides out 5. It is X5's responsibility to stay with 5 if he goes baseline. If 5 comes high, then we may switch, but I really don't want to. X5 must work to get on the ballside of the floor.

(Diagram 16)   When the ball is in the middle of the floor, there is no helpside so we must front both low post positions. When the ball goes to the wing, then X5 must get to the help position and X4 is in a full front position between man and ball.

Diagram 15

Diagram 17

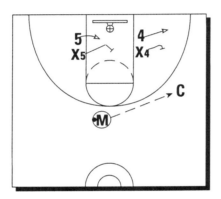

Diagram 16

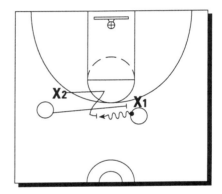

Diagram 18

(Diagram 17)   When the ball is passed to the wing, the defense retreats to the side of the pass and fronts the cutter to the baseline.

(Diagram 18)   Defend the screen on the ball. We used to always double-team. But as Coach Knight says, when you double-team, you create opportunities for both teams. So, this year we had good guards and we showed and recovered. X2 shows and recovers. We do not switch. We make the dribbler take a different path and then recover. X1 can go behind, but don't go more than one man removed. The third way is that X1 can slide through.

(Diagram 19)   If we double, X2 must get out in the path of the dribbler.

(Diagram 20)   Box-out. The coach shoots and defense boxes-out.

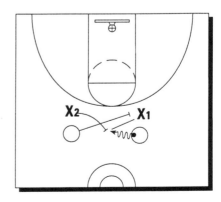

Diagram 19

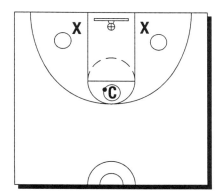

Diagram 20

because we are a pressure team. We also caused about 18 turnovers a game.

Question: What is your rule for doubling down on the post?

Answer: (Diagram 22) First of all, we don't do it because I want to front the low post, but sometimes the defense gets caught behind. If X5 is behind and the ball goes in, our rule is that X2 goes half way. Any offensive move by 5 and X2 goes all the way. If 2 is a great shooter, X2 must be able to get back to guard him.

(Diagram 21)   Deny. The coach fakes and/or passes to either side, one player is in "deny," the other in "help."

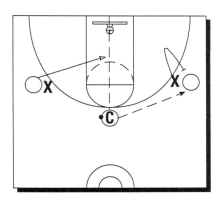

Diagram 21

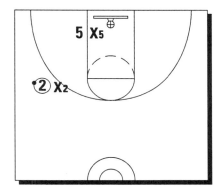

Diagram 22

(Diagram 23)   You can double-down from three different areas.

Now we work 5-on-5 and we talk about **no major sins**. The biggest one is failure to box-out. Another major sin is a failure to front the low-post. I emphasize the word **low**. If I can get you one full stride off of the block, we don't front. We will 3/4 you low or high depending on where the ball is. A major sin is trailing a man in low. If your man goes low, you must go with him. Another sin is to allow an easy change of sides and the last is the failure to get a hand up on the shot. The last three years we held our opponents to field goal percentages of: 1997, 38.7%; 1996, 37.9%, 1995, 39.9%. That's pretty good

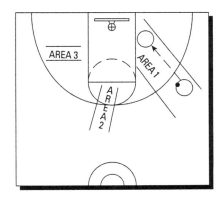

Diagram 23

(Diagram 24)   Guarding the high post. We start on the ballside. On the pass, the defense swings the left arm through as he goes behind and he reestablishes himself on the other side.

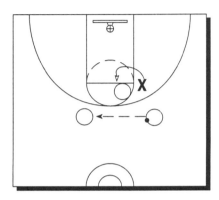

Diagram 24

(Diagram 25)   If the high post gets the ball, we play between him and the basket and we want him to dribble. There are two ways to guard him. Get up on him and make him dribble or back up and let him alone. The worst thing is to get caught half way between.

Diagram 25

(Diagram 26)   If the ball is on the wing and there is dribble penetration, X5 is not in the double-team if he is at the middle or high post. He is not in the help

position because he is only one pass away. The help must come from the other side of the floor.

Diagram 26

Question: Will you show the movement of people on your secondary break?

Answer: (Diagram 27) The ball starts in the corner and is reversed. 4 moves with the ball. 3 moves in and sets a rear screen for 5 for the lob. If 5 doesn't get the lob, then 3 steps out for the pass from 2 and looks in to 4 and 5 for the duck-in. That was my contribution while I was an assistant at North Carolina. Makes me feel good when I see anyone run it.

Diagram 27

(Diagram 28)   If 4 could not get the ball, that means he is fronted. So, if 5 doesn't get the lob and the pass goes to 3, then 5 screens for 4, who comes back across the lane.

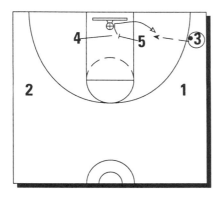

Diagram 28

(Diagram 29)   4 seals and there is no defense in the middle. 3 can pass to either 4 or 5.

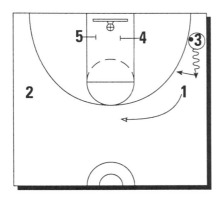

Diagram 29

(Diagram 30)   A variation. 2 can backdoor. Or, after 5 passes to 2, 5 and 1 double-screen for 3, who gets the pass from 2.

(Diagram 31)   Another variation. You can run the flex.

Diagram 30

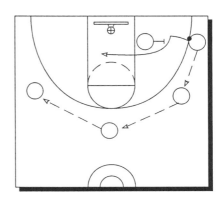

Diagram 31

(Diagram 32)   Corner. 5 will screen away for 2. 3 passes to 2 at the top. 4 and 5 set a staggered screen for 3, who goes to the corner for the pass from 2.

Diagram 32

(Diagram 33)   Another option. 2 backscreens for 5 and then gets a pass from 1. 2 dribbles across the top and passes in to 5 at the post.

(Diagram 34)   Isolation. 1 dribbles away, 4 down-screens for 2 who takes the three-point shot.

Diagram 35

Diagram 33

Diagram 36

Diagram 34

(Diagram 37)   If 5 isn't open, 2 and 3 should be open for the three-point shot.

(Diagram 35)   Here is a play from the box set. 1 dribbles to the wing. 4 cuts away from the ball. 3 sets a screen for 5 who comes high. 1 then reverses the dribble and 1 and 5 run the screen and roll.

(Diagram 36)   An option to this is for 4 to screen down for 2 while 3 backscreens for 5 as 1 comes off of 5's screen.

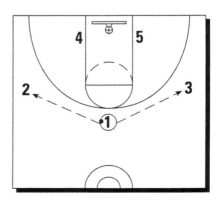

Diagram 37